BARRON'S POCKET GUIDE TO STUDY TIPS

Fifth Edition

BARRON'S

BARRON'S
POCKET GUIDE TO
STUDY TIPS

Fifth Edition

George Ehrenhaft

Former English Chair
Mamaroneck High School, Mamaroneck, New York

William H. Armstrong

Winner of the National School Bell Award for distinguished
interpretation in the field of education and author of the
Newbery Medal award-winning book *Sounder.*

All inquiries should be addressed to:
Barron's Educational Series, Inc.
250 Wireless Blvd.
Hauppauge, New York 11788
http://www.barronseduc.com

ISBN-13: 978-0-7641-2693-2
ISBN-10: 0-7641-2693-8

Library of Congess Catalog Card No. 2003045127

Library of Congress Cataloging-in-Publication Data
Ehrenhaft, George.
    A pocket guide to study tips / George Ehrenhaft,
William H. Armstrong, M. Willard Lampe II.—5th ed.
        p. cm.
    At head of title: Barron's.
    Armstrong's name appears first on earlier ed.
    ISBN 0-7641-2693-8 (alk. paper)
    1. Study skills. I. Title: Barron's a pocket guide to correct study tips.
II. Armstrong, William Howard, 1914– III. Lampe, M. Willard.
IV. Title.

LB1049.A72   2004
371.3′028′1—dc22   2003045127

PRINTED IN CHINA
9 8 7 6 5 4 3 2

CONTENTS

PREFACE

Welcome to the world of studying.

Whether you go to middle school or high school, attend a trade school, a college, or even graduate school, this book is sure to help. No, it won't necessarily turn you into the class valedictorian, but it will help you make the most of the countless hours you spend in the classroom, doing homework, writing papers, studying—doing whatever is necessary to achieve academic success. The book is crowded with useful, eye-opening tips based on the experience of thousands of students who have successfully navigated through courses of every kind in schools at every level.

In its pages, you'll find suggestions to help you better manage your time, to study more productively, to read faster and with greater understanding, to build your vocabulary, to gain the satisfaction and rewards that come from doing the best you can. You'll also find, among other things, practical information on how to use the library, how to be a good test taker, and how to motivate yourself for success.

In short, the book will help you learn how to learn—an admirable and important goal that in the long run can make a big difference not only in school but in life.

Chapter 1

Introduction: From These Roots

Learning is not easy. It never has been, and it never will be, despite the fond hopes of every student. Learning involves too much to be easy. It requires *perception, thought,* and *communication*—three natural gifts that determine to a great degree how successful you are as a student and as a learner.

THE GIFT OF CREATIVE PROBLEM SOLVING

Perception is the gift that enables you to become acquainted with the world around you. History offers illustrations of men who used their perceptive powers to achieve success. The story of Joseph in the Book of Genesis is one of the world's great success stories. Joseph was a slave and a prisoner in the stone quarries, an alien—completely alone in a strange land and numbered among the dead by his kinsmen. His chance audience with the Pharaoh came because Joseph had a reputation as a dreamer and an interpreter of dreams. But Joseph was more than a dreamer. Had it not been for keen perception, Joseph might have been sent back to the stone quarries after he had interpreted the Pharaoh's dream to mean seven years of plenty followed by seven years of famine. Joseph gave purpose to what he had perceived by suggesting that the Pharaoh prepare for the famine by storing grain during the years of plenty. The Pharaoh made Joseph his second-in-command and put him in charge of the whole program of preparation for the years of famine. Joseph saw with his eyes and his mind, and acted upon the purpose he had visualized. He exercised keen perception—perception that sees through to the end of a problem.

There is also a wonderful story of a young woman who arrived at a newspaper office in response to a help wanted ad. Much to her dismay there were twenty-two candidates ahead of her in line. A keen sense of perception solved her problem. She wrote on the back of an envelope: "Dear Sir, I am twenty-third in line. Please don't hire anyone until you have talked to me." She then folded the envelope and asked the person in front of her to pass it forward to the person doing the interviewing. The interviewer read the note and continued to speak with each applicant, but the young woman twenty-third in line got the job because of her sharp perceptive sense.

Another story illustrates the power of a strong perception. Five days before an important French exam, the teacher filled the classroom chalkboard with material—verbs, sentences in English, sentences in French, lists of words. She taught a total of sixty students who daily sat in her classroom for nearly an hour. When the examination was passed out, there was a loud chorus of groans. Where had they seen this before? It had been right in front of them for five days. Two students earned a perfect score on the exam. They had used their perceptive powers. Everyone else received grades close to those they customarily earned.

The conclusion? Perception is the gift that acquaints you with everything in the world around you. It is a precious gift, to be used fully, constantly, and wisely. When you look, make sure you *see*.

THE GIFT OF THOUGHT

Perception without thought brings neither conscious purpose nor action. The gift of thought is the one without which all other gifts would lie dormant. Your whole education is designed to bring growth to your ability to think. That ability will serve you well each year of your life.

The gift of thought enables the mind to deal in abstractions. Sounds—the words "I love you," for example—are abstractions that can convey and evoke deep feelings. Humans have the further ability to record their thoughts in writing. In fact, the gift of thought makes possible much of what we treasure—material things, ranging from the first flint hatchets used by people living in caves to cutting-edge computer chips, and also immaterial things—feelings and morals, beliefs and values, qualities and standards. In a word, the gift of thought gives us our humanity.

THE GIFT OF COMMUNICATION

Communication and *community* come from the same root word, and without the ability to communicate, community would be impossible. Through communication you will receive your education, and the extent to which you develop the ability to communicate with others will help to determine success or failure. The memory of mankind—its total knowledge and beliefs—is communicated mostly through the medium of language.

Winston Churchill, Britain's leader during World War II, was one of history's great masters of communication. His ability to communicate stirred first the British and then the entire freedom-loving world into action against Hitler. An American war correspondent wrote, "Winston Churchill has mobilized the English language and sent it into battle." Indeed, he had done just that—and he won. When he became prime minister in England's "darkest hour," he communicated to his people what they knew, but feared to utter: "I have nothing to offer but blood and toil, tears and sweat." When Belgium surrendered, France had fallen, and the German army stood on the French coast and stared menacingly across at the white cliffs of Dover, Churchill communicated to his countrymen the defiant and resolute feeling that needed to be given voice:

> We shall defend our island, whatever the cost may be. We shall fight on the beaches. We shall fight on the landing grounds. We shall fight on the fields and in the streets. We shall fight in the hills. We shall never surrender. Let us brace ourselves to our duties, and so bear ourselves that, if the British Empire and Commonwealth last for a thousand years, men will say: This was their finest hour.[1]

It is reasonable to say that this one man did more than any other to win World War II. The world may never require of you such exertion of your gift of communication, but you must never cease working to increase the power of this great gift. Success in high school and college will in large measure be determined by your ability to communicate to teachers and others what you have learned.

Perception, thought, and communication—these make possible the memory of the past, provide the

[1]Winston Churchill, *The Second World War*, 6 vols. (Boston: Houghton Mifflin Co., 1949), 2:25.

vision and dream of the future. And these are the chief ingredients of learning, the basic reasons for education.

The three gifts of perception, thought and communication, when combined with the willingness to work hard, constitute the formula to make the time you spend on your studies count for something personally rewarding and significant.

Chapter 2

The Classroom: Atmosphere for Achievement

TRUE CONFESSIONS

1. If you were the teacher and had to face a class of students like yourself, would you be pleased? Tell the truth.

2. If you were asked to contribute to an article entitled, "How to Drive Teachers Crazy," what would you write?

3. If you scrupulously followed all the school's rules and those of your individual teachers, would you be treated scornfully by your friends? If so, how would you handle the situation?

IMPORTANT ELEMENTS OF CLASSROOM SUCCESS

The two important elements of classroom success are attitudes—yours toward your teachers and your work, and your teachers' toward you. Another is your style of work—good habits make for good work and good attitudes and go a long way toward creating the atmosphere for achievement. The contribution that you make toward maintaining an environment of learning will be appreciated by your teachers and no doubt will be used in determining your grades.

PARTNERSHIP WITH THE TEACHER

If you want to succeed, make the teacher your partner. Two simple tests can give you a good idea of how profitable such a partnership can be. First, estimate what the class would be like if every other student acted and responded the same way as you. Would there be a general air of indifference, inattention, and lethargy? Or would there prevail a sense of responsibility and a willingness to learn? Would class time be eaten up with pointless, inane questions and comments, or would the tone be set by intelligent and well-organized discussion?

The answers to these questions depend largely on the quality of the relationship between teacher and students. Ideally, the partnership should be effective and productive. It's in your best interest to make it so because a thriving student-teacher partnership can be one of the great educational experiences of your life, one that you will fondly look back on again and again in the years to come.

Now examine the strength or weakness of this important joint venture by the second test—put yourself in the teacher's place. Is your work the quality that you would like if you were the teacher? Do you respond to correction and help as you yourself would like? If you were the teacher would you pick yourself as one of the most diligent and cooperative members of the class? You may not be the smartest person in the class, but you can be the most responsive and appreciative.

Teachers know that they are not teaching to all the people in any given class. Some students are there for the social ride, some because their parents require it, some because it's a state requirement, and some are there because they want to learn. If you were the teacher, in which of the groups would you place yourself? And if you were the teacher, one of the most complimentary things you could ever say about one of your students would be, "That person wants to learn." What do your teachers say of you?

THE INFLUENCE OF YOUR TEACHERS

"The teacher's influence," wrote Henry Adams, "reaches eternity, no one knows where it stops."

How you use your teachers is going to influence greatly your success in the classroom. Books of biography and autobiography are saturated with such influence that reached past the classroom into life. Thomas Jefferson wrote: "It was my good fortune, and what probably fixed the destinies of my life, that Dr. Wm. Small—a man profound in most of the branches of science, with a happy talent of communication, and an enlarged liberal mind—was my teacher." And Charles Darwin, writing of his life: "I have not yet mentioned a circumstance which influenced my whole career more than any other. This was my friendship with Professor Henslow—I became known as the boy who walks with Henslow."

Of course it's not necessary to befriend all your teachers in order to benefit from their instruction. Most teachers have earned graduate degrees in their fields, and therefore, have a good deal to teach you. Although having a degree is no guarantee of teaching talent, it is likely that your teachers want to be effective purveyors of knowledge. Although some teachers are hard to learn from, make it your business to learn what they have to offer, regardless of your personal feelings toward them. When students say that they can't learn from teachers they don't like, they reveal more about their maturity than about the quality of instruction.

In some courses your teacher will assign you an interim or final grade based solely on your scores on tests and quizzes. Sometimes class participation is also used. In other courses, though, teachers take into account several subjective criteria such as attitude, effort, and even the way you behave in class. Because many intangibles may be factored into your grade, it makes sense to do your best at all times, demonstrate that you care about the course, and—especially in large schools and large classes—show the teacher that you are more than just an occupant of a particular seat. Let the teacher know you as a unique individual. You may well find that your teacher cares more than you think. It's true that for some, teaching is merely a job—to cover one chapter a week from pages 95–130 and give a quiz on Friday. For many others, however, teaching is a calling. They regard teaching as a noble profession, and care greatly not only about their subject matter but about their students. "Show me the person you have made of yourself," wrote one English teacher to his students. "Let me see its full size. For how can I judge what you know, what you say, what you do, what you make, unless in the context of the whole person?"*

Even though you may feel occasionally that the work in a course is beyond you, don't despair. Most teachers respect students who try hard, and they will go

---

*Ken Macrorie, *A Vulnerable Teacher* (Rochelle Park, NJ: Hayden, 1974), 38.

out of their way to offer extra help. Sometimes teachers deliberately attempt to push you to your intellectual limits by making their courses extremely rigorous. Ken Macrorie, formerly a professor of English at Western Michigan University, recalls overhearing a conversation between a teacher and a student.

"This course is killing me," said the hapless student. "I don't understand the assignments. Can't you tell me more about what I should do? I get home, read the book, and start to write my paper, and I don't know what I should say. There's a great high wall in front of me. I start climbing it but then I fall back. I climb again, same thing, I'm never sure what I should be doing, but I want to climb the wall."

"That's the way I want you to feel," said the teacher with his sweet smile. (39)

HINTS ON ATTITUDE

Some of the things that you take for granted and seem insignificant and trivial are actually of greatest importance in making the classroom your arena of achievement. As the following hints imply, the way you behave in the classroom will affect the way you feel and think about your work, and also the way your teacher feels and thinks about you.

➤ Accept that learning is something no one can do for you. Learning is a lonely business, not a social affair. Even in the classroom, in the midst of your classmates, you will be learning on your own. If you expect the class to be a social affair, you are bound to be disappointed.

Learning anything of value is difficult—hard, often tedious work; but remember, it also has moments of joy and exhilaration arising from the feeling of achievement and self-satisfaction.

➤ Expect your teacher to require excellence. The teachers you'll remember as the ones who taught you the best are those who required honest work and never compromised the integrity of the class. They never disguised the true aim of the class behind a front of meaningless give-and-take or the absurdity of useless argument.

➤ Ask questions, but be aware that your questions reveal much about your attitude. By your questions you show that you are sincere in your desire to learn and are not merely "going through the motions" of doing assignments. If you are assigned a composition, don't ask, "How long does it have to be?" Ask instead, "What do you want us to include?" If you are not satisfied with a grade on written work, don't walk up to the teacher and protest, "Why'd you mark me off on this?" Ask instead, "How could I have improved this answer?" In each of these cases the former question carries negative implications, implications of hostility toward the teacher, while the latter question implies a sincere desire to improve.

➤ Behave respectfully in class. Nothing can destroy the rapport of student and teacher so quickly as a boorish manner. Arrive in class on time, don't yawn, sleep, or start looking at your watch halfway through the period. Don't start putting on your jacket and gathering up your books before the period ends. What would a coach think of a player who slacked off before the game was over? The way you carry your books, your body language, the manner in which you enter and leave the classroom—all these contribute to the way your teachers see you. A little common sense goes a long way: Leave your snacks and drinks at the door unless the teacher permits eating in class. Similarly, don't chew gum, wear your baseball cap, apply makeup, carry a blaring radio, or bring your cell phone or beeper to class. In short, look and act the part of a student.

Like you, teachers want to be treated with respect. There's no need for you to fawn and grovel, but to make a good impression, merely be polite and friendly, and most teachers will respond in kind. When you come late to class, be courteous enough at the end of the period to explain why. When you have returned from an absence, show enough concern to ask the teacher what you have missed and to pick up the homework or other assignments. Like other people, teachers have bad days. Occasionally a class drags, discussion is desultory, students' eyes glaze over with boredom. Most teachers know very well when a lesson seems to be stuck. Make it your challenge to come to the rescue. Ask a thoughtful question or make a provocative, but relevant, comment. If you can be the catalyst that wakes up a slumbering class, everyone will be grateful, including your teacher, who won't forget your effort.

A little observation will reveal that the best students are those who maintain a high standard of classroom manners. They are aware that what is being done in the classroom is to help them learn. They are conscious of the continuing judgment that the interested and devoted teacher makes. Perhaps, save on isolated occasions, the student's only means of expressing gratitude and appreciation is through courtesy—from which all good classroom manners grow.

Accepting classroom instructions and following them puts you in the "atmosphere for achievement." Good habits are as easy to follow as bad ones, a good attitude as easy to develop as a bad one. The bad produce negative vibes; the good, good ones. Nothing could be simpler. It's your choice, so choose wisely.

POP QUIZ: WHAT KIND OF STUDENT ARE YOU?

How would you describe your participation in class? How do you rate your overall attitude toward school? Do you have any of the following traits?

➤ Are you the unprepared bluffer—the person who attempts to cover up lack of preparation by asking irrelevant questions or volunteering unreliable information?

➤ Are you the winger—a person who "wings it," and like a fluttering magpie, interrupts constantly, often before giving any thought to what you plan to say and sometimes even repeating what others have already said, thereby adding nothing to the class's progress?

➤ Are you the sensitive hopeful, the person who has prepared sufficiently to contribute, but is afraid of what the teacher and other students will think of your comment or question?

➤ Are you the accomplished leader, the person who has prepared the assignment, reviewed the essentials, established a point of view for possible discussion, and now has the initiative to speak out intelligently in class?

BE A CLASSROOM LEADER. HERE'S HOW

To be a positive force in any class, try to develop a supportive and enthusiastic attitude. Easier said than done, of course, but here are some steps to take:

➤ Go to class with your assignments prepared. While this
  instruction may seem obvious, many students prepare
  themselves haphazardly or not at all. To check the status of your preparation, ask yourself the following
  questions:

Am I pleased with what I have done? Let the work
represent the best you have to offer. Be proud of it.
Anything less reflects indifference or lack of ability.
Don't be satisfied with mediocrity.

Will my work satisfy the teacher? Even if you can't
finish the assignment, let the work you've done reflect
a high level of effort and responsibility. Follow
carefully the teacher's instructions regarding format,
paper quality, heading, length, organization, and any
other details of presentation.

*Will the work be considered among the best in the
class?* Others may have more mastery of the subject,
but no one can prevent you from making your best
effort. Teachers quickly learn their students' capabilities
and assess their work accordingly. A good effort, even
if you miss some answers, will be recognized and
appreciated.

To judge the quality of your preparation for class
discussion, ask yourself these questions:

1. *Do I know enough to make a positive contribution?*
   Since teachers often follow the textbook, you can
   sometimes predict what will be discussed in class. If
   you fear speaking up in class, anticipate one or two
   topics you think likely for discussion and prepare
   for those topics. Knowledge will make you secure
   and help to overcome your fear. You also will learn
   that sincere and honest comments are not met by
   critical judgments. You probably will find, with a

little inquiry, that you are not the only responsible student who fears speaking up.

2. *Do I answer direct questions with confidence?* Don't begin to answer questions by belittling what you are about to say. To start off with "Isn't it true that . . .?" or "Doesn't the book say?" casts doubt even before you have stated your point. Other "don'ts" include such introductions as "I don't know but," "I heard or read somewhere," "I'm not sure, but I think." Design your answer to give your listeners assurance that you know what you are talking about. Try to make a quick blueprint before you start, particularly as to how you will end your answer. You will find it a painful experience if you shred a splendid answer by tacking on insignificant details merely because you have not anticipated a climax and a quick closing. Imagine your recitation as a one-minute drama that is to be properly staged; or imagine that for the period of your individual recitation you are the director of a meeting, controlling your audience and speaking so clearly that no one can help understanding.

3. *How will my oral participation be judged by the teacher and my fellow students?* If you ask yourself the first two questions and can answer them honestly with a resounding YES, you will have answered this third question. Everyone will judge your comments favorably; all will judge you to be an accomplished leader!

➤ Go to class with the proper tools. Take pens, pencils, lab notebook, laptop, textbooks, assignment pad, calculator, compass—whatever you need for that class. If in doubt, ask the teacher what to bring with you. Coming without or with the wrong tools tells the teacher, in effect, "I AM NOT INTERESTED IN YOUR CLASS!" This is not a message that a teacher wants to hear. If you were playing center field, and inning after inning went out without your glove, do you think your coach would keep you on the team for very long? Imagine going to a music lesson and forgetting to take your instrument or music. Arriving at a class without the tools will very quickly put you off the team or out of the lesson.

➤ Follow instructions. Write down, *clearly,* your assignments in a division of your notebook set aside for assignments or in a special assignment pad. Make sure you write down and follow the general instructions your teacher gives about the format for work done in the course. If your teacher asks, for example, for your name to be in the upper right-hand corner of the paper, put it there, every time.

LOOKING BACK

1. You are writing an essay on the topic, "How to Win Friends and Influence Teachers." What are three common sense suggestions you just read about that you might incorporate into your essay?

2. As you examine the many hints for successful classroom behavior in Chapter 2, which one would you single out as being the most important? Explain the reasons for your choice.

3. As you think about the quality of your own class participation, which of the guidelines in this chapter do you find easiest to follow? Which the hardest? What do you think it would take to make the most difficult one easier?

Chapter 3
Study Time: Design for Success

TRUE CONFESSIONS

1. On Monday morning you must turn in a long historical research paper on the Vietnam War. Is it likely that you will submit it on time? How do you know?

2. Have you ever made a plan for budgeting your time? If not, are you willing to try? If you have tried in the past, did it work? If not, what caused it to fail? Are you game to try once again?

3. On December 22 your English teacher distributes a list of American novels, telling you to select one for reading during the upcoming vacation. Are you likely to get the book on December 23? December 29? or January 3? Explain.

   One of your classmates who is certain to start on the book the night before the written report is due explains by saying, "I like to live dangerously." What other possible reasons are there for such a practice?

YOUR MOST IMPORTANT TOOL FOR LEARNING—TIME

The point of this chapter is that "all genuine learning is self-education." The time you spend in classrooms and labs with teachers and aides is not unimportant, but it can't compare in value to the time you spend alone reading and studying. Group learning can be enjoyable; you can learn a great deal from your peers, but the learning that lasts and lasts is that which you do on your own. Basically, because studying is a solitary and often difficult business, it's easy to think of things to do instead. To keep mind and body in shape, it's important to hang out with friends, listen to music, cruise the Internet, shoot hoops, take naps. But if you use these activities as a substitute or as an escape from studying, you are squandering the one thing that the great philosopher-emperor of Rome, Marcus Aurelius, called "the only thing of which a man can be deprived"—the present.

The Greek philosopher, Epicurus, pointed out that we ourselves are the deprivers: "But you, who are not master of tomorrow, postpone your happiness: life is wasted in procrastination." Indeed, procrastination is one of the most ruthless destroyers of time and in severe cases can lead someone into a life of missed opportunites and pathetic "might-have-been's."

HELP YOURSELF. PROCRASTINATE NO MORE

Sometimes procrastination is mistaken for laziness. You may even joke about how lazy you are. "I do my best work under pressure," you might say, or "I can't write this paper until I feel inspired." Such excuses may be signs of laziness, but the causes for postponing work may be far more complex and psychologically rooted than that. In a recent book, *It's About Time* (Viking Penguin, 1996), the authors Jack McGuire and Linda Sapadin speculate that the causes of procrastination vary from person to person. Some people are *perfectionists*, so desperately afraid of the slightest failure that they put off starting or finishing a task or project. *Dreamers*, on the other hand, rarely get going because their grandiose ideas are way beyond their grasp. They expect great things of themselves but are often disappointed. *Worriers*, who prefer to do nothing rather than risk running into problems, need reassurance from others before starting projects. *Defiers* feel resentful and manipulated when asked to perform an unpleasant task; they resist authority, carry out their responsibilities grudgingly, work slowly and often do a poor job. *Crisis makers* ignore important work until the last minute, then work like the dickens, apparently getting a kick out of living life on the edge. Finally, *overdoers* are the proverbial decapitated chickens who run around aimlessly. They don't accomplish much although they always seem busy and complain that they have too much to do.

Whether you are a major or a minor procrastinator, there are many techniques available to help you overcome a tendency to put off or totally ignore disagreeable tasks. If you recognize that you have a problem, then you can take appropriate steps to lick it. For example, pick out a single goal to concentrate on. Choose a small task, one that can be completed in less than half an hour—washing the car or tidying up your desk. If the job you are putting off is a large one—writing a research paper, for instance—think of the job as a series of small steps, each one requiring a limited amount of time. Then, each day for a couple of weeks, devote thirty minutes to getting the paper done. Don't wait until you "feel like doing it." Set aside the same thirty-minute period day after day—possibly a half an hour just before dinner or when you get home from school. After each session you are bound to feel less anxious about the whole job, and when you have the end of the job clearly in view, your relief may be palpable. To keep you going from day to day, reward yourself every step of the way. Treat yourself to some popcorn, listen to some music, take a bike ride—do anything that you consider special.

Another technique that many procrastinators find helpful is to keep a list of things to do. On a small index card write down all the tasks you need to complete during the next few days. Assign each one a priority. As you finish each one, cross it off. Even if you manage to accomplish only a few of the important tasks within the allotted time, you will have come a long way from your previous paralysis. Changing behavior takes time, but if you are determined to alleviate the anxiety and panic that procrastinators often experience, each small step counts as a giant leap for you. To keep up your momentum, never think of the chores you have as burdens. Rather, consider them things that must be done, things you choose to do because of the dire consequences of not doing them.

TIME IS OUR MOST PRECIOUS RESOURCE

There is a traditional way of perceiving time which indicates that it can be controlled, and that way is to look at time as a valuable personal possession. If you were told there was an unbreakable limit to the amount of money you had to spend—that once it was gone, you would never get another penny—it would probably make you very careful about how you disposed of it. You would do your best to ensure that the finite amount available was directed into getting what you really wanted out of life.

Yet faced with the same situation with respect to time, wastrels throw it carelessly away, figuring that there will always be more time tomorrow or next week. It goes against nature to take deliberate steps to control your use of time. Who, after all, would want to sap life of its charming spontaneity, and who wants to be enslaved by the clock?

Perhaps we resist surrendering ourselves to time's demands because we associate the organization of time with business and the factory. Control of time and motion for increased productivity, while improving the efficiency of workers and managers, smacks of robotics—transforming humans into automatons. What's more, taking steps to use time more productively sounds a great deal like more and harder work, although the truth is that this is contrary to the chief aims of modern time-management techniques.

Far from making work harder, the systematic allocation of time makes work easier. The world of poor time management consists of screaming deadlines, nagging problems, irritating harassments, and unpleasant surprises. Well-organized time managers get their work done with less wear and tear on their emotions and less strain on their health.

The underlying purpose of time management is to spring loose more "disposable" time that may be directed toward meeting one's life objectives. These objectives might include anything from learning to play a musical instrument, to playing Ultimate Frisbee, to seeing the Taj Mahal.

What the workaholic forgets and the would-be manager of time should always keep in mind is what one might be doing outside of work. Possibilities are limited only by our imagination; they might include walking out in the weather of sunlit days and storms, watching the seasons change, seeing children grow and maybe even helping the process along, being there to comfort a troubled friend. If you consistently choose work over these alternatives, then you really do have a problem managing time.

In any case, the principles of time management apply to all of life, not just the relatively small portion of it that is spent in working. Though they are commonly taught to managers and supervisors, the techniques for conserving time work equally well for Olympic athletes, students, self-employed people, retirees, and anyone else who seeks to get the most out of life.[1]

FINDING WHERE THE HOURS GO

Because self-discovery and self-evaluation are the only really effective means of convincing yourself where your time goes, make a time chart of your waking hours for one week, being completely honest with yourself, and record in as much detail as possible what you do. Keep a simple chart that looks like this:

---

[1]Adapted from *The Royal Bank Letter.* Reprinted with permission of the Royal Bank of Canada.

TIME USE CHART

MONDAY, SEPTEMBER 5

Hours	
A.M.	Awoke at 7:30; arrived in school 8:00
8:00–9:00	Ate breakfast in cafeteria; talked with friends 8:30–9:00
9:00–10:00	Chemistry class
10:00–11:00	Free period—went to guidance office to pick up bulletin about taking SAT IIs; chatted with secretary
11:00–12:00	History class
P.M.	Lunch for half an hour
12:00–1:00	Can't remember what I did until 1:00 P.M.
1:00–2:00	English class
2:00–3:00	Math class
3:00–4:00	3:00–3:30 helped to hang pictures for art show in school gallery
	3:30–4:00 went home; had snack
4:00–5:00	Met friend and browsed at Blockbuster
5:00–6:00	Read English assignment 25 minutes; listened to music; read a magazine article on life after death
6:00–7:00	Dinner
7:00–8:00	Shot hoops in backyard 20 minutes
8:00–9:00	Studied for math test
9:00–10:00	Phone calls; chemistry homework
10:00–11:00	Watched television; went to bed at 11:15

TOTAL: 15 hours and 45 minutes

Time in class	4
Time studying outside of class	_____
Time in social activity and recreation (talking, video store, telephone, music, etc.)	_____
Time otherwise accounted for	_____
Time not accounted for	_____

Do the same for each school day. At the end of a week, add up the totals. If your allotment of time satisfies you, that's fine. But if the totals show that you have squandered a great deal of time or that you have devoted more hours than you should to one activity or another, make an effort to balance your time. Be confident that you can rearrange and reapportion each day, in particular during those unscheduled hours that you can fill as you choose. If one week's trial does not convince you, carry the experiment through a second or third week.

Psychologists and efficiency experts have done much research in the advantage of organized time. The results of this research are very convincing. They show the tremendous value in time saving. They show the effectiveness of work approached with a definite job in mind rather than the question "What next?" Research has shown that the energy saved through good organization is directed toward the job at hand. Consequently, one of the significant benefits of organization, system, and a well-worked-out schedule for study, is the power that organization makes available.

BUSY, BUT WELL ORGANIZED

Once you have a fairly precise idea of how you spend your time, you can move on to setting priorities. The purpose of setting priorities is not so much to determine what is important as it is to eliminate what is not. On examination you may find that some of the routines you practice are not worth the time you put into them. Lists of priorities should be checked against a list of long-term objectives. Any task that does not advance toward these goals is of questionable importance.

In the hustle and bustle of everyday life, it is difficult to determine which tasks are more important than others. It is therefore advisable to adopt a system that makes you stop and think about each item. It may sound slightly neurotic, but some busy people use color-coded file folders to sort out their priorities—red for what must be done immediately, green for what must be done within the day, yellow for what must be done within the week.

If we spend too much time on inconsequential matters because we overestimate how important they are, we also do so because of our own psychology. It is human nature to do the quick and easy tasks before the harder ones. We are quite capable of deluding ourselves about what really matters. All of us know how much more important it can seem to go shopping or repair a bicycle than to sit down and write an essay on *Macbeth* or study for a chemistry test.

The trouble with doing even legitimate small jobs first is that they tend to multiply, taking time away from work on long-range goals and planning. It is, however, not so simple to stick to the big important things of life because the small ones keep interfering.

Crises erupt that distract us from working towards the things that really count.

When faced with an apparently urgent problem, the important questions to ask are: "Is this so urgently important that it supersedes the importance of what I am now doing?" and "Does this require my personal attention, or can it be done just as well by someone else?"

If a problem does prove to be of surpassing urgency, it automatically leap-frogs to the top of your priority list. This means that you should work on it until it is finished. After that, you can turn your attention back to the item that was formerly first on your list.

But here the world intervenes again. It is all very well to say that we must systematically go about disposing of our priorities, but our time is riddled with interruptions. No wonder some of the big things don't get done.

The fact is, however, that many interruptions are avoidable. It is human nature to invite them, especially to elude a struggle with a tough assignment or to put off some unsavory task. For instance, do you often find ways to postpone writing thank you notes or making phone calls that you'd rather not make? Do you sometimes drop a major piece of work to start a minor one? If so, you are like countless other people— people who would probably benefit from a schedule that systematically apportions their time.

How do you design a schedule that will help you avoid problems like those noted above? Here is a recommendation: Equip yourself with a weekly planner—a book not unlike the one that your teachers probably use for lesson plans—in which you can enter all relevant data. In a planner, the days of the week will be divided into enough periods to take care of your classes, free periods, pre- and after-school activities, with space left over for late afternoon, evening, and weekend planning. In appearance, a page may look something like the model on the following two pages, except that it would be six times larger, each space being roomy enough for you to write in assignments or what to study for each class. (The entries on this model schedule pertain to a high school sophomore with a full academic program and extracurricular activities.)

If for some reason this particular schedule doesn't suit you, there are literally hundreds of other forms for telling you at a glance what you need to do and when to do it. The shelves of office supply stores are crowded with planning books, pads, blotters, and calendars. Or go on-line, search for "Weekly Planners," and you'll be swamped with forms that can be downloaded and printed using Adobe Acrobat, rtf format (MSWord), and other programs.

TIME SCHEDULE

Subject Period Time	Monday	Tuesday	Wednesday	Thursday	Friday	Saturday	Sunday
Early A.M. Band practice 7:15–8:15	Band practice	Band practice	Band practice	Band practice	Band practice		Have fun and prepare for the week ahead
Homeroom 8:30–9:00	Homeroom	Homeroom	Homeroom	Homeroom	Homeroom		
Math 9:00–10:00	Math, pgs. 1–5, Ex. 2, Prob. 1–8	Math	Math	Math	Math	Study and homework for Monday	
English 10:00–11:00	English Macbeth Act I, pgs. 1–34	English	English	English	English		
Free period 11:00–12:00	Study Math for Tues. ——— Lunch	Study Math for Wed. ——— Lunch	Study Math for Thurs. ——— Lunch	Study Math for Fri. ——— Lunch	Biology Lab ——— Lunch		
Biology 12:00–1:00	Biology	Biology	Biology	Biology	Biology	Recreation, excercise, part-time job	
French 1:00–2:00	French	French	French	French	French		
Social Studies 2:00–3:00	Social Studies Chapter 3, pgs. 65–90	Social Studies	Social Studies	Social Studies	Social Studies		
After school 3:00–5:00	Track practice	Track practice	Track practice	Track practice	Track practice		
Home and dinner 5:00–7:00	Home and dinner	Home and dinner	Home and dinner	Home and dinner	Home and dinner		
Homework 7:00–9:00	Homework for Tues.	Homework for Wed.	Homework for Thurs.	Homework for Fri.	Volunteer for safe rides 8:00–11:00		
9:00–11:00	Read, relax, review	Same	Same	Same			

TIME SCHEDULE

Twelve Precious Hours	Monday	Tuesday	Wednesday	Thursday	Friday	Saturday	Sunday
8:00–9:00	8:00–8:30 Bus to school Review one subject						
9:00–10:00	Chemistry Class						
10:00–11:00	English Class						
11:00–12:00	Study Chem. for Tues.	Study Chem. for Wed.	Study Chem. for Thurs.	Study for Chem. test on Fri.	Study Chem. for Mon.	Study English for Mon.	
1:00–2:00	Math Class					Good study time	
2:00–3:00	History Class						
3:00 4:00	Home and Exercise						
4:00–5:00	Recreation			Study for Chemistry Test			
5:00–6:00	Study Math for Tues.	Study Math for Wed.	Study Math for Thurs.	Study Math for Fri.	Study Math for Mon.		
7:00–8:00	Study Hist. for Tues.	Study Hist. for Wed.	Study Hist. for Thurs.	Study Hist. for Fri.	Study Hist. for Mon.		
8:00–9:00	Study Eng. for Tues.	Study Eng. for Wed.	Study Eng. for Thurs.	Study Eng. for Fri.	Recreation		
9:00–10:00	Relax and Read	Listen to Music					
	Comments All work finished	Comments	Comments	Comments	Comments A good week Grades up	Comments	Comments

Or you might prefer a more compact model, one that's easier to carry around, and one without space for noting assignments. Of course, one copy of such a schedule in front of your notebook and another copy posted where you study would suffice, perhaps with minor changes, for the entire school year. Such a schedule is usually divided into twelve working hours between 8:00 a.m. and 10:00 p.m., leaving an hour free for lunch and one for dinner. Such a schedule might resemble the model on page 29.

There is much to commend each type of schedule, but many students prefer the latter. Only one day, Monday, is filled in fully. Several things are very important if a schedule is to work effectively. Notice that the period from 11:00–12:00 is used to study the same subject each day except Friday. The same is true for 5:00–6:00, 7:00–8:00, and 8:00–9:00. Research has shown that doing the same thing at the same time each day makes the work seem much easier because it does away with the energy-consuming self-conflict and the confusion of deciding "What next?" It becomes a part of you—not a force outside with which you have to contend.

The schedule also shows you there is much time that can be used for the things you want to do—perhaps more, actually, than you have ever thought available. Two interesting results have been noted from the study of time usage. First, the more one has to do the easier it is to make a workable schedule and follow it. Second, students who plan carefully study fewer hours and often earn higher grades than those who don't restrict their studying to specific time slots. At all costs, avoid deluding yourself into believing that you study all the time. Don't be a person who works without a schedule, bombs a test or quiz, and then whimpers, "But I studied for three hours!" What could have happened is that this hapless whiner sat with a book for three hours, perhaps daydreamed a bit, listened to music, was distracted by the television, and never got into the subject.

A popular alternative to a plan book of any size is an electronic organizer. People in many fields—business, the arts, journalism, law, academia, the sciences—have digitized their schedules. With a handy pocket-size Palm Pilot or other computer, they keep track of their daily appointments, names and addresses, dates to remember, and any additional information that will help them keep their lives running smoothly. CEOs, military brass, and high government officials may have human aides and staff members to guide them through the day, but the rest of us need to rely on ourselves to keep our work schedules in order.

If neither a published nor a preprogrammed electronic planner suits your unique schedule, you can always design your own. Computer software, including almost every desktop publishing program, contains grids for making charts for any purpose. Merely choose a grid and begin filling in the boxes. If you run out of space, enlarge the boxes or use a smaller typeface. More boxes can easily be added, using the proper commands. The point is that people who follow a schedule of work train themselves to concentrate. Problems in concentration are, in fact, problems in the effective use of time. The person who sets a limit of time to complete a job makes a choice between getting the job done or dreaming in a halfhearted way for an equally indefinite period of time.

The first of all good study habits is the proper use of time. A well-organized schedule, followed until it becomes a natural part of living, improves your ability to concentrate. From the combined results of these two comes the power of work; and from the power of work well, the sky's the limit!

You have the power to bring productive and effective order into your life. The suggestions that follow can make a time schedule work for you.

MAKING YOUR SCHEDULE WORK

➤ Give your schedule a fair chance. After you have evaluated your loss of time without a schedule and have prepared a working schedule, give yourself a month or more to develop the habit of alternating activities. Go from something light to something heavy, from something hard to something easy. Go from a deadly class to an activity you enjoy. Study a subject you like, then a subject you hate, and so on. Reward yourself for getting through a particularly onerous task with a treat of some kind—a handful of Oreos, an extra ten minutes of your favorite music, or maybe reading a few more pages of this book.

➤ Choose a specific place to do your work. Place is as important as time in making your schedule effective. If you study in the library at school or in the student commons, try to sit at the same carrel or table. Bring pencils, paper, books—whatever you need to work. After getting situated, discipline yourself not to move until you've completed a certain block of work. If you study at home, find a quiet spot, well-lighted, and facing away from the window. Put all distractions out of reach and sight if possible. Your friend's picture, magazines, unanswered letters, will pull you away and waste your time because you will lose your power of concentration.

If it is noisy at home, study in the public library. The setting, the quiet, the presence of books and other people deep in concentration could help you put your schedule into effect.

Do not kid yourself by thinking that you can study and listen to music, catch snatches of television, or listen to people talk. It cannot be done, and this has been proved by numerous tests and experiments. There is no common ground where study, relaxation, and sociability meet. There is a place for study and a place for relaxation and sociability. If you attempt to make them the same, your study schedule won't work.

➤ Study the same thing at the same time each day. This further strengthens the good habit of action by second nature. It also eliminates the exception—always troublesome and causing some delay. You are prepared mentally for the thing you are used to doing with regularity. Mental preparation is the first step toward concentration.

➤ Fit your schedule to your needs. You know your capacities. One subject will take you longer than another. Learn to measure your concentration span. If necessary, build regular breaks into your schedule—five-minute respites during which to take your eyes and mind off the work you are doing.

➤ Don't overdo it while making your first schedule. If you turn yourself into a relentless grind for two weeks, your schedule may become such a drag that you won't benefit from its true purpose—to make your work easier and to free you from drudgery.

➤ Don't be afraid to change your schedule to take care of emergencies and unexpected variations. An important part of an education is learning how to choose between conflicting interests. When faced with a change, however, try to keep the pattern of the day and week as nearly regular as possible. For example, if you have a chance to play basketball on Thursday afternoon between four and five, decide when to study for the chemistry test. Not to do so will put you in a hole and also defeat the purpose of having a schedule in the first place.

These suggestions can help set you on the right track, but be prepared to work out your own schemes to fit your personality and circumstances. The exact methods are less important than your recognition that time is your most valuable resource, and that it should be allocated according to a plan that puts first things first. The paradox of time management is that greater control means greater freedom to do things you want to do. By making the most of your time, you can go a long way toward sucking the marrow out of life and in the process, being the best student you can be.

LOOKING BACK

1. What do you see as some advantages of keeping a schedule? What are some disadvantages?

2. It may seem paradoxical that students who have less time to study often manage to do better in school than others. How can this be explained?

3. What advice would you give to a friend who says, "I don't make schedules because I know I can't live up to them"?

Chapter 4

The Art of Studying

TRUE CONFESSIONS

In response to the question of how they go about studying for tests in a major subject, this is what a handful of students said:

1. "How do I study? Reluctantly, reluctantly . . ."

2. "I flip the book's pages quickly, stopping only on those sections that look unfamiliar, and I reread them carefully. I don't waste time on what I already know."

3. "I look over my answers to the homework questions, review the quizzes we had during the marking period, and spend an hour discussing possible test questions with the brightest kid in the class."

4. "If the test covers two or three units in our biology book, I will read them over, scan the questions at the end of the chapters, and then check over my class and lab notes."

5. "I pray earnestly!"

Which answer most closely resembles what you might have said?

LEARNING TO STUDY

Several years ago a psychologist was asked to help Maxwell Air Force Base officers improve their efficiency in studying. As he began his work, he discovered a remarkable thing: "When a number of them [who requested] help were asked if they had forgotten how to study, almost every one replied, 'No—I never learned.'" [1]

In fact, study skills *per se* are rarely taught in school. Therefore, it's odd that students are often told to "study" this or that, as though everyone has at one time or other been instructed in how to do it. Nothing, however, is further from the truth.

TRIED-AND-TRUE STUDY METHODS

Had they been taught the art of studying, students would know that there are many techniques, each varying in complexity and effectiveness, and each suitable for particular purposes at particular times. Nevertheless, all are intended to help students understand and accurately recall meaningful information from sources of every kind, from books and lectures to class discussions and films.

➤ Almost every effective study technique contains an element of "previewing." *Previewing* is an apt term, for as you look over a body of information, say, a chapter of a textbook, you begin to discern highlights that reveal the content and organization of the material. To preview effectively, read the introductory paragraphs, the bold-face type, and any summary, review, or study questions

---

[1] Thomas F. Staton, *How to Study,* 4th ed. (Nashville: McQuiddy Printing Co., 1954), preface.

that may appear at the end. If the material contains none of these highlights, preview the material by reading the first one or two sentences of each paragraph. Much of the time, these "topic sentences" will tell you what the remainder of the paragraph is about. By skimming in this way, you will quickly gain an overview of the scope and sequence of the chapter.

To some extent, studying is like going on a trip. As you prepare, you may consult a map to find the best way to reach your destination. When you have planned the route, you begin to gather whatever is necessary to successfully complete the trip. For a trip by car, you'll need wheels, a licensed driver, gas, a way to pay for snacks and tolls, and a supply of CDs to wile away the time. On a journey through an assignment for school, you will need paper and pen, perhaps a computer, the correct text, and a quiet, distraction-free place to plop yourself for an extended period of uninterrupted time. A good preview, like a good map, will help you begin to sort out the important material from the chaff. It will also substantially increase your ability to put the information you read into meaningful units and will improve your ability to remember it.

➤ The second part of an effective method is *reading* the assignment. Read it carefully but quickly, reading for ideas. As you read for ideas, take notes in your own words or underline the key phrases in your textbook, if you have your own copy. You will find, if you have done the preliminary survey, that reading will go fairly quickly, more quickly than you are accustomed to reading. The reason for your increased speed is that the preview has started you thinking about the topic you are studying and has put the major areas of discussion in your mind, thus enhancing your ability to sort out the information and make sense of it. In order to read the assignment quickly and thoroughly, stay alert and take an active part in the process. If you remain passive, letting the words wash over you, you will not be able to find the main ideas quickly, and you will have to reread the assignment more than once, thereby losing the time you saved by having done the preview!

➤ The third step is *review*. After reading the material, reflect on what you have read. Reflecting is not rereading but rather a mental activity in which you try to recall major ideas and themes. Ask yourself such questions as these: "What was the major idea?" "What minor ideas were included?" "What material was used to support or illustrate the major idea?" If you can accurately answer these questions, you have understood the substance of the material, and you may have anticipated the questions that your teacher may raise during the next class period or on a quiz or exam.

An experiment in a Connecticut high school, during which a group of juniors recorded their questions in writing, showed that after six weeks of practice, the students had anticipated and prepared for eighty percent of the questions asked by their teacher in class. Experiments with other groups showed just the opposite: Students using a study method that failed to include an organized questioning process averaged nine points lower on identical tests.

One productive study technique, then, employs three major parts: *a preliminary survey, a careful but quick reading for key ideas,* and *a review.* In all honesty, though, an altogether different method—see the techniques detailed on the following pages—may be equally, or even more effective, for you. Try each of them, and see which produces the best results.

SQ3R

The name of this technique is derived from five steps: Survey, Question, Read, Recite, Review. In a nutshell, here is how SQ3R works for a typical homework assignment that consists of reading a chapter from the textbook of the course:

SURVEY: Reading boldface type, topic sentences, summary paragraphs, review questions, will give you an idea of the contents of the assignment.

QUESTION: After you have completed the survey, ask yourself what will be the important information contained in the assignment. Questioning will also help you to link the information in the assignment to what you already know. An easy way to create the questions is to turn the boldface type or the topic sentences into questions.

READ: Read for ideas; especially, to answer the questions you have created. Read one section at a time, and then go to the next step.

RECITE: Answer the questions you have asked, without looking at your notes or at the textbook. After you have finished answering the questions, go on to the next section of the assignment, read it, and answer the questions you have asked. Continue reading and reciting until you have finished the assignment.

REVIEW: After you have finished the assignment, look away from the book, go
over your notes, and get a comprehensive grasp of the complete
assigment.

A variation of SQ3R was devised to help Air Force
officers improve their study habits. Called PQRST, it
also consists of five parts: Preview, Question, Read,
State, Test.

Here is the gist of it.

PQRST

PREVIEW: Read the topic headings, the summary paragraphs, the review questions, or if these are not present, the
topic sentences of the paragraphs.
Try to associate this assignment to
previous work in class or to previous
assignments.

QUESTION: Ask yourself what is important in the
assignment. Try to turn the topic
headings into questions.

READ: Read the assignment carefully but
quickly, looking for key ideas. Take
notes or highlight key passages in
the textbook. Be judicious both in
notetaking and in highlighting. Non-
specific notetaking is time-consuming
and ultimately useless because it
does not organize your notes or your
thinking. Too much highlighting also

is non-specific and does not organize your thinking; you will lose the key ideas in the mass of bright yellow highlighter.

STATE: Answer the questions you created at the beginning. State what was important that you neglected to ask questions about.

TEST: Review your knowledge of the assignment. Ask yourself questions, and answer them. Be as detailed as is necessary, but avoid getting bogged down with so much detail that you lose the key ideas.

Here is a method of studying that gives you an accurate picture of how well you know the material.
It also obliges you to think about it, not just casually look it over:

INDEX STUDY SYSTEM[2]

➤ While reading your textbook or reviewing your notes, think of questions about the material. Imagine you are the teacher; what questions would you ask the class?

➤ Write each question on an index card; also write down any terms that you should probably know. Record the answer or explanations on the other side. Use your own words whenever possible.

---

[2]Created by Joe Landsberger, University of St. Thomas, St. Paul, Minnesota.

➤ Give your stack of cards a good shuffle, so that you can't figure out answers based on their location in the deck.

➤ Read the first card in the deck. Try to answer the question or explain the term. If you know it, pat yourself on the back and put the card at the bottom of the deck. If you miss the answer, insert the card somewhere in the middle of the deck so you'll come back to it soon.

➤ Proceed through the cards until you have all the material down pat.

Extra study tips:

— Take your cards with you wherever you go. Test yourself whenever you have a few unoccupied minutes.

— If you think you know an answer but can't put it into words, consider it a wrong answer. Being able to explain it is the only sure way to tell that you have mastered the information.

— Consider testing yourself where nobody can see you (and think that you have lost your mind). Alone, you can say the answers out loud. That's the best way to be sure that you can explain them.

— Study with a classmate. Sharing ideas and trading information helps you learn.

Still another method is called Four Steps to Mastery. An explanation of its parts follows.

4S = M
(Four Steps Equal MASTERY)

PRELIMINARY SURVEY: Recall yesterday's assignment, and associate it to the new assignment. Read topic headings, summary paragraphs, study questions, or if the textbook lacks these, the topic sentences of the paragraphs.

READING THE ASSIGNMENT: Read for ideas, do not read word by word. Turn the units of thought of the chapter into questions.

QUICK REVIEW: Retrace your steps quickly through the assignment by skimming, looking for the main ideas.

SUMMARIZE THE ASSIGNMENT: Write, if you can, a summary that contains all the important information found in the assignment. If you lack the time to write the summary, prepare it mentally.

Finally, here is a study system that goes by the acronymn M.U.R.D.E.R., borrowed from Joe Landsberger, University of St. Thomas, St. Paul, Minnesota.

M.U.R.D.E.R.

➤ **Mood:** Get into a positive mood. Choose a good time and place to study, and approach the study session with an upbeat attitude.

➤ **Understand:** Make a note of any information that puzzles you.

➤ **Recall:** After studying a chapter or an assignment, put what you have learned into your own words.

➤ **Digest:** Go back to what you did not understand and reconsider the information. If you still don't get it, ask a classmate or your teacher for help as soon as you can.

➤ **Expand:** Ask yourself three kinds of questions about the material:
- If I could speak to the author, what would I ask or what criticism would I offer?
- How can I apply this material to me personally or to what I am interested in?
- How can I make this information interesting and understandable to others?

➤ **Review:** Go over the material once, twice, three times, or however often it takes to master it.

The best study methods will cause you to think carefully about your assignments and put information into new categories. They will enable you to make the relationships among pieces of information stand out and make your own sense of what you read. In making sense out of the assignment, you will have made the assignment part of you and thus much easier to remember. The study methods also have the benefit of organizing vast quantities of information into manageable units, so that when you review for quizzes and exams, you will be studying from well-organized notes that will quickly tell you what you need to know and will not be forced to create order out of chaos in the limited amount of time available at exam time.

TIPS FOR GOOD STUDY HABITS

➤ Use your own experience to judge which study method works best for you.

➤ Concentrate as you study. Do whatever you need to do to make sure that you understand what you read. Do not allow yourself to go passively over what you do not know; instead, try to psyche yourself up to be enthusiastic about what you are learning.

➤ Set a goal each time you sit down to study—not merely to fill up half an hour, but to answer fifteen questions, write three complete paragraphs, finish the lab report that is due on Monday, and so on. Set your goal high enough to make it a challenge. If your expectations are too high, however, you'll feel frustrated by failure. But excessively low expectations will waste your effort and time.

➤ Work in a nondistracting environment. If a nearby frisbee game, the chatter of friends, or an overheated room keeps you from concentrating, vacate that space. If you can't move, grin and bear it, but try the next time to find a place free of distraction.

➤ Pay attention to all the visual and semantic clues in your textbooks. Textbooks are not written to be read as one reads a novel. They are organized to present a specific amount of material in a definite way. Authors put in illustrations, diagrams, maps, and charts to highlight important information. Authors also use phrases and words such as *generally* and *the two main reasons* . . . and many others to introduce major points. If you pay attention to graphic and semantic clues, you will be better able to identify what is important in what you read.

➤ Arrange for variety in your studying. Try not to study in blocks of time longer than 60 minutes. After an hour switch to a new subject or switch what you are doing, perhaps moving from reading to writing. This variety will help you maintain your concentration and keep a high level of efficiency.

➤ Prepare a worksheet for each assignment. For example, a worksheet for a reading assignment might consist of the following steps:

4S = M WORKSHEET

Step 1: *Preliminary Survey*

    a. What do you know already about this assignment from what you have learned in class?

    b. Read the summary at the end of the chapter and make a list of topics covered by the assignment.

    c. If there are study questions instead of a summary, read and learn from the questions what topics the assignment covers. Write a list of the topics.

Step 2: *Reading the Assignment*
  a. Read the assignment *actively,* looking for the topics you have listed in part b or c of step one above. Turn major thought units of the chapter into questions.
  b. Write the page number(s) on which you find the topics you have listed or on which you find the answers to the study questions.
  c. Take notes in outline form, using the $^1/_3$–$^2/_3$ format on your page or computer screen (see Chapter 7, pages 97–102, for details).
  d. If you draw a map of the chapter, make sure to allow space for revising and highlighting your map (see Chapter 7, pages 103–109, for a discussion of mapping).

Step 3: *Quick Review*
  a. Answer orally the study questions found at the end of the chapter.
  b. Orally, recite the topics covered in the assignment (if there are no study questions).
  c. Write down the topics covered in the assignment that you were unable to predict during your Preliminary Survey.
  d. Write down questions you think your teacher might ask on a test.

Step 4: *Summarizing the Assignment*
  a. Write a summary of all the important information found in the assignment.
  b. If you lack the time to write the summary, prepare it mentally.

Using these guidelines, prepare a worksheet for each assignment. After completing each worksheet, insert it in your notebook directly in front of the pages containing your class notes. It will serve as a handy introduction to material you may need to study for major tests and will enable you to prepare yourself more efficiently.

If you prefer to take notes on a personal computer or a laptop, create a template of a study worksheet. As you read, fill in the answers to the questions. When you are finished, save your work and print a copy to insert in your notebook. Then, even when you are far away from your computer, you will have material to read and review.

LOOKING BACK

1. While trying the SQ3R method, which of the five steps—Survey, Question, Read, Recite, and Review—did you find the most useful and productive? Was one step considerably harder than the others? Was one step easier?

2. Do you find the PQRST method more effective or less effective than the SQ3R method? Please explain why. Tell why you would (or would not) use either of these methods in the future.

3. If you had to explain the preview techniques to beginners, what would you say? Which features of previewing would you highlight?

4. All schools offer a variety of courses, but it is rare for a school to give a course called "How to Study." Can you explain this omission? If your school were to add such a course to its curriculum, would you take it? Why or why not?

Chapter 5
Studying for Different Courses

TRUE CONFESSIONS

1. The major subject areas in high school are English, social studies, mathematics, science, and foreign languages. Which of those areas give you the most trouble? Explain the reasons for your difficulty.

2. Statistics show that boys tend do better than girls on the math section of the SAT. In contrast, girls score higher than boys on the verbal section. How can this be explained? Do these facts surprise you, or do they merely confirm what you already knew or have observed?

3. Visitors to countries where English is a foreign tongue have doors of opportunity opened to them when they can speak and read the local language. Peace Corps volunteers begin their training with a total immersion course in the language of their host country. Military officers attend a foreign language school in Monterey, California, before being posted to many overseas assignments. And multinational corporations are ever on the lookout for bilingual employees to work in countries around the world.

Do you aspire to spend time abroad? If so, are you ready for the hard work it takes to master a foreign language?

SUCCESS BEGINS WITH INTEREST

The word *educate* is closely related to the word *educe*. In the oldest pedagogic sense of the term, this meant drawing out of a person something potential or latent. We can, after all, learn only in relation to what we already know. Again, contrary to common misconceptions, this means that, if we don't know very much, our capability for learning is not very great.[1]

The desire to learn, to know, to become educated, comes from within. No one can learn for you, no one can become educated for you. When it comes to acquiring an interest in knowing, you are on your own. If you are lucky, you have a curious mind and a love of learning, and you probably think that school is a fairly decent place to be—better, say, than a bowling alley. On the other hand, if school bores you, perhaps you'd rather be bowling.

Nevertheless, as a person who someday might like to do more than knock down pins all day, your current responsibility is to *try* to become interested in your studies.

No one can be expected to be enamored of every course and every assignment in school. To do well in a subject you dislike, in fact, takes willpower, resilience, and determination—three characteristics generally valued in our culture. The good news is that students who, in spite of themselves, accept the challenge of improving their performance in a subject that ordinarily turns them off sometimes reap unexpected rewards—a surprising affection for the subject, for

---

[1] Neil Postman and Charles Weingartner, *Teaching as a Subversive Activity* (New York: Delta, 1969), 62.

example. Feelings of drudgery vanish, replaced by appreciation, and respect. But don't take this author's word. Find out for yourself by making a massive effort in your least favorite subject.

RELISH FOREIGN LANGUAGES

Speech, man's greatest invention, is the thing that makes us what we call "human" rather than "animal," the thing that provides a memory for mankind and the basis of all culture and civilization. This heritage is just as significant in Hebrew, Greek, Latin, French, German, Italian, Spanish, Chinese, and Japanese as it is in English. You can, therefore, approach the study of another language from the point of view that language study is one of the most broadening and cultural elements of your education.

Whether you are trying to learn Spanish, Chinese, Urdu, or any other language, there are many techniques for sharpening your skill. Whatever methods you favor, they all begin with attitude. In other words, the desire to learn must burn inside you. Without the passion, in no time at all you may find yourself throwing in the towel.

Once resolved to become as fluent as possible in the language of your choice, you might try several of the following suggestions, or adapt them to suit your needs and circumstances:

➤ Tune to foreign language radio stations or foreign language cable channels. They broadcast the news, show movies, advertise products, engage in gossip, tell stories, play pop and folk songs. (Although you may not understand every word, you'll be hearing the language the way native speakers use it.)

➤ Go to foreign movies. Try to avoid reading the subtitles unless you really are clueless about the meaning of the dialogue.

➤ Invite your foreign language teacher to lunch. Find a friend to join you, and speak only in the language from appetizer to dessert.

➤ Check out books, records, cassettes, and other materials from the library in town, in school, or, if available, in the office of the foreign language department. Your teacher may also have some materials that you might borrow.

➤ Get on the Internet and join a chat group in the language of your choice. On-line, you can easily start a correspondence with a student in a far-off land.

➤ Every day the Internet contains newspapers from around the world. Make it a habit to peruse the headlines of papers in Paris, Munich, Rome, Tokyo, or almost any other major city.

➤ Practice reading aloud, with or without an audience. As your confidence grows, invite spectators who know the language and can help you analyze your pronunciation.

➤ If you get the chance to travel, take advantage of the opportunity to use the language as much as you can. In the United States, visit foreign consulates where the language is spoken. (Some consulates hand out lots of free literature, run lending libraries, show movies, and so forth.) Going abroad? Fly the native airline, talk to immigration and airport personnel, hotel and restaurant staff, fellow travelers, and other passengers. While abroad, visit the universities, youth clubs, and other places where people of your age will be happy to engage you in conversation.

Of course, learning a foreign language can't be all fun and games. There will come a time when, to hasten the process, you'll have to buckle down and start memorizing. You learned your first language slowly and with a great amount of repetition and practice. You used sounds over and over again—practice and more practice. In time, you could think in terms of words without having to say them out loud. As you learn a new language, practice, practice, and more practice is going to be a very important part of the program.

From rules of grammar you will learn how the words are arranged in sentences to impart meaning. You may learn to read some of the language and speak it before you learn the technical elements of grammar. You certainly did this with your first language. Learning the fundamentals of grammar is, perhaps, a sound way to start learning a second language, but many schools, including your own, may use a combination of teaching techniques to help you learn quickly and correctly.

To Memorize: Write and Recite

➤ Memorization is the key to learning vocabulary and the forms of various parts of speech, especially nouns, verbs, and adjectives. The first step in memorizing is to determine what it is that you need to learn. Certainly, your teacher will tell you precisely what you ought to know.

➤ The next step: Write down what you need to know. To build vocabulary, write the words on cards, the foreign word on one side, the English definition on the reverse. Or write words and their meanings in parallel columns on notebook paper. Study the words by covering either column and quizzing yourself.

➤ The third step in memory work is to recite *out loud* the whole stack of cards or lists until you know them perfectly without looking. In the case of a list, start by breaking the list up into small groups, seven items to a group; learn the first group, then go on to the second. When you have learned the second, go back over the first and second together; then proceed to the third group, and so on, until you have learned all the words. Then put the list aside, and after eight to twenty-four hours, review the list *out loud,* again in the small groups, until you can run through the list perfectly once more without looking. The best time for such recitation and review may be immediately before going to bed—(Your mind may continue to review the list while you sleep!)—and upon awaking. The fourth step is once again to review orally the material to be learned within two days, and then within seven days. If you follow this procedure, the words may stay with you forever.

➤ Say the rules of grammar out loud until you know them by heart. Then use the rules constantly. Make them part of you. It may also help to compare and contrast the rules of grammar of a foreign language with the rules of grammar for English.

➤ Practice in listening and speaking will develop your oral command of the language. Your teacher is likely to be a good model. Also, pay attention to your fellow students; as they recite, recite silently along with them, note their errors and the teachers' corrections.

➤ Reading and translating are two similar but distinct skills. Both require you to understand what a passage says and means. To translate, you must be able to write accurately in English what the passage says. To read, you must understand, in the language itself, what a passage says. Fortunately, the same study techniques improve both skills. Read phrase by phrase rather than word by word, and guess at the vocabulary from context before looking up new words in a dictionary. Keep lists of words and idiomatic expressions you had to look up three or more times, and memorize them.

Hints for Language Study

1. Imitate fluent speakers as much as you can. Imitate your teacher and use your school's language lab.
2. Memorize vocabulary and forms until you know them and can recall them accurately, and study the grammar of English and the language you are learning.
3. Study *out loud* as much as you can.
4. Space your studying effectively. Break assignments up into small units, and review after every two or three units. Break your study time into periods of about twenty minutes. After each period, take a five-minute break from hard studying, to review quickly or even to get up and move around a bit.
5. *Study every day.* When you are learning a foreign language, you are embarking on a journey through an unknown wilderness. Study every day, or you may lose your way.

No doubt the most effective way to improve foreign language skills is to use the language as often as possible. In reality, however, many people avoid speaking the language because they fear making mistakes. They can't express themselves easily, they are bashful, and most of all, they are afraid of being laughed at. But if you can overcome any inhibitions you may feel and give yourself a chance to shine, take the plunge. Begin with some of the suggestions in this chapter. They could take you far, and once you have succeeded a couple of times, there may be no stopping you!

ENGLISH GIVES MEANING TO FEELING

By now you must have noticed that this book emphasizes the importance of words and how important it is to learn and use them correctly and wisely. Reading and writing, after all, are the foundation of most learning. Words, and the beauty and power that can be coaxed from them, have made possible—for better or worse—the achievements and influence of figures like Lincoln, Lenin, Churchill, and Martin Luther King, Jr. Words can move us to tears and to action, and they give humankind the unique ability to express ideas and utter thoughts that have never been uttered before.

In your English courses, you are given the opportunity to develop your word power—as a reader, a writer, a speaker, and a listener. If your assignment requires that a sentence be written or spoken, make it the best sentence. If a course requires reading a novel, story or poem, or listening to a speech or oral recitation, use your head, but give your heart a chance. This is the meaning of feeling.

> To follow knowledge like a sinking star
> Beyond the utmost bounds of human thought.[2]

---

[2]Alfred Lord Tennyson, "Ulysses," *Collected Poems* (London: Macmillan Co., 1842), 72.

Literature

In English courses you will be asked to analyze literature. You will devote most of your time to fiction, but you also will read poetry, drama, essays, and non-fiction, such as biography and cultural history. As you read a work of literature, you will often be asked to know *what* the author has written, *how* the author has written it, and what *your response* has been to it.

As tools to express ideas about how authors write, your teachers and texts will use terms of literary criticism. Pay careful attention to terms such as *irony, tone, point of view, theme, plot, symbol,* and *figures of speech.* Make notes in your notebook explaining these kinds of terms and citing specific references to the work you are then reading. If you own the book you are reading, put notes in the margins.

Below are worksheets to use as you read different kinds of literature. Use them *before you read* to help your mind get set for reading critically, *while you read* to help you take notes, and *after you have read* to organize your review for tests.

WORKSHEET FOR A NOVEL

1. Who is the author? When and where did the author live? Knowing the historical and cultural context in which the author lived may shed light on the meaning and purpose of the novel.
2. What is the novel's title? Where and when does the story take place?
3. Who are the major characters? What are their most important characteristics? How do the characters relate to one another? What function does each

character play in the story –hero? villain? source of conflict? lover? victim? antagonist?

4. Is the narrator the main character, a secondary character in the story, or an observer? Is the narrator omniscient or partly omniscient? (To put it another way, is the story told in first person or third person?)

5. How is the novel organized or structured? Is it chronological? Is it a recollection of the past? Does its structure reflect character, theme, conflict, setting, or some other aspect of the novel?

6. Is there anything distinctive about the author's use of language? About the tone of the novel? About the use of description and/or dialogue? Is the story told realistically? Is it pure fantasy? Or does it contain elements of both the real and the unreal?

7. What are some of the novel's most important themes? In one sentence,what ideas is the author trying to convey?

WORKSHEET FOR A SHORT STORY

1. What is the title of the story? When was the story written? Who is the author?

2. Where and when does the story take place?

3. Who tells the story? Is the narrator a character in the story? Is the narrator omniscent? Partly omniscient?

4. Who is the main character? What are that person's chief characteristics? Who are the secondary characters? What role do they play in the story? Which characters, if any, change during the course of the story?

5. What is the conflict in the story? Is it resolved? How? Does its resolution contribute to the story's overall meaning?

6. Is the author's use of language distinctive in any way?
7. What is the story's climax?
8. What is the theme or main purpose of the story? What does it say about life or the human condition?
9. What is the significance of the story's title?

WORKSHEET FOR A PLAY

1. What is the title? Who wrote the play? When?
2. Where and when does the action take place?
3. What is the role, if any, of stage directions in the script?
4. Who are the main characters? How would you describe them? How are they affected by the setting, by the circumstances in which they find themselves, and by the other characters?
5. What, if anything, do you learn about events leading up to the opening scene?
6. How is the play organized? How much time passes between the beginning and the end?
7. What is the conflict or problem that the play presents? How is it resolved?
8. Do figurative language, symbolism, irony, or any other literary technique contribute to the point of the play?
9. Is the play tragic, comic, semi-serious, historical, social, or some combination of these or other qualities?
10. Can you state in a sentence what the play's main theme is?

WORKSHEET FOR A POEM

---

1. Who is the speaker, and to whom is the speaker talking?
2. What is the background of the poem? What circumstances have led up to it?
3. What happens during the poem?
4. What is the speaker's purpose and/or tone?
5. How does the language of the poem contribute to its meaning?
6. How is the poem organized?
7. Do patterns of rhyme and rhythm contribute to the meaning and effect of the poem?
8. What themes or motifs does the poem contain?

WORKSHEET FOR AN ESSAY

---

1. What are the title, author, and date of the essay?
2. What is the essay's main idea? What is the author trying to illustrate, argue, or prove?
3. What is the essay's main organizational mode? Description? Narration? Process analysis? Cause and effect? Argumentation? Comparison and contrast? Definition? Other?
4. Is there anything distinctive about the author's use of language? How does the language fit the subject matter and purpose of the essay?
5. What is the tone of the essay? How does the tone fit the subject matter and purpose of the essay?

Expository Writing

In English classes you'll be asked to write essays on the literature you are reading or on a subject either assigned by the teacher or of your own choosing. As you write, you will be demonstrating what you know about the topic, the quality of your thinking, and your ability to write clearly, compellingly and correctly. In a sense, then, composing an essay is the culmination of your training in English.

For your essay writing to be forceful, you need to organize your thoughts carefully, present your arguments in a logical manner, and write sentences that are not only grammatical but also interesting to read. To organize your thoughts, create a brief outline, either on paper or in your mind, before writing; and as you create the outline, review the order of your ideas to check for a logical arrangement. To write sentences that are interesting to read, vary their structure. Use both short and long sentences. Try to incorporate simple sentences along with compound and complex ones. A string of sentences each with the same or similar structure makes for monotonous reading. Variety can inject life into dull prose. Try it!

Usage and Grammar

In addition to the study of literature and to the development of your skills as a writer, you will study usage and grammar in English class. Although usage and grammar are often used interchangeably, usage describes the actual written and spoken language, and standard usage is that language used by educated people, many of whom occupy positions of respect in society. Grammar, on the other hand, is a set of rules, based on Latin, that describes or defines the way language is to be used. In your English class, you will probably receive some instruction in both usage and grammar. Like any complex system of rules, grammar takes time to master. Perseverance helps, but avoid getting bogged down trying to memorize every detail. Rather, save your energy for clearing up those problems in English usage that seem to recur in your speech and writing. When a paper is returned to you with a grade and a comment, it may often be marked up with various symbols that indicate errors. For example, your teacher may have pointed out a problem in agreement, or a faulty reference, or an incomplete sentence, or a comma splice. (Sometimes the number of possibilities for error seems infinite.) In order to correct the errors it helps considerably to know grammatical terminology. For instance, in the following sentence there is a problem with the agreement between subject and verb.

> <u>Delivery</u> (singular subject) of today's newspapers and magazines <u>have been</u> (plural verb) delayed.

Perhaps your ear will tell you that something is amiss in this sentence, but if not, you might easily figure out the problem if you knew the grammatical rule that subjects and verbs must agree in number and were familiar with the concepts of *subject, verb, singular*, and *plural*. It would help, too, if you knew that any noun that lies within a prepositional phrase (of today's newspapers and magazines) may never be the subject of a sentence.

The grammar textbook that you use in school may be of the traditional sort and use such terms as these, or it may not follow tradition and use other terms to describe the components of sentences. Regardless of the style, it will use terminology to name the functions of words and parts of sentences; and it will be advantageous to know them.

One way to learn grammatical terms is to commit them to memory, just as you would memorize the parts of the human anatomy or the pieces that comprise an internal combustion engine. Unless you use the terms regularly, however, they're not apt to stick. Instead of memorizing, then, buy a good grammar book to keep by your side. Consult it as you would a dictionary or thesaurus. Whenever your papers are returned with errors marked, consult the book or arrange a writing conference with your teacher to discuss the problems. If the same errors recur on paper after paper, then it's time to approach the problem diligently and systematically. In your notebook make lists of those errors, devise and study flashcards, ask your teacher for grammatical exercises. By paying close attention to the few errors you find yourself making consistently, you are certain to eliminate them from your writing. Concentrating on a handful of errors is a far more realistic approach than trying to grasp all the complexities of English grammar in one fell swoop.

Turn to Chapter 11 for more details on grammar and usage. *P.184*

HISTORY—THE WISDOM OF THE AGES

The ancient historian Herodotus probably never asked what history was good for; he considered it the ultimate form of entertainment. Thucydides, who came soon after, found in history a deeper and more useful good—lessons for the future from incidents of the past. He and many others down through the ages recorded events when they saw the desirability of preserving their collective story for the generations that would be born after they were gone. "History makes men wise," said Francis Bacon. Also believing that history and intelligence are related, Supreme Court Justice Oliver Wendell Holmes observed that, "A page of history is worth a volume of logic." Thinking it foolish to ignore history, George Santayana wrote, "Those who cannot remember the past are condemned to repeat it."

Each generation rewrites the history of the world in light of the problems it faces. No one living, say, during American's colonial period could have conceived of a world preoccupied with such issues as terrorism and global warming. Nor can we in the twenty-first century really understand life in eighteenth-century America, although as a result of studying it, we can appreciate what it probably was like. Imagine, for instance, life at a snail's pace, when it took weeks to travel from Boston to New York and months for a letter mailed in Philadelphia to be delivered in London or Paris.

Students sometimes miss the beauty of history because they study it piecemeal. They are aware only of its parts—the names, dates, events, and people. They have lots of trivial facts at their command but lack understanding of interrelationships. They don't have a handle on the geographical or cultural implications of historical events. They don't see themselves as an integral part in the unfolding drama of history, and worse, they have a blurred vision of their own role in the world and its future.

Well-educated and well-informed people can put themselves into history—not by performing great world-shaking deeds but simply by thinking historically and by studying the documents of history. A grasp of history enables you to make up your own mind about issues of the day instead of relying on the opinions of others. Was it right for the United States to invade Iraq in early 2003? Or was it a grievous mistake? Your understanding of history will give you an answer. Was it wise for America to send men to the moon in the 1960s and 1970s, or was it a pointless adventure? Your knowledge of our history since then will lead you to a thoughtful answer.

And so on. In school, studying history will enable you to marshall facts to support your opinions. You will be able to assess your sources when you do research, judging whether they are eyewitness accounts (primary sources) or secondhand accounts (secondary sources). You also will be able to determine the bias of your source and judge the validity of the information it contains.

To succeed as a student of history you will need to pay particular attention to facts, trends, and patterns, for without them you will be unable to support your arguments in your essays. Use the *who, where, when, what*, and *why* method for remembering details of your history lesson. Put the person in the right place at the right time, know *what* was done and *why* it was done. The five w's make a complete picture; they bring the parts of the puzzle together.

For example: Early in World War II, Hitler, frustrated by his Luftwaffe's failure to subdue Britain from the air during the spring and autumn of 1940, turned east and invaded Russia in June of 1941, in violation of the Nazi–Soviet nonaggression pact he had signed with Stalin. In so doing, Hitler created a two-front war, a situation his generals had hoped to avoid. The five w's also make an outline through which the entire dramatic story of Hitler's fateful blunder will come back to you.

If you practice the *who, where, when, what,* and *why* method for remembering your history lesson, you will find that many details, once lost, will remain with you. The five w's method of creating a complete picture of events is used by newspaper writers to present a clear story, and by lawyers to present clear and complete evidence to juries in court. Use it for studying your history lesson.

Hints for Studying History

1. Keep a list of important names, dates, events, and ideas in your notebook at the front of the section of notes.
2. Use a study method, as discussed in Chapter 5. History is the academic discipline best suited to the use of study methods.
3. Use a worksheet to summarize the contents of your textbook. Use the sample work sheet that follows, or adapt it as you see fit.

WORKSHEET FOR TEXTBOOK ASSIGNMENTS IN HISTORY

---

1. What does a preview tell me abou the contents of the assignment?
2. What can I find out about this assignment from a quick scan of the boldface type?
3. What do the study questions at the and of the chapter tell me about the assignment?
4. How does this assignment relate to previous assignments?
5. Read the assignments and take notes, using the $1/3$–$2/3$ format (see Chapter 7).

6. What topics of importance was I unable to predict in Part 2 and 3?
7. What are the important names, dates, in this assignment? *Remember* the five *w's—who, where, when, what, why.*
8. What questions will my teacher ask on tests about this assignment?

As part of your study of history, you may be asked to write research papers; and in doing the research for these, you will need to pay attention to the special demands the academic discipline of history places upon you. In addition to the regular requirements of research, you will need to weigh the validity of your sources. Primary sources are documents, letters, papers, speeches, and the like, that were written by people directly involved in the process or event you are investigating. These documents are eyewitness accounts, so to speak. Because they were written by people close to the origin of the event, these documents are to be considered of greater value than opinions written by men and women not directly involved. Newspaper or magazine articles, and books written by men and women who did not take part in the event are called secondary sources.

If, for example, you were doing a research paper on President Harry Truman's decision to drop the atomic bomb on Hiroshima and Nagasaki, primary sources would be notes, letters, and memoranda written by the president and his military, scientific, and political advisors. Secondary sources would include such works as *Danger and Survival* by McGeorge Bundy and *Truman*, a biography by David McCullough.

You may find it helpful to use worksheets in addition to your regular note-taking method when you are doing your research, so as to help you distinguish your primary sources from your secondary ones, and to weigh the importance of each source. Below are two sample worksheets.

WORKSHEET FOR PRIMARY SOURCES IN HISTORY

1. Who is the author of this document?
2. What do I know about the author?
3. When did the author write the document?
4. What sort of document is this? (Letter, speech, *etc.*)
5. For what purpose did the author write?
6. What can I expect to get out of this document?
7. What does this document say? (Write your notes according to the system you have already determined to use—on notecards, for example.)
8. Does this document meet my expectations, as I expressed them in my answer to Question 6? If not, why not?
9. What topics does this document encourage me to study in other sources or texts?

WORKSHEET FOR SECONDARY SOURCES IN HISTORY

1. Who is the author of this work? When did the author write this work?
2. Does this author present a balanced argument? Or is his argument biased? If so, how?
3. For what purpose am I reading this work?
4. Make notes, according to the system you already have determined to use—on notecards, for example.

5. What other secondary sources does this work suggest I read?
6. What primary sources does this work suggest I read?

MATHEMATICS—GOING FOR IT BIG TIME

The ancient fascination and feeling for numbers have been passed down to us through the millenia. Centuries ago people sitting in a cave may have counted their fingers and discovered the number 10. And thus mathematics was born. If our ancestors had only four fingers, the structure of mathematics might be completely different. On the banks of the Euphrates River, about five thousand years ago, a people we call Sumerians assigned particular significance to the number 10, and today our decimal system is based on that all-important number.

The pages of history make it very clear that feeling for mathematics never slackened once numbers were discovered. The ancient Egyptians used a forty-inch measuring reed (called the *canon*) to lay out the Great Pyramid, which covers thirteen acres. The ancient Babylonians measured and laid out irrigation ditches and discovered geometry—the measuring of the earth. So this is mathematics, simple and mystic, practical and romantic, measuring the height of a newborn child in inches and the distance to a star in light years—one about twenty-one inches, the other 5,880 billion miles.

Mathematics can serve you profitably and give you much pleasure, or you can serve it as a resentful slave, waiting to finish the last required course. The basic step for you, as with all subjects, is to develop an interest in the intrinsic value of mathematics and in its importance to our lives.

To appreciate the value of mathematics, it is best to approach it as a way of looking at things, The poet sees the world in one light, the mathematician in another, and it follows that if you enjoy looking at things in literature through the eyes of the poet, you are capable of looking at things as seen through the eyes of the mathematician.

In addition to making the world around you more interesting, mathematics can serve you in the following ways.

➤ It can improve your ability to think clearly and precisely. Although there is a great deal of memorization and recall in the study of mathematics, there is also the application of knowledge, the applying of old patterns to new things, calling on you to use your hunch or best guess to find a new relationship that was not anticipated when you began a problem.

➤ The study of mathematics can improve your powers of observation. No reading requires keener observation of exactly what is written and precisely what is being asked.

➤ The study of mathematics and its history can provide an appreciation for the marvelous workings of the mind of man. We could learn how some 2,200 years ago, Eratosthenes, with a deep well in Syrene, Upper Egypt and a post hole at Alexandria, 574 miles away, and an angle of 70° 12″ to the sun, calculated the circumference of the earth to be 24,662 miles—missing by only 195 miles, or an error of less than one percent. Or we could study Euclid, whose geometry was used longer than any other work except for the Bible; or Archimedes, perhaps one of the half-dozen greatest thinkers who ever lived. Or we could study the work of earth's space scientists, who, with the aid of computers, can determine the exact moment when a speeding asteroid will crash headlong onto the surface of the planet Jupiter, millions of miles away.

But our feeling for arithmetic, algebra, or geometry cannot long survive based only on the history of mathematics. A practical approach is necessary—a study of our own skills and an understanding of the language of mathematics.

There are tests available in the basic skills—handling of decimals, word problems—that can be used to identify areas of weakness. Such tests include SAT I and the ACT, samples of which are available in bookstores everywhere. Your math teacher may also be able to give you drills, exercises, and tests. You also could keep track of the mistakes you make on homework papers. Once you have identified trouble areas, you can take sensible steps to be aware of your problems and check your work on them carefully.

A real feeling for mathematics will develop with understanding of words and definitions. Although the scope of mathematics has increased more in the past fifty years than it did in twenty-two centuries from Euclid to Einstein, the vocabulary has grown even faster. The old words—addition and multiplication—are still in use, but new words and phrases—transformations, imaginary numbers, spreadsheets, composition, quantifiers, matrices—are now appearing in math books. You will need to use the definitions found in the particular book you are studying, so the index should be used as a guide to review basic words until you know them.

There are several things you also can do to enhance your performance in mathematics classes.

➤ Take note of the format of the textbooks you use. These books may have visual aids to help you identify significant ideas: different colors of print, shaded areas, or boxes. Your textbooks also will have sample problems, with all the steps included, in order to show you the necessary steps in the correct process of reaching an answer. And, of course, there will be many problems for you to solve by using the procedures illustrated by the sample problems. In many recent textbooks there is an answer key at the back so that you may check your work for accuracy.

➤ Pay close attention in class to what your teacher is saying and doing, and make careful notes. (Be sure to label your paper as class notes, and be sure to put the date at the top.) Copy down the problems your teacher solves on the board, since they will probably be problems containing the essence of the topic under discussion. (These problems may also be typical of problems you will find on quizzes and tests.) To avoid potential confusion when you study, keep separate sections in your notebook for class notes and for homework.

➤ As soon as you can after math class, neatly rewrite the notes you took in class that day, separating the important material from the scratch work. Then review your notes regularly. You will also gain ground if you rework the problems your teacher put on the board during class. If you can't do this soon after class, try to get to it before beginning your homework. By solving these problems again, you will be reinforcing all the knowledge you have gained from that day's class.

➤ Try to be as neat as you can when taking notes in class, when completing assignments, and when taking tests. Write your symbols clearly and large enough to be read easily. Also, try to be complete, showing the work you have done to reach the answer. Finally, when you are doing homework, leave space for your corrections, so that if your solution is wrong, you can correct the error on the page.

➤ Read your text carefully; read with paper and pencil in hand; and as you read, notice the visual aids in the text and what they are highlighting. When you come across a sample problem, cover the solution with paper and solve the problem yourself. Then check your solution with the one in the text to make sure that you have the correct answer and that you have included all the proper steps.

➤ Do all homework assignments only after reading your text, solving the sample problems correctly, and reviewing your notes from class. You can never review enough. After you have solved an assigned problem, compare your answer with the one in the answer key at the back of the textbook. If your answer is incorrect, solve the problem again, and compare your answer again. If you still are incorrect, put a star beside the problem on your homework paper, and ask your teacher about that problem at the start of your next class.

➤ Perhaps most important of all, keep all old quizzes and tests. Quizzes will show what your teacher thinks is important and will identify typical problems. Use these quizzes as guides for studying for tests, and solve the problems on them again as part of your test preparation. Because tests on a chapter of the textbook will identify problems of major significance, you will benefit if you use them as study guides for unit tests and exams.

➤ Finally, practice math on a calculator. Calculators eliminate arithmetical errors and enable you, among other things, to use logarithms, find standard deviations, and calculate maximums and minimums. Mastering the functions of a calculator saves lots of time and trouble, and has transformed many a student's attitude toward learning and studying math.

Along with calculators, computers have changed the face of mathematics instruction. Even if computer instruction is not part of your school's curriculum, you can teach yourself how to use spreadsheets and graphing programs. Computers give you insights into organizing and visualizing mathematical problems and information, not to mention new and attractive ways to present solutions.

Although calculators and computers are marvelous tools, they can't do the learning for you. Don't be lulled into complacency by their power and incredible speed. As tools of learning they are indispensible, but they can't take the place of the human brain—not yet, at any rate.

➤ Help with math is available on many Internet sites. For example, if you are stuck on a problem or have questions about a particular math topic, just ask Dr. Math. The good doc can be found at *mathforum.org* and has material for students working at every level from basic arithmetic to calculus. Whether you want to know about functions, fractions, or fractals, you'll find information at the forum. You can also ask particular questions about math, but the folks who answer them will decline doing your math homework for you. Instead, they'll suggest places you can seek electronic help.

THE ROMANCE OF SCIENCE

Science courses from bio to physics, from general science to oceanography deepen appreciation of the world and add new dimensions to life. The study of science demands an exactness in reasoning, a precision in observation, and a thoroughness in execution similar to those required in mathematics; for, of course, mathematics is the tool of science.

Common to all scientific studies is a method of inquiry, usually called the scientific method. The scientific method has three basic parts: *the creation of hypotheses, the collection of data by experimentation,* and *an analysis to test the validity of the hypotheses.* These parts need not come in the order given, but for any scientific inquiry to be complete, the scientist must perform all three parts.

There are some things you can do in science class to improve the quality of your studying, things that are useful in any of the sciences.

➤ Do a quick survey of the chapters of your textbook. Is there a preliminary paragraph in the chapters that tells you what you will be learning? Are important terms printed in boldface type or in italics? Are units of the chapters numbered? Are there study questions at the end of the chapters, or perhaps summaries or review outlines? Are there visual aids to help signal important information (such things as boxes, shaded areas, different colors of print)?

➤ Look at the back of the textbook for a glossary and an index. The glossary will be helpful when you are learning new technical terms, the index will help you find a topic easily when you are reviewing. Check also for appendices. Many textbooks contain several kinds of charts, lists of important scientific laws, formulas, and other types of information. Check also for an answer key if your textbook contains problems to solve.

➤ Follow all instructions carefully when you are doing laboratory work. Take careful notes in a laboratory notebook, and make sure not to mingle your lab notes with the notes you take in class or from your textbook. Write clearly in your notebook. Illegible or incomplete lab notes may interfere with your understanding of the experiment or demonstration.

Although most science courses involve lab work and use of the scientific method, each course also has its distinctive demands.

In Biology

1. Become acquainted with systems of classifying living organisms and with the criteria used to sort living things into special groups. What, for example, distinguishes humans from simians? Or fish from whales?
2. Keep a list of biological terms and definitions in your notebook. This list may become lengthy in a short time, but terminology is a crucial part of a scientific education, especially in biology, which may in fact have more terms than any other science.
3. Pay close attention to the details of the drawings that your teacher puts on the board and that are in your textbook. Make sure that the drawings you put in your notes are both accurate and clear.

In Chemistry

1. Recognize that it is very important to know and to understand the procedures to be used in chemistry.

Learn *why* you are following a certain procedure, since merely memorizing the steps in a procedure will not usually give you sufficient knowledge to adapt it to new situations or experiments.

2. Most of the work you do in problem solving in the first year of your study of chemistry will require some knowledge of algebra. If you haven't already studied algebra when you begin chemistry, don't give up. Even without a background in algebra, you will be able to keep up in class if you work hard to understand and apply the procedures used in problem solving as they are explained in your textbook or by your teacher. Also, many chemistry textbooks contain an appendix that explains the mathematics necessary for chemistry. If you need extra help with the mathematics, look for such an appendix, or ask your teacher for extra help.

3. When reading your textbook, take notes and work out the equations given in the text.

In Physics

1. As in chemistry, in physics it is necessary for you to understand why you are using procedures and performing operations. Mere memorization of steps won't be sufficient.

2. Algebra is almost essential when you study physics. In fact, in many schools a course in algebra is a prerequisite for taking physics. If your algebra skills are rusty or non-existent, do something about it. Borrow an algebra review book from the library or the math department in your school and study it carefully. If you need help, consult with your teacher or with any math whizzes who happen to be in your class.

3. In class write the problems your teacher puts on the board clearly in your notebook, making sure to label them as class notes. It is likely these problems will be similar to the problems you will see on tests.

4. As you read your assignments, do so with paper and pencil, and practice working out problems and equations. As much as you can, practice solving problems and working out equations. Such efforts are never wasted.

LOOKING BACK

1. Mission Impossible? Imagine yourself being responsible for introducing biology to a group of young kids—all about eleven years old. You have one week to do it. What plan might you develop in order to give the group not only a taste of biology but the enthusiasm to learn more about it?

2. What does the quotation "No mathematician can be a complete mathematician unless he is also some- thing of a poet" mean to you? What possible rela- tionship is there between mathematics and poetry?

3. While this chapter has different approaches for helping you to study more effectively in the major subject areas, there are some suggestions that are common to all subjects. Can you name three of them?

Chapter 6
Listening:
An Easy Way to Learn

TRUE CONFESSIONS

"I never remember the names of people introduced to me."

"I didn't get what you said because I was thinking of what I planned to say."

"I forgot the due date for the book report. Did Mrs. Benson tell us when it had to be handed in?"

If these statements sound like you, don't despair. Take heart that you are one among many who have never thought: "God gave us two ears and one mouth. So he probably wants us to spend twice as much time listening as we do speaking."[1] Fortunately, it's possible to change your listening habits; you can train yourself, successfully, to listen better.

THE MOST DIFFICULT OF ALL LEARNING PROCESSES

It is a paradox that for most students listening is both the easiest path to learning and the hardest study skill to master. Listening must be self-taught, because it is a difficult skill for a teacher to teach.

---

[1]*Christopher News Notes.* No. 234, undated.

Why do people find listening so difficult? For four major reasons: 1) Listeners must coordinate their mental processes with others, namely with speakers, 2) listeners must move through topics and grasp meanings at the same rate as the people doing the talking, 3) listeners must follow speakers' lines of argument even if they disagree with speakers' conclusions, and 4) listening is something you must do on your own—no one can do it for you.

THE PROBLEM OF COORDINATION

Much of what you do in school is done on your own. Although you may be surrounded by crowds, you read, think, and observe by yourself. When your eyes wander across the pages of a book, you, and only you are in control of what you see and absorb. When you open a book, your abilities, desires, and interests, along with your willpower, determine both what happens inside your head and the quality of the experience.

If you permit your mind to wander while you read, you are free to do so, knowing that you can always go back and reread what you missed. When listening, however, you can't replay the speaker's words. You must get them the first time. That takes concentration, which means that, regardless of how dull you think the speaker may be, you must keep other thoughts out of your mind and pay attention to what the speaker is saying. Later, you are free to think anything you want, evaluate what you heard, and draw your own conclusions. But if you allow random thoughts to drift into your head while listening, you might as well have been somewhere else.

THE PROBLEM OF SPEAKING RATE

When you read, your eyes and brain limit your speed. When you write, your fingers and hand control the number of words you can spill onto the page or record on a computer screen. Thought travels at lightning speed. But when you start to train yourself to be a good listener, you can't go any faster than the speaker can talk; you can think many times faster than anyone speaks. Therefore, only by concentrating intensely can you force yourself to pay attention. This can be accomplished if you spend time thinking around the topic—"listening between the lines," as it is sometimes called.

It's possible, for instance, to train yourself to anticipate a speaker's next point, to summarize what you have heard, to question in silence the accuracy and importance of the words being spoken. Put the speaker's ideas into your own words, and if the speaker happens to be your bio or math teacher, try to figure out a quiz or exam question that could be developed from the words being said. If you can train yourself to do this, you will save time by not having to read and study what you already know. As a bonus, you'll find yourself becoming more interested in the subject matter and more responsive to the teacher—something that your teacher is sure to notice and appreciate.

THE PROBLEM OF WORKING ON YOUR OWN

Another stumbling block in the way of those who would become good listeners is tradition. Years were spent teaching you to read, and you accepted it as basic to your future learning and success in school.

Typically, however, you may now spend far more time learning by listening than learning by reading. Finding yourself in this situation is probably a bit puzzling. Countless times during your schooling you've probably been told to "pay attention" or "listen up." Perhaps you did so dutifully, perhaps not, but either way it's likely that you were never actually taught to do so.

The distortions that arise from careless or shoddy listening sometimes cause misunderstandings, some of them worth a chuckle or two. As a child you probably played a party game called Telephone in which a message is whispered from one person to another. Invariably the words became garbled and lost their original meaning, giving everyone a hearty laugh. Amusing, yes, but this innocent game illustrates the difficulties of listening accurately.

Consider the words of the Pledge of Allegiance. As the columnist William Safire reports, every day schoolchildren place their hands over their hearts and pledge allegiance to the flag, "and to the republic of Richard Stans," the most saluted man in America. Other kids say "I pledge a legion to the flag" or "I led the pigeons to the flag." Similarly, some children have asked "Who's José?" when they sing the opening line of the national anthem, "José, can you see, by the dawn's early light . . . ?" Another such distortion concerns the words shouted by John Wilkes Booth after he had shot Abraham Lincoln in Ford's Theater on the night of April 14, 1865. History has understood the words to be "Sic semper tyrannis," the state motto of Virginia. But a flagman on the Chicago, Aurora and Elgin Railroad gave Carl Sandburg another version. He had heard it differently: "This man Booth," said the flagman, "he shot the President, jumped down onto the stage and hallooed, 'I'm sick, send fer McGinnis!' "

FEW DO BUT MANY CAN

The late Columbia University Professor Jacques Barzun observed that only the rarest minority ever become experts in the art of listening: "Nothing is more rare: listening seems to be the hardest thing in the world. . . . In a lifetime one is lucky to meet six or seven people who know how to listen. . . ." [2]

Psychologists and educators agree. Through a series of extensive tests given after lectures, recordings, and discussions, they have compiled statistics that show that very few people are able to retain even half of what they have heard.

Nevertheless, listening well is invaluable. Businesspeople and attorneys, executives and physicians, teachers and politicians, and especially successful students understand that good listening skills are assets not only on the job but in life. And the good news is that listening is not only teachable, but that you can learn to do it on your own. In fact, communications specialists estimate that motivated people can double their listening proficiency with a few months' effort.

THE CLASSROOM AS A PROVING GROUND

On the next pages you'll find ideas for training yourself to listen both in the classroom and elsewhere. You'll also find several common practices to avoid. Before proceeding, however, remember what your efforts may lead to: 1) better grades, 2) more efficient use of time, 3) greater enthusiasm for your courses, and 4) increased personal satisfaction.

---

[2] Jacques Barzun, *Teacher in America* (Boston: Little, Brown, & Co., 1945), 124.

To be sure, achieving these goals is hard work, but consider this: Using a tape recorder, an educational researcher compared teachers' oral presentations in class with questions on quizzes and exams given by those teachers. In one history course, the researcher found that eighty percent of the material asked for at testing time had recently been presented orally during classroom lessons. In addition, some of the insightful questions asked by students in the class were almost identical to the questions found later on tests.

The percentage for science and mathematics classes was even higher. In several cases, demonstrations and associated instruction had presented the course so thoroughly that good listeners, capable of taking sufficiently detailed notes, could have performed well without using either text or source book. Even in English classes, questions dealing with literature interpretation showed that the answers had been discussed in class.

If you still question the chance to improve your grades by improving your ability to listen, try this simple experiment. As the class is being taught, write down what you think will be possible test questions. When testing time comes, see how many of your questions appear. If you give it a fair trial, you will need no further convincing.

TAKING NOTES: THE ULTIMATE KEY TO SUCCESS*

Following naturally from good listening habits is skill in taking notes. Good note-taking requires action on your part: attentive listening, one-track thinking about what you hear, and active writing of key ideas.

---

* Also see Chapter 7 for more on note-taking.

The format and organization of your notes are important. You won't go wrong using the following tried and true method, which applies equally to note-taking on paper or on a laptop computer: Put the date at the top of each page. Write the topic of the day on the top of the first page. Divide the paper into two columns using about one third of the width for the left column. Write your notes only in the right-hand, wider column.

Emphasize important points by indenting, leaving spaces vertically, underlining, or using boldface type or italics on your computer. These are quick and easy methods of indicating importance.

Listen for key ideas, and write them down in your own words. Avoid writing down every word of the speaker; you will become a nonthinking "scribble-maniac" if you try to take such dictation. Notes in your own words will have more meaning when you review them later. Recall of material covered will be much easier, for putting notes in your own words has made them your personal knowledge.

If you are writing by hand, don't erase if you have made an error. Simply draw a single line through the mistaken material. Such a practice is quicker than erasing and has the added benefit of leaving information on the page; you might find that it becomes useful later.

As soon as possible after a class, read your notes. As you read, fill in any gaps you may have left. Use the left-hand column on the page to highlight information, writing there the important names, dates, technical information, or any other significant terms. Such reading is a kind of review that will serve to fix the material firmly in your mind, making study for tests and exams much easier. Ideally, you should review your notes within twenty-four hours of taking them.

As you read your notes and highlight them, think actively about what you are reading. When you have finished, ask yourself questions about what you have read: what was this lesson about? what are the important points to remember? what might be on the next test? It may help to write these questions at the end of your notes, for they will serve to organize any review you may do before quizzes and exams.

Note-taking, like learning to listen, requires practice. Even though you think all the material you need is in the textbook or handouts, notes taken in class may make the reading easier by indicating those points your instructor considers important. Note-taking and listening complement each another. To become a good listener there is no better practice than note-taking. To lighten the burden of study outside of class—and to earn high grades at the same time—there is little that rewards more than thoughtful, constant, informative note-taking in class.

LISTENING AIDS FOR LECTURES AND DISCUSSIONS

➤ Estimate how much of the course material is taught in class, so you may see clearly the value of good listening.

➤ Accept responsibility for gaining as much as you can by listening in class. Don't assume that it is solely up to the teacher to get the lesson through to you. Teaching and learning is a partnership, and each partner must carry a share of the load.

➤ Listen for key words and clue phrases. Key words are those that carry great meaning and so serve as a kind of trigger for your memory. Clue phrases are the words that alert you to important information that follows; e.g., "this is important," "the three principle results are," or "don't be shocked to find this on Firday's quiz."

➤ Come to class prepared to take notes—with pen or pencil, a notebook or a laptop with a charged battery.

➤ Ahead of time, prepare a work sheet to organize your thoughts and your note-taking. Such pre-planning will start you thinking about the topic even before the lesson begins. A worksheet that many have found successful is this:

WORKSHEET FOR NOTE-TAKING FROM LECTURES

I. Ask questions on topics from prior lessons, about which you need more information or explanation. Put your teacher's answers in the appropriate place in your notes.

II. Preview

Write down in the space below what the lesson is going to be about. If you are not sure, ask your teacher.

Take a minute to reflect on the subject and predict what topics will be covered.

III. Notes

Using the $^1/_3$–$^2/_3$ format, write your notes. *Write key phrases and ideas only.*

Do not take dictation.

Leave the left-hand $^1/_3$ of paper blank—to highlight important ideas or to fill in when teacher amplifies an idea.

Take notes in your own words in the right-hand ²/₃ of the page.

IV. Question

Review your notes and:

1. Write questions to test your knowledge of what you have heard.

2. Write down questions about things you are not sure you understand, questions you need your teacher to answer at the beginning of the next class.

➤ Make your listening three-dimensional: use your eyes, ears, and mind actively to pursue knowledge. Keep your eyes on the speaker and on what is written on the board. Keep your ears critically attuned so you may note what is important in the lecture and what is good or bad in the class discussion. Keep your mind on the topic.

➤ If the teacher has given more than the textbook offers, by all means, use it in your test and homework answers. You can be fairly sure that the part of the answer the teacher will value most is the part you got from listening.

LISTENING ERRORS TO AVOID

Almost all the stupid, repetitive, and time wasting activity of the classroom that robs people of the right to learn, arises from actions of people who, as described by Professor Barzun, are "afraid to lend their mind to another's thought, as if it would come back to them bruised and bent."[3] Here are a few listening "don'ts" for the classroom:

1. Don't interrupt in the middle of an explanation to say that you don't understand. If you wait until it's finished, you may have your question answered without having to ask it.

2. Don't be too fast with a related question. Until you have trained yourself to a degree of efficiency in listening, you may often find that your question has already been answered.

3. Don't display such impatience to speak, by frantically waving or tilting forward in your desk, as though the world's future depends on what you have to say. Before you signal to speak, ask yourself, "Is this worth listening to?"—a far more important question than, "Is this worth saying?" For example, that you saw *Macbeth* on television does not add to the class's knowledge of *Macbeth*. But if the scenery for Act II, Scene III, was unusual, both teacher and class might enjoy a brief description of it.

4. Don't ever believe that speaking is more important than listening. It was Voltaire who said, "Men employ speech only to conceal their thoughts." And Socrates, one of the world's great philosophers, had the reputation of being the most patient and inquisitive listener in all Athens.

5. An in ability to listen often makes the bore, so well defined by Ambrose Bierce, "A person who talks when you wish him to listen."

---

[3]Barzun, *Teacher in America* (Boston: Little, Brown, & Co., 1945), 232.

DAILY EXERCISES IN LISTENING

All the waking hours of the day provide opportunities for practice to improve one's ability to listen. The requests made by parents that go unheard, the sounds of the world around you—the song of a bird, the interesting conversation of the two people seated next to you, the name of the person to whom you have just been introduced. The last is the one almost universal test of a poor listener. You are introduced to Tom McCabe or Joan Banks—simple sounds—yet five minutes later you say, "I'm sorry, but I missed your name." You heard the name with your ears only—your mind was making a critical assessment, your eyes were busy with the color of a sweater or a hairstyle, perhaps you were trying to place the person geographically. All these things could have followed the initial listening, but they replaced it instead. Here are some practices that will help you develop your ability to listen outside the classroom.

➤ Make a resolution each morning for two weeks that during the day no one will have to repeat a single thing said to you.

➤ Practice selectivity. As you go to and from school, or wherever you go, or whatever you are doing, there are many sounds around you. Practice picking out those you wish to hear. Close your mind to all others. John Kieran, the naturalist, could sit amid cheering thousands at a football game in the heart of New York City and pick out the "honk, honk" of a Canada goose flying south high against the November sky.

➤ Start hearing the things you really enjoy. Do you really have to play the latest Phish CD a dozen times to learn the words? The answer is "No." Test yourself—you can master the whole number with two playings.

➤ Form a team with a friend. Read each other poetry, sports scores, or whatever is of interest, and see what percentage the listener can repeat correctly.

➤ Books on tape are excellent for self-teaching. They are available at many libraries, or can be bought or rented.

➤ Develop a consciousness of your own speaking so that you will be clearly heard and understood. This will make a profound indirect contribution to your own listening ability.

LOOKING BACK

1. Here are four factors that hinder good listening:

   a. You have to coordinate your mental processes with those of the speaker.
   b. You must follow the speaker's line of argument.
   c. You must teach yourself how to listen.
   d. One typical listening error we make is interrupting in the middle of an explanation to say we don't understand. Another is believing that speaking is more important than listening. What are two other "don'ts" that were listed in this chapter?

2. What are three steps to take after a class to get the most from the notes you took?

Chapter 7
Note-Taking: Summaries, Outlines, Maps

TRUE CONFESSIONS

1. As you prepare to take quizzes and exams, can you depend on your own notes for complete and reliable information? What is the strongest point of your note-taking? The weakest?

2. Sir Francis Bacon wrote, "To spend too much time in studies is sloth." Was Bacon in need of a cold shower when he said those words, or did he have a legitmate idea in mind? How do you interpret his words?

3. Samuel Johnson, the great eighteenth-century man of letters, called note-taking a "necessary evil." Tell why you agree or disagree with Johnson.

KINDS OF NOTES

Once you have chosen a method of studying that works for you, you'd be doing yourself a favor by developing note-taking techniques that keep a clear record of what you are supposed to know. Good notes will ultimately reduce the amount of rereading you'll need to do and make important information easier to remember.

There are three basic kinds of note-taking:
1) summaries, 2) outlines, and 3) maps. All three techniques graphically represent the basic structure and

meaning of the material you must study. Each is compact, clear, and systematic, but each also has its unique features.

FORMAT

Whatever style of note-taking you favor, pay close attention to the format. If you indent, space, underscore, capitalize, or otherwise highlight key information on each page of your notes, do it consistently so that it will stand out from the rest when you sit down to study.

When you write summaries and outlines, divide the paper or computer screen into two columns, using about one-third of the width for the left-hand column. Write your notes only in the wider column. Save the left side to highlight key names, terms, dates, or noteworthy ideas you want to keep fresh in your mind as you review the material. The left column leaves room for adding notes later from your reading, from classwork, from the Internet, or any other sources of information.

WRITING SUMMARIES, PRÉCIS, AND SYNOPSES

A summary—also called a précis or synopsis— condenses the main points of a body of material. The most useful summaries 1) omit no important ideas, 2) introduce no ideas that are not in the material, 3) leave out editorial statements and generalities, 4) accurately convey the tone and point of view of the author, and 5) are written in your own words.

As you write summaries, beware of using disparate ideas taken from the text without relating them to one another. Groupings of unrelated sentences are not summaries but rather chopped-up versions of the original that may cause you to scratch your head when you go back weeks or even months later to review for an exam or to write a paper. For your own benefit, use transitions to tie ideas together. You won't go wrong if you remember that a summary should be a small, coherent composition, beginning with a topic sentence and including major and minor ideas all clearly identified.

A summary, précis, or synopsis offers several advantages: (1) a clear set of notes for review, (2) an improved ability to think and condense, (3) practice in recognizing the main points in what you read (what is important), (4) a good memory aid (your own words are easier to remember than someone else's), and (5) practice in organizing and writing smooth and complete short compositions.

Summary writing starts as a challenge. Reducing sentences to phrases, phrases to meaningful words, will require practice and the study of summaries written by others. Examine the essays in reference books; they really are summaries and are the best examples you can find to emulate. Economy of words can become an important part of your learning, as well as a real time saver. The length of a summary will vary according to your purpose and the expectations of your teachers. However, for your own review summaries, try to keep them below one-third of the size of the original text. If after extensive practice you can reduce them to one-fifth, it is even better. A well-written summary is a test of how completely you have understood a paragraph, a chapter, an assignment, or a book; and of how concisely and clearly you have been able to shorten it without loss of meaning.

Examine the text that follows. It is a summary of a chapter from a book about applying to college. Note the format, especially the items in the left column.

CRITERIA FOR COLLEGE ADMISSION

Select colleges use similar criteria	Most selective colleges use similar criteria for admitting students. First is grades in college prep courses. Then scores on standardized admissions tests (SATs or ACTs). Other factors include recommendations from teachers and counselors, extracurricular activities, the application essay, an interview with an alumnus or a member of the faculty, special talents or achievements in athletics, music, art, and almost any other field. Students who are "legacies" (family members who attended the college) and students with unusual backgrounds or who come from far-off places may also be given preferential treatment.
Some criteria given more weight than others; varies among colleges	Some colleges give more weight to test scores than to other factors. Other colleges count grades, rank in class, and the application essay as the most important criteria. The needs of a college also may play a part. If most of the swim team or marching band graduated last year, high school swimmers and musicians may have an advantage when it comes to admissions. Some students find that the college admissions system is fickle and unpredictable, almost beyond understanding. Nevertheless it seems to work. Every year hundreds of thousands of high school graduates successfully find their way into colleges they have chosen and that have chosen them.
Needs of a college make admissions unpredictable	
System works in spite of complications	

FINDING MODELS OF CONDENSING

If you have difficulty summarizing, even after honest attempts at practice, you will find it helpful to examine some models of condensing.

Look in a young person's encyclopedia, such as *World Book* or *Encarta.* Read about the history of your state or city. Read several biographies. Note carefully the division of topics, the choice of words, and the use of graphic material in dealing with population, industry, and resources. If you can find a one-volume encyclopedia, such as the *Columbia Encyclopedia,* compare the facts of an article with an article about the same topic found in a ten-volume work.

Equally as valuable as seeing how material is summarized is to learn what summaries exist ready at hand to help you. Are you enjoying your algebra class? Is the study of chemistry proving difficult for you? Are you confused about "Jacksonian Democracy" as it is presented in your textbook? Look up *algebra* in the encyclopedia. Here you will find the course, its principal parts, the methods of solving equations, and illustrations to clarify difficult problems. From a four-page summary your whole conception of the course may be changed. You may really understand for the first time what algebra is all about. Do the same for your chemistry. The enlightenment resulting from such a brief inquiry can change both your attitude, your understanding, and your mark. Check "Jacksonian Democracy" in a young person's encyclopedia, then in a larger one, or in an encyclopedia of history.

Perhaps you have more than once been in a situation similar to the student who, reading Homer's *Iliad* in poetry translation, could not follow the thread of the story. After much persuasion, he looked up the *Iliad* in the encyclopedia. There he found it summarized by books. Book II, which was causing the reader so much trouble, was summarized in nine lines; and the whole twenty-four books, the thread of the story plainly given, in three-and-a-half pages. From this time on, the student did not have to be persuaded to use the summaries available to him. He was able to read the *Iliad* and enjoy it. He discovered that the reference shelf in the library was filled with study aids, waiting to be used to clarify and to save time.

Books of facts, general encyclopedias, encyclopedias of specific subjects—history, literature, science—all contain summarized material that can provide quick clarification. Atlases, handbooks, dictionaries of all kinds, beckon from the reference shelf in the library. The use of carbon-14 to explain that Cro-Magnon man's campfire in a cave in France burned 11,000 years ago sounds complicated and difficult. Look it up in a reference book. The whole process is summarized in half a column.

Weekly news magazines and book reviews often provide excellent examples of good summarizing. The table of contents of books, single-page condensations of school subjects, Barron's *Book Notes,* can all be used to help you better understand how you can make your own summary.

THE ART OF OUTLINING

Outlining, like summary writing and mapping, improves the clarity of your thinking, promotes good organization, and boosts your ability to recall the chief components of a mass of information or a lengthy text.

In effect, an outline serves as a blueprint of ideas, a plan that 1) shows the order in which ideas are arranged, and 2) illuminates the ideas' relative importance.

The standard outline form follows five specific rules: (1) A title is placed at the beginning, but is not numbered or lettered as part of the outline. (2) Roman numerals are used to designate main topics. (3) Subtopics are designated in descending order by capital letters, Arabic numerals, then small letters, then Arabic numerals in parentheses, followed by small letters in parentheses. (4) Subtopics are indented to the right of the main topic, and divisions of the subtopics are indented to the right of the subtopics. All topics of equal rank are in the same column: all main topics on the left, subtopics indented from the main topic, divisions of subtopics indented from the subtopics, and so on. When indented, the letter of the subtopic is placed in the space directly under the first letter of the first word of the main topic, the numerals of the divisions of the subtopic are put in the space under the first letter of the first word of the subtopics and so on. (5) There are always two or more subtopics because subtopics are divisions of the topic above them, and whenever you divide anything, the minimum number of parts is two.

Outlines can do wonders when you need to organize a jumble of material and put an assortment of ideas into a logical sequence. An outline just for its own sake has little intrinsic value, but it can't be beat as a study aid and as a guide for writing a lengthy paper. Preparing some sort of outline can help you to arrange ideas and prevent both you and your readers from getting lost.

What follows illustrates the standard form for a formal outline.

CORRECT OUTLINE FORM

Title: Safe Biking

I. The right bicycle
    A. The proper fit
    B. Safety equipment
        1. Mirrors, reflectors, and lights
        2 Bike helmet
        3. Pedal straps, toeclips
II. Bike inspection
    A. Before every ride
        1. Tires
            (a) Inflation
            (b) Wheel attachment
            (c) Wheel alignment
        2. Brakes
            (a) Brake shoes
            (b) Cable tightness
    B. After every ride
        1. Dirt and water removal
        2. Bike security
        3. Storage
III. Long-term care of a bike
    A. Inspections and adjustments
        1. Weekly
            (a) Loose spokes
            (b) Suspension fork bolts
        2. Monthly
            (a) Chain and cassette
            (b) Derailleurs

        (c) Loose nuts and bolts
           (1) Seatpost binder lever or bolts
           (2) Handlebar clamp bolt
           (3) Bar-end clamp bolts
           (4) Fender, rack, and light attachments
    3. Quarterly
        (a) Brake levers and calipers
        (b) Crankset
        (c) Pedals and toeclips
  C. Lubrication
    1. Regreasing
        (a) Bottom bracket bearings
        (b) Wheel bearings
        (c) Pedal threads and bearings
    2. Lubricating
        (a) Wheel quick releases
        (b) Seatpost
        (c) Handlebar stem
IV. Safe riding
  A. Rules of the road/trail
    1. Following traffic laws
    2. Hand signals
  B. Awareness of dangers
    1. Riding with no hands
    2. Potholes, soft shoulders, drain grates, etc.
    3. Inconsiderate motorists

A formal outline isn't necessary every time you put ideas in order. Informal outlines—for example, a list of ideas ranked in order of importance—may serve your purpose just as well. While outlines are used most often for planning ahead or for summarizing a body of material, get into the habit of using them to check the organization of your own work. After writing a paper in, say, English or social studies, outline it in order to determine whether you have sufficiently and logically supported your major ideas. An outline will also reveal your paper's organizational flaws. You may discover, for instance, that your first idea might better be placed somewhere in the middle of your paper. Or perhaps that concluding statement might serve as a knockout opening. In other words, an outline can open your eyes to problems that you might otherwise overlook.

Outlines usually fall into one of several reasonable orders. Items may be arranged logically in: (1) Time (chronological) order—such as biography or sequence of events. (2) Numerical order—according to size or number. An outline of steel-producing states would probably start with the one producing the most and go to the one producing the least or vice versa. (3) Alphabetical order—a rather arbitrary order used for convenience. For example, steel-producing states could be outlined alphabetically. (4) Place order—according to location. If one wished to emphasize the regional distribution of steel-producing states, place order could be used.

The key word is *logically,* as it pertains to the purpose of the outline. The arrangement of ideas is a personal matter. The important thing is to have a sensible reason for the arrangement.

The practices of outlining for study and review will usually be no more than the condensation of textbook material. This will not be difficult because most textbooks are arranged in logical patterns of sequence and relationship. As in the case of summaries, encyclopedias often provide excellent models of outlining.

Many good encyclopedias contain articles that cover two or three pages with an outline of the article. These and your social studies textbook should afford sufficient examples to help you become expert. Your greatest problem at first will be reducing your outline to sensible proportions. There is frequently an inclination to include too much.

ALTERNATIVE METHODS OF NOTE-TAKING

Working notes for review and recall may take several forms. Some students use summary texts. A summary text is a one-sentence statement of a section, chapter, or assignment, recorded daily to give a bird's-eye view of things to know from the course material.

1. Parallel columns are useful for making comparisons and contrasts:

	Mississippi	*Amazon*	*Nile*
Location:	USA	Peru, Brazil	Sudan, Egypt
Length:	3,860 miles (w. Missouri R.)	4,000 miles	4,160 miles
Features:	Spring floods/ levees	Rain forest	Irrigation of arid land
Terminus	Gulf of Mexico	Atlantic Ocean	Mediterranean Sea

2. Columns may be used for classifications:

Classical Historians	*American Dramatists*
Herodotus	Eugene O'Neill
Thucydides	Arthur Miller
Polybus	Tennessee Williams

3. Another pattern is the multiple column:

Who?	When?	What?
Charles Darwin	1850	*Origin of the Species*
Mark Twain	1884	*Huckleberry Finn*
Franklin Roosevelt	1933	Began the "New Deal"

How you condense and organize bits of information is up to you, of course. Be clever, ingenious, artistic . . . whatever. But be consistent in order to make sense of your jottings when the time comes for you to review the content of the course for a final exam or other purpose. None of these note-taking techniques will necessarily turn an average student into a super-scholar, but along with habitual summary writing and outlining, they could steer you in that direction.

MAPPING

The third major type of note-taking is mapping. Mapping is drawing a diagram of the information you are condensing.

Many people find it easier to remember pictures than words. These people will find mapping a very good form of note-taking, because it uses their capacity to remember forms and shapes.

You may be someone with a better memory for pictures than for words. Try this simple test. Think of a time in class you had difficulty remembering something you had read. You couldn't remember the information, but you could visualize where it was in your book, perhaps even to the point of identifying what preceded it and what followed it on the page. If you have had such an experience, or numerous such experiences, you will be able to use mapping to good advantage.

To draw a map of a chapter of a text, start with a clean sheet of paper, put the title of your map on the page, and draw a box around it. On our sample of a map, we will put the title in the center of the page. To illustrate map-making, we will refer to the contents of Chapter 6, on Listening, pages 79–91.

A map begins with a just a title. At each step in the mapping process, the title grows appendages and eventually looks like the scheme of a complex operation. But don't be put off by its intricate appearance. Each step simply adds more details. Keep track of the map's growth and you'll observe that each addition consists of highlights derived from a different section of the chapter. The complete map, then, will give you a reasonably thorough overview of Chapter 6.

Step 1: To draw a map of the chapter, start with a clean sheet of paper, put the title of the map on the page, and draw a box around it.

LISTENING:
An easy way
to learn

Step 2: Decide where to add new material to the map. For this illustration, we have chosen to begin at the twelve o'clock position and then add new information in a clockwise path.

Step 3: Determine the first topic of major importance and write it on the map, connecting it to the title with a line.

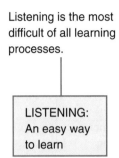

Step 4: This step divides the first topic of major importance into two subtopics, labeled (1) and (2) on the map.

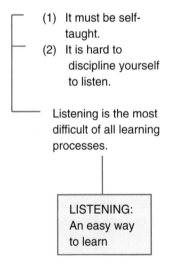

Step 5: Now add the second major topic of importance ("Four stumbling blocks . . .") along with its four subdivisions, labeled (1), (2), (3), and (4).

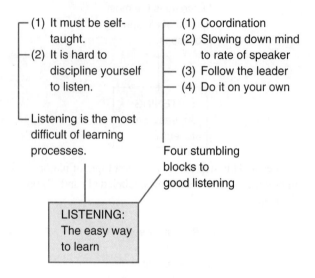

- (1) It must be self-taught.
- (2) It is hard to discipline yourself to listen.

Listening is the most difficult of learning processes.

- (1) Coordination
- (2) Slowing down mind to rate of speaker
- (3) Follow the leader
- (4) Do it on your own

Four stumbling blocks to good listening

LISTENING: The easy way to learn

Follow this process for each major topic and its subdivisions, moving around the page in a clockwise direction.

Steps 6, 7, 8. Continue to add major topics of importance along with their subdivisions.

Final Step: With the addition of the sixth major topic and its subdivisions, the map has reached its final form:

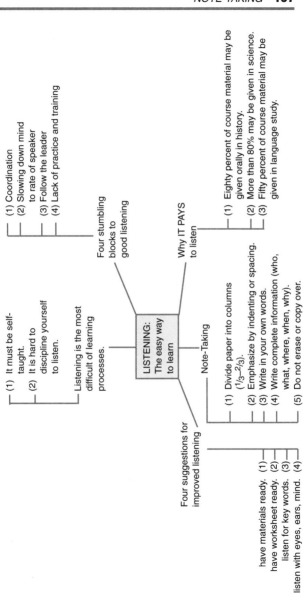

LISTENING: The easy way to learn

Four stumbling blocks to good listening
(1) Coordination
(2) Slowing down mind to rate of speaker
(3) Follow the leader
(4) Lack of practice and training

Why IT PAYS to listen
(1) Eighty percent of course material may be given orally in history.
(2) More than 80% may be given in science.
(3) Fifty percent of course material may be given in language study.

Listening is the most difficult of learning processes.
(1) It must be self-taught.
(2) It is hard to discipline yourself to listen.

Note-Taking
(1) Divide paper into columns ($\frac{1}{3}$–$\frac{2}{3}$).
(2) Emphasize by indenting or spacing.
(3) Write in your own words.
(4) Write complete information (who, what, where, when, why).
(5) Do not erase or copy over.

Four suggestions for improved listening
(1) have materials ready.
(2) have worksheet ready.
(3) listen for key words.
(4) listen with eyes, ears, mind.

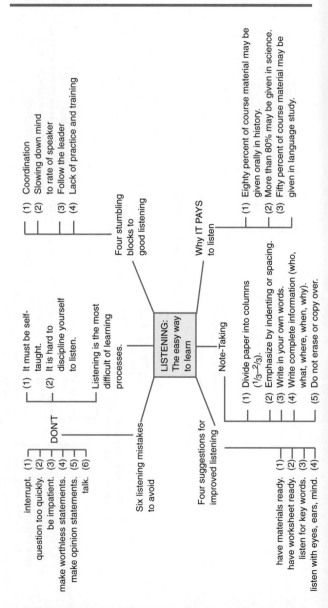

Four stumbling blocks to good listening
(1) Coordination
(2) Slowing down mind to rate of speaker
(3) Follow the leader
(4) Lack of practice and training

Why IT PAYS to listen
(1) Eighty percent of course material may be given orally in history.
(2) More than 80% may be given in science.
(3) Fifty percent of course material may be given in language study.

LISTENING: The easy way to learn

Listening is the most difficult of learning processes.

DON'T
(1) It must be self-taught.
(2) It is hard to discipline yourself to listen.

Note-Taking
(1) Divide paper into columns (1/3–2/3).
(2) Emphasize by indenting or spacing.
(3) Write in your own words.
(4) Write complete information (who, what, where, when, why).
(5) Do not erase or copy over.

Six listening mistakes to avoid
DON'T
(1) interrupt.
(2) question too quickly.
(3) be impatient.
(4) make worthless statements.
(5) make opinion statements.
(6) talk.

Four suggestions for improved listening
(1) have materials ready.
(2) have worksheet ready.
(3) listen for key words.
(4) listen with eyes, ears, mind.

Mapping may take any form you wish—feel free to use whatever shapes you find that make sense to you. You may use colors to code the areas, or you may use any eye path that is comfortable for you.

You need not make such tentacled things as our sample maps. Many people have great success using overlapping circles or geometric shapes—triangles for three part ideas, squares for four, and so on. The only object of a map is to present information clearly to you, so that you can understand and remember easily what you have read.

Mapping may be used for class notes as well as for notes from reading. With a little practice, you will find that it can be very helpful.

WRITING BETTER SUMMARIES

➤ Get into the habit of summarizing what you read and study. Use pleasurable reading—newspapers, magazines, stories—as your training ground for studying and reading for school. Whatever you read, try visualizing how you might summarize it. The more you practice, the easier summary writing gets. When you can quickly summarize what others hardly grasp, think how you can impress your teachers and friends.

➤ Train yourself to replace the author's words with your own, but not just an equivalent word. Try to select an equally impressive synonym or a better one. This makes your summary so personal that recall is almost automatic.

➤ Practice economy of words. Link parallel details together. Use the semicolon to emphasize in one sentence
what is expressed in the original text in three. Learn to
link ideas in series for easy recall. Practicing economy
of words is an aid to separating main points from
nonessential introductory and illustrative material.

➤ Avoid generalizing in your summaries. Avoid unnecessary lead-ins and repetitive conclusions. Differentiate
between fact and opinion. If you happen to be writing
about the end of the Cold War, there's no need to
remind yourself (or your teacher) that Russia was an
adversary of the United States and its allies. That fact
is too well-known and obvious to state in a concise
summary. Nor do you need to say that the Soviet Union
was the evil empire and deserved to be defeated. That
may be your opinion, but if the idea does not appear in
the material you're summarizing, leave it out.

➤ Learn to distinguish between fragmentation and sum-
marization. Fragmentation is bringing together ideas
from an assignment and recording them in a haphazard
manner. A good summary is a miniature theme containing all the elements—unity, coherence, and emphasis.

➤ Do not content yourself with reading one or two summaries and accepting them as models. Compare the
summaries you write with ones on similar topics in
encyclopedias. The reference shelf in a library is a
good storehouse of models.

➤ When you write your summaries, make sure that you
follow the $\frac{1}{3} - \frac{2}{3}$ format on the page, saving the left-
hand column for highlighting when you review your
notes.

BETTER OUTLINES

➤ Observe carefully the standard outline form. Any changes, transpositions, or incorrect indentations may mislead you or diminish your understanding of the topic.

➤ Avoid the most common error in outlining—leaving off the title or designating it as a main topic.

➤ Be sure your outline clearly shows: (1) the arrangement of ideas; and (2) the relative importance of the ideas.

➤ Remember that a subtopic results from division of a topic. Therefore, there will always be at least two subtopics—*A* and *B, 1* and *2, a* and *b*. Nothing that is divided can remain whole (one); it will become two, three, etc., depending upon its separate parts.

➤ Know the orders of outlines: (1) time, (2) numerical, (3) alphabetical, and (4) place. Use common sense to determine sequences. If you can reasonably explain the order you have used, your outline is probably in good order.

➤ Use the outline as an aid to memory, a blueprint for easy recall, an organizational frame for written tests, term papers, and themes.

➤ Remember to use the $\frac{1}{3} - \frac{2}{3}$ format for your outline, leaving the left-hand column for highlighting when you review.

BETTER MAPPING

➤ Plan your map ahead of time. For example, will it contain radiating lines, or will it look like a wall of building blocks?

➤ Use shapes that are meaningful—triangles are good for three-part ideas, concentric circles for sets and subsets, octagons for things not to do, since we associate that shape with stop signs.

➤ Use color coding if you can—one topic completely in blue, another in red, another in black, and so forth.

➤ Make sure the units of the map are distinct and clearly separated from one another.

➤ Write the words so that you need not rotate the paper to read them.

LOOKING BACK

1. The facing page contains World History notes from a student's notebook. They deal with a lesson on Mao Zedong, the powerful Chinese leader of post-World War II. As you examine them, point out (a) their strengths, (b) their weaknesses; then suggest ways in which the notes could be improved.

2. According to a friend of yours, "Mr. Reardon always asks for an outline along with our English compositions. I write the composition first, then make up the outline for old Reardon. He never gets wise to my short cut!"

   How good is that technique? Before you answer, try it out both ways—writing the outline before and after you do your next writing assignment.

World History 104   February 9

Mao Zedong

- ambitious for country's growth
- looked in four different directions: Korea, Vietnam, Tibet
                                              Nationalist China

- North Korea / U.S.
- Foothold after Armistice
- Mao was a veritable thorn in the side of the United
      States when it came to Vietnam. He sent arms,
      soldiers, and officers to help the Communist
      Vietnamese combat the French and then the
      United States.
- Tibet conquest - gateway India
- First "protest"
- attack religion
- Takeover followed
- Taiwan ever since 1949
- American fleet a headache

Chapter 8

Reading: The Key to Understanding

TRUE CONFESSIONS

1. I'm a fast reader, all right," Sarah said. "The only trouble is that I can't remember what I read."

   Is Sarah's problem your problem? Have you ever "read" an entire page or chapter in a book without being able to remember anything it says? Is there an easy cure for this common experience?

2. Generally, we read different material in different ways. For example, you might approach your chemistry book with more determination than you would read the television listings.

   On a scale of 1–10 (10 being the highest level of concentration), how closely would you typically read each of the following?

A love letter addressed to you	_____
A poem you found in a magazine	_____
The sports page of your school newspaper	_____
A novel for English class	_____
A chapter on reading faster and with greater understanding	_____
Directions for using a Walkman	_____
The back of a cereal box	_____
Information on how to apply to college	_____
A letter of commendation from your math teacher	_____

3. "Reading is to the mind what exercise is to the body," said the eighteenth-century essayist Joseph Addison. Do you agree or disagree? Do you buy the argument that two or three hundred years ago reading was more important than it is today because we have many other forms of communication undreamt of back then?

THE NATURE OF READING

By the time you finished elementary school you might well have said, "I know how to read," but research has shown that even the most literate and educated adults can always learn to read better. Listen to Johann Wolfgang von Goethe, poet, novelist, and philosopher: "The dear good people don't know how long it takes to learn to read. I've been at it eighty years, and can't say yet that I've reached the goal."

Henry David Thoreau, in his classic, *Walden,* or *Life in the Woods,* includes an essay on reading, which says in part: (the italics are the author's):

> To read well—that is, to read true books in a true spirit—is a *noble exercise,* and one that will *task the reader more than any exercise* which the customs of the day esteem. *It* requires *training* such as the *athletes underwent,* the *steady intention almost* of the *whole life* to this object. *Books must be read as deliberately and reservedly as they* were *written.*[1]

---

[1] Henry David Thoreau, *Walden*, or *Life in the Woods* (New York: The Heritage Press, 1939), 110.

Continuing in the same essay, he writes:

> Most men have learned to read to serve a paltry
> convenience, as they have learned to cipher (count)
> in order to keep accounts and not be cheated in
> trade; but *of reading as a noble intellectual exercise
> they know little or nothing, yet this only is reading in
> a high sense,* not that which lulls as a luxury and
> suffers the nobler faculties to sleep the while, but
> *what we have to stand* on top-toe to read and
> *devote our most alert* and *wakeful* hours to.[2]

Reading Problems

How well do you understand what you read? Do you
understand everything, or does your comprhension
depend on what you are reading and for what purpose?
Or have you, perhaps, developed all sorts of ingenious
techniques to avoid reading altogether? Do you say that
you are too tired or that you have a headache? Do you
pretend to read but sit there and let your mind wander?
Some people avoid reading because they don't feel
confident about their ability but they are too proud to
admit it. Others avoid reading because they don't
remember enough of what they read; to them, reading
seems like a waste of time. Some readers begin reading
a story or a newspaper but quickly lose interest.

Sometimes a reading problem is a matter of eye-
sight, solved for a few dollars by buying a pair of
reading glasses. Sometimes, of course, the problem
may be more serious. Recognizing that you have a
reading problem, however slight, is the first step in
solving it. The fact that you are reading this book,

---

[2]Ibid, 110.

however, suggests that (1) you want to be a better reader, and (2) the measures for improved reading described in this chapter can help you to become one.

The Reading Habit

A crucial practice for improving your reading is to get into the habit of thinking about what you read, talking to other people about it, and comparing your thoughts with theirs. Of course, if you find the reading material dull, silly, or pretentious, there's not much to think or talk about. That's why your very first task is to get your hands on material that will grab your interest. What interests you? If you have a hard time answering that question, stop at the library and walk around for half an hour looking at books and magazines. The variety is remarkable, and, unless your brain is more dead than alive, you will surely find something to engage you, something that can be integrated into your life.

As a student you must spend a good deal of time reading. As long as you have to do it, why not make the most of it? If the reading matter is worth your while in the first place, focus intently on what it says. Make an effort to remember as much as possible, and try to apply or associate what you are reading to your own experience. To a greater or lesser extent you probably do these things already, especially when the reading is important to you, although few people can read at full throttle all the time. When the reading you have to do doesn't deserve your undivided attention and energy, skim the material to find particular facts or references to something of interest. While skimming, read rapidly, picking out essential ideas without paying much attention to accompanying details. When reading something important, however, read more slowly and carefully. Pick out main ideas and look for major supporting details. Take your time. Think about what the words say. Chances are the words were not chosen carelessly. Rather, the author picked them for the sole purpose of conveying ideas to you, the reader. But reserve your highest level of reading intensity for matters that absorb you intellectually, emotionally, and perhaps in other ways, too.

What to Look For

With a page of text in front of them, mature readers look for more than the letters that make up words. They look at individual words, of course, but view them only as the means to express ideas. People who get the most out of reading know that words are merely symbols and labels used to convey thought. Some thoughts are stupid and inane, some meaningful and profound, and others somewhere in between. Regardless of how significant the words may be, reading a piece of prose word by word can hinder the flow of the author's ideas. (Chances are you are not one of those habitual word-by-word readers. If you were, you probably wouldn't have come this far into this book. In fact, this and every other sentence printed in these pages would have made very little sense to you.) But if you find yourself now and then concentrating exclusively on each word, you can overcome the tendency by habitually starting off your reading with a quick bird's-eye view of the material. The theory is that if you know roughly what a passage is about, you are more likely to cruise through it.

To see how this works, turn back to the passage by Thoreau earlier in this chapter. Skim it rapidly and try to pick up from the italicized sections its main thought, namely: *Reading is a noble intellectual exercise, requiring more training than most people are willing to devote to it.* Now go back and read both paragraphs more slowly. Perhaps you'll notice that Thoreau's organization and purpose practically jump off the page.

The surest way to obtain a bird's-eye view is to quickly find the core of the paragraph, an idea that most often appears in a topic sentence near the beginning, although sometimes it shows up at the end or somewhere in the middle. Sometimes, too, the topic sentence is not stated at all but is so strongly implied that it's hard to miss.

Going over a paragraph for its central thought removes the hesitant awkwardness that occurs when reading word by word. A couple of examples will show you how quickly comprehension follows when you know what to look for in a paragraph. (Italics added by the author):

> *How should you read?* As you please. If you please yourself by reading fast, read fast; if you read slowly and do not feel like reading faster, read slowly. Pascal does not say we are apt to read too fast or too slowly, but he blames only an excess. Montaigne complains of a formal way of reading. "My thoughts go to sleep when they are seated," he says, "so they and I walk." Honest industry merely jogs along, curiosity flies on Mercury's pinions. Passionate reading not only flies, it skips, but it does so only because it can choose, which is a high intellectual achievement. How do you read the timetable? You skip till you come to your place; then you are indifferent to the whole world and engrossed by your train, its departure, arrival, and

connections. The same thing with any formula for
the production of the philosopher's stone.

Whatever we read from *intense curiosity* gives
us the *model of how we should always read.*
Plodding along page after page with an equal
attention to each word *results in attention to mere
words. Attention* to *words never produces thought,*
but very promptly results in distractions, so that an
honorable effort is brought to nought by its own ill-
advised conscientiousness.[3]

Suppose for a moment that a reader had accidentally
failed to read the initial question (quite possible for the
word-by-word reader). In that case, the whole paragraph would be a muddle in the reader's mind because
the paragraph consists of an answer to an unknown
question.

Note the essentials of the topic sentence in this expository paragraph (again the italics are the author's):

Among the many kinds of material we must find in
books, at least *three* are readily distinguished:
happenings, facts, and principles. Happenings—the
narratives of *what* has *occurred*—concern us in *all
forms of fiction,* whether as plays, novels, or stories.
And *happenings* are a major part of all *history* and
biography. Throughout such narratives and in almost
all *sorts of writing* we encounter *facts* that may lack
narrative connection: dates, names, locations,
definitions, descriptions of processes. Less concrete
than either happenings or facts, and often *harder* to
remember, are *principles:* the *translation* of *facts* into
statements of *law,* the *interpretation* of *happenings*

[3]Ernest Dimnet, *The Art of Thinking* (New York: Simon and
Schuster, Inc., 1928).

as *cause* and *effect, or* the attempts to explain
human experience in the *form* of *theories.*[4]

The topic sentence is made to alert the reader; the
signal word *three* gives the clue. The body of the
paragraph explains what *happenings, facts,* and *principles* are. The reader who knows what to look for will
not have to reread this paragraph.

Here is a summary paragraph for this part of the
chapter. Will it help you remember what to look for in
your reading?

Summary Paragraph

What does the good reader look for? First, for the only
thing that can be gleaned from the printed page,
thoughts. Second, the reader looks for action on a wide
screen—moving quickly over the page, getting a bird's-
eye view. Third, a good reader knows the form of dis-
course, patterns of paragraphs, and structure of
sentences so thoroughly that they add to the action of
reading by almost literally jumping from the page to
meet the reader. Finally, the reader looks with an eye
to selection and classification of the kinds of material
found in books—happenings, facts, and principles. What
all good readers look for in their reading causes them to
think, and indeed, all effective reading is thinking.

UNDERSTANDING MORE

You probably wouldn't be reading this unless you had
at least the trace of a desire to become a better reader.
In other words, you may wish to comprehend more of

---

[4] E. Wayne Marjarum, *How to Use a Book* (New Brunswick: Rutgers
Univ. Press, 1947), 4.

what you read and to remember it longer. With that in mind, here are some steps you might consider:

First, define your purpose. Greater comprehension and longer retention are by-products of *purpose*. That is, understanding often depends on why you are reading the material in the first place. If you pick up something to read casually while waiting for the bus, you are less likely to take the material seriously and therefore, will probably forget it sooner. Faced with an assignment from a teacher, however, the incentive is likely to be greater, not only to read more diligently but to try to remember the material longer. The importance of the assignment itself will generally dictate the seriousness with which you approach it. On a given day, a few pages of a novel for English class may engage you less than the chapter in your biology text on which you'll have a quiz on Friday. In short, the purpose will govern what you do: 1) skim it, 2) read it carefully, or 3) read with great intensity.

If your purpose is to locate information, skimming will suffice; but mastery that demands gathering facts and understanding their interrelationship, forming opinions backed by substantial evidence, might well dictate skimming first—followed by careful or intensive reading.

A second strategy for better comprehension and easier retention is to condition yourself for positive rather than negative results. Faced with a difficult passage or assignment, readers sometimes start by expecting *not* to be able to understand and remember. This prepares the mind psychologically for defeat. Expect to understand and remember, and for a while it is excellent training to speak aloud to one's self: "I am going to remember this after one reading." Would the runner win the race if at the starting gun he said to himself, "I know I can't win"?

Would high jumpers clear the bars if they said just before they left the ground, "I know I won't clear it"? Purpose plus confidence will, with the reader's help, interact to insure comprehension and retention.

A third aid to comprehension and retention is to read with questions in mind. The right questions can result in helping you enclose what you are reading with experience or association, thus making information so personal as to make forgetting impossible.

Ask questions such as: What would you have done at the Battle of Thermopylae? Would you have enjoyed walking and talking with Milton as he felt his way along his garden path with his cane? Could the author have stated this rule more clearly? The example seems rather vague, what could I use as a better one?

"There is no such thing as an interesting book or assignment"; to paraphrase Emerson, "there are only interested readers." And it might be added that only interesting questions make interested readers. How is this assignment related to the preceding one? Will what I already know about the topic make it easier for me to remember the facts I am now adding? And when a section or chapter is finished, self-recitation questions about main topics and how successfully, or unsuccessfully, the author has presented them will increase your ability to remember more of what you have read.

Retaining what is read is aided by finding some unifying association or significance. Facts and ideas can be very dull, but if some relationship can be established, what might have turned you off can become truly scintillating.

Remembering Longer

Into much of the reading done in school must be introduced the learning skill that causes many students to shudder—memorization. Fear it not. Instead, think of memory work as a challenge or as an offer you can't refuse.

The first step in improving your powers of memory and putting them to work in your reading is to define the kinds of ideas you remember with less difficulty than others—whether happenings, facts, or principles, and the element in each that helps you remember. Some people remember color, others motion, still others cannot remember numbers when they are spelled out. General U. S. Grant could not remember the names of three consecutive towns he passed while marching, but on a topographical map he could memorize dozens of towns and their location in a matter of seconds. Alexander the Great could not remember the names of some of his close acquaintances, but he could memorize poetry with almost no effort.

Psychologists generally agree that each of us has not one memory power but many. By testing whether it is faces, places, dates, designs, pictures from reality, pictures from imagination, association with the physical or mental world that we remember more easily, we can find our memory strengths and use them as the association frames upon which to hang what is to be remembered.

One very simple but effective test is to think quickly of a person you met recently. Say, for instance, you talked to a girl at the mall on Saturday. How do you remember her? By what she was doing? By the place where you saw her first? By who was with her? By the color of her sweater or jacket? By some number—packages she was carrying, what time it was, words spoken? By what she really looked like?—(reality). By what you thought she might have looked like?—(imagination). Which do you remember more distinctly—her hair color? (physical)—or what she said? (mental). Apply the same test to a character you meet in your reading.

When association and memory are not sufficient because the facts to be remembered are so numerous, the reader's last recourse is to take notes. If you own the book you are reading, marginal notes and the designation of important points by some system of marking suited to your purpose and kept consistent can be invaluable.

One of the simplest methods of designating degrees of importance is to use one, two, or three vertical lines: | for important, || for very important, and ||| for must remember. Some students use a (?) question mark to indicate further study needed; some use T or Ex. to signal likely test or examination material. One splendid practice for marginal notes is to write the main thought of a paragraph in a brief question beside the paragraph. Some students try to summarize with such brevity as to include the summary at the end of each paragraph.

Note-taking on what you read forces you to think and to be constantly alert for the essentials. Such notes can be kept in better order and made available for quick use if taken on 3×5 index cards. These can be filed by subject or book for any desired reference or project, and are far more easily arranged than pages of a looseleaf notebook or binder.

A review of summary writing and outlining will afford you two methods of taking notes on what you read. There are, however, two additional types of reading notes sometimes used: (1) question and answer and (2) word and phrase list. The question-and-answer method states the question in full and then gives key words or phrases to indicate the answer. For example:

I. What does a good summary contain?
   A. Principal ideas
   B. Author's point of view
   C. Student's vocabulary

II. What are the steps in making a summary?
   A.
   B.
   C.

Once practiced, the question-and-answer method leads to clear-cut distinctions between what is and what isn't important.

Writing a list of words and phrases may sometimes suffice. This sort of informal outline is useful when reviewing quickly for a quiz or exam. For example, this chapter might be summarized as follows:

READING: FASTER WITH MORE UNDERSTANDING

LOOK FOR
Bird's-eye view
Thoughts
Main topics

COMPREHENSION
Writer's aim
Questions on material
Happenings
Facts
Principles

RETENTION
Memory powers
Application and
   association
Marginal notes
Written notes

INCREASING SPEED
Self-tests
Conscious purpose
Hollow triangle
Mechanics
Cautions

READING FASTER

Another area for improvement in reading has to do with the speed. Fast readers are more accurate and remember more than slow readers. And in the process, of course, they save time. Slow readers often lose their train of thought, and often their place on the page. Fast readers read several words at a glance and are consequently dealing only in thoughts. Slow readers tend to read word by word.

There are many self-tests available for measuring your reading speed and comprehension. Your English teacher may be able to provide you one, or perhaps even administer such a test. The results should be instructive. If you have reading difficulties, the test will probably pinpoint areas where specific practices can help.

How do we read? First of all, every reader faces the problem of coordinating the mind and the eye. The mind is capable of receiving ideas much more rapidly than the eye is able to receive and relay them. Thus, the problem of mind-wandering arises. If you don't discipline your mind, it tends to wander—and suddenly you have lost your place on the page. The slower you read the more difficult it is to control the mind; therefore, rapid reading is training the eye to speed up and the mind to accept the eye's pace.

Our eyes move across the page by a series of quick stops, not in a flowing, even movement. These stops are called fixations, and whether you see one word or several at a fixation determines your speed. (Some of the fastest speed readers can take in a whole line of type in one fell swoop, and the speediest of them all can scan a whole page in a few seconds. But they are world-class speedsters, performing feats that escape most ordinary mortals.) Good readers who remember much of what they read make two or three fixations per line of print— a perfectly attainable goal for most students. At that speed, ideas can be quickly understood and remembered. Slow readers pause briefly at each word and sometimes glance backward, returning to previously read words. This practice is called regression and is something to avoid. It causes considerable confusion and is one most damaging symptoms of reading without purpose. Good readers sweep from the end of the finished line downward and to the beginning of the next with no difficulty; slow readers will often make two or three false starts on beginning a line, and frequently reread the line just read or skip the one they should read. This, of course, is not completely the fault of the eye. Until the eye and the brain are working together, troublesome habits of reading will prevail. Mechanical practices will help, but the determined effort to concentrate on increasing speed and comprehension, and a willingness to make each assignment a practice in better reading habits, will prove a great aid.

Measure your "recognition span," the number of words you see at a fixation, with an index card or some other semi-stiff material from which you cut out a hollow triangle. Make the base wide enough to take in six or eight words. Place it on the line and move from top to bottom to determine how many words you see at a fixation. It may be used for a few minutes' practice each day, or as a test from time to time to measure improvement. Progress may also be noted on a chart on which you can enter the number of pages (of similar type material) that you can read in a 15-minute period. If you are putting serious effort into reading improvement this test might be done weekly.

Careful self-analysis will dictate the methods you choose. Beware of developing speed without comprehension. Nervous haste has driven many students to accelerate their reading but at the same time diminish their recollection of what they've read. Let the purpose help determine the speed. Concentrate on eliminating habits common to slow readers, and the increase in speed will usually take care of itself.

Above all, keep in mind that 1) most study problems have a reading problem at their roots, 2) improvement in reading is a lifetime process, and 3) if you read a great deal, you will become a better reader; and similarly, if you choose not to read, you're probably making a life-altering mistake.

PRACTICES FOR READING BETTER

➤ Psyche yourself to achieve positive results.

➤ Know that good readers do the following:
  – concentrate on the material
  – remember as much as possible
  – apply or associate what they read to their personal experience

➤ Use the style of reading appropriate to the material:
  – skimming
  – careful reading
  – intensive reading

➤ Get into the habit of looking for:
  – thoughts
  – the bird's-eye view
  – main topics
  – ways to memorize

➤ To improve comprehension and retention:
  – Read as though you are having a conversation with the author
  – Remember your purpose
  – Read with questions in mind
  – Associate what you read with personal experience
  – Take notes

➤ Try to speed up without losing comprehension
  – Test yourself to measure speed and keep track of improvement
  – Know how your eyes function as you read
  – Avoid the practices typical of slow readers
  – Practice expanding the number of words you see at a fixation
  – Remember that increasing speed without understanding is counterproductive

LOOKING BACK

1. Why is so much emphasis placed on speed in reading? If you can absorb material only by reading slowly, can you think of any reasons why you should bother to increase your speed?

2. A useful aid to increasing comprehension is to ask specific questions about what you are reading. Did you ask yourself any questions as you read this chapter?

3. Many people keep reading journals in which they record reactions, ideas, associations—anything at all that their reading evokes. Events in a story, for example, sometimes inspire students to recount personal experiences in their journals. Would you be inclined to keep such a journal?

Chapter 9
Words: Using Them Well

TRUE CONFESSIONS

1. There is an old joke about a man who looked up the meaning of "to be frugal" and found out that one of the dictionary definitions was "to save." One day, while riding a ferry, he fell into the water and shouted as loud as he could, "Frugal me, frugal me!"

   Have you ever misused a word that way?

2. What word did you look up in a dictionary lately? Why did you want to know its meaning? How have you used it since you discovered its meaning?

3. A high school senior asked: "Why are teachers always pushing us to use big words? Can't I say the simple word 'cut' or must I use a four-syllable word such as 'laceration'? After all, Ernest Hemingway specialized in words of one syllable, and he was one of America's greatest writers."

   How might a teacher answer that question?

WHY STUDY WORDS?

The purpose of this chapter is to help you increase your vocabulary, adapt it to a more meaningful use, and through that improved use, elevate your grades in school and raise your SAT I scores. As a by-product of a richer vocabulary, you may also take greater delight in the reading that you do for class and for pleasure. Reading not only strengthens your knowledge of word connotations and nuances of meaning, it adds immeasurably to your personal vocabulary.

In this chapter on vocabulary growth you'll find ideas for using a dictionary, suggestions for keeping lists of new words and for putting new words to work. But these are the back-door methods necessary for those who have somehow missed the excitement of entering word study by the front door—namely through their natural fascination with words. As the poet, W. H. Auden, put it, people who aspire to be writers or poets will know they've chosen the right profession if they "like to hang around words and overhear them whisper to one another."[1]

THE QUALITIES OF WORDS

Words are the tools of thinking. Beginning with the grunts and exclamations of our remote ancestors, words, these symbols of thought, have flowered into their many uses to provide man with a history totally different from the lower primates. Writes J. Donald Adams:

> In words we reflected all the delights and miseries of human existence. Words are one of the most living things of man's creation; indeed, one might argue that they have more vitality than anything else we have fashioned. What else is there that seems to lead an independent life? Words do; they acquire strength and lose it; they may, like people,

---

[1] As quoted by John Ciardi, "Manner of Speaking," *Saturday Review* 55 (March 11, 1972): 14.

become transformed in character; like certain
persons, they may gather evil about them, or like
others, prod our wits and lift our hearts.[2]

How particular sounds came to represent particular
things is also part of the fascinating story of words. In
Plato's shortest dialogue, *Cratylus,* covering only four
pages, Socrates speculates on the origin of words. He
suggests that many names indicate the nature of the
thing named—some names express rest while others
show an affinity for motion. The sound of *l* seems to
suggest the *lull* that *lures* toward the *lunar* world of
rest. How many words with *l* can you list?—leisure,
lullaby, lassitude, lazy—the lengthening *list* makes one
listless. Over against the rest-inducing *l* stands *r,*
suggesting motion—run, race, rowdy, rodeo, rattle,
ruin, ripple. Ripple, the last mentioned, suggests that
some words echo the sound of the thing for which they
stand. (The ripples crept quietly under the over-
hanging bank. The brook babbled its protest to the
rocks as it raced along.)

WORD ORIGINS

Etymology is the study of the origin and development
of a word, says your dictionary, tracing a word as far
back as possible. The word etymology comes from two
Greek words—*etymon*, meaning "true sense," and
logy, meaning "the study of." Etymology usually
proceeds by the method of linguistic comparisons,
indeed, an exciting means of discovering the romance
behind our everyday language. Add to this the origin

---

[2]J. Donald Adams, *The Magic and Mystery of Words* (New York:
Holt, Rinehart and Winston, 1963), 36.

of names, and word study takes on an absorbing and fascinating quality found in few subjects.

Think briefly of several names around you. Perhaps there is a mountain named Hawk's Peak, another named Candlewood. Long ago indigenous people may have watched the hawks soar above the peak, brushing the sky with their wings, and named the mountain. And having gone to gather pitch pine to light the frontier cabin, substituting the pine torch for candles, the pioneers named the mountain where they found the candle wood—Candlewood Mountain.

Etymology, begun with the familiar that lies before your very eyes, and extended to your dictionary, will not only enrich your vocabulary, but will make you word conscious, help you spell correctly, and indirectly improve your ability to read with greater comprehension.

To create a picture of the origin of a single word is to journey into a remote past. The evolution of words reaches far back in time, perhaps eighty thousand years. For many thousands of years signs and grunts named things men saw—slowly language evolved from these mere names of concrete things to expressions of abstract ideas.

About four thousand years ago man advanced his evolution of speech and words into a new epoch; he began to write. First he scratched strangely and crudely on stone, perhaps also with a pointed stick in the sand; afterwards on bits of hardened clay, and finally his materials included papyrus, parchment, and paper. How did he begin? Doubtless with a picture. Slowly the picture came to represent an idea. The idea came to be represented by a symbol—a symbol that could be read and uttered. This was a written word.

Ever since the time of Socrates there have been many theories about the origins of words and names. Was the Native American who looked out from his campsite high on the Blue Ridge Mountains naming the beautiful valley below? Was he echoing the sound of earth and sky caressing at the edge of the vast panorama? Or was he raising his arms in awesome devotion to the daughter-of-the-skies? Anyway, the word he made was—Shen-an-doah, Shenandoah. Is there a single valley on the earth more beautifully named? And what of Je-ru-sa-lem—that beautiful, musical word? How came the word—the name—from David's harp or the wind whispering among the promontory rocks?

WORD PARTS

The excitement of words! A thousand word games, histories, and stories are all about you daily. Do not let the fascination of words be clouded or lost. Every word was in its beginning a stroke of genius. And according to Emerson, "Every word was once a poem." "Uttering a word," said the philosopher Ludwig Wittgenstein, "is like striking a note on the keyboard of the imagination." Words convey most of our ideas and thoughts. Without them we can think only in concrete terms—we can picture an object, a rock, for instance; but we cannot picture an abstraction, such as love. To express the idea of "love" we need words.

The putting together of words to produce distinctive and understandable prose demands sentences that deal quietly and justly with the common feelings of men, and give beauty and loftiness to things of the everyday world—things which, if not lifted up, are sometimes lost in the drab words of grocery lists, small complaints in little language, and repetitions stamped with dullness.

Some of the earth's benefactors came to greatness through their ability to give color, simplicity, enduring strength, and nobility to words. In analyzing the qualities that made Abraham Lincoln great, Benjamin P. Thomas wrote:

> Mastery of language may have been that ultimate factor without which he would have failed. For the self-taught man who once would have given all he owned and gone into debt for the gift of lyric utterance had touched the summits of eloquence. Yet this, like his other achievements, had not come by mere chance. Patient self-training, informed reflection, profound study of a few great works of English literature, esteem for the rhythmic beauty that may be coaxed from language, all these had endowed him with the faculty to write well and to speak well, so that at last, when profound emotions deep within him had felt the impulse of new-born nobility of purpose, they had welled forth—and would well forth once more—in imperishable words.[3]

How then can you put your love of words into action—"to write well and to speak well"? There are four steps: use a dictionary, learn the roots from which many words come, learn prefixes and suffixes, and *use* the words you have learned.

1. USE A DICTIONARY

The first step is to make friends with the dictionary, to make it your lifelong companion. The word

---

[3]Benjamin P. Thomas, *Abraham Lincoln* (New York: Alfred A. Knopf, Inc., 1950), 500.

"dictionary" is derived from the Latin word *dictio,* meaning *to speak*, or *to point out in words*; the dictionary is a book that speaks to us about words. It tells us: a. what are the origins of words, b. how to pronounce them, c. what parts of speech they are, d. how to spell them, e. what their meanings are, f. similar words (synonyms), g. words that have opposite meanings (antonyms). Practice using your dictionary in as thorough a manner as possible. Do not hurry through the entry for the word. Read all the meanings of the word—not merely the first. Try looking at the word *sound* or *round.* The entry for either of these words is very long. You will be surprised to find how many different uses each of these words has.

Most word-processing programs contain dictionaries as well as a thesaurus of synonyms. The dictionary will check your spelling, although it cannot differentiate among misused words. It won't tell you, for instance, whether you have improperly used *their, they're,* or *there* in a sentence, but it will send you a signal if you have written *thier.* It is the thesaurus, however, that will offer suggestions for words to enrich your writing and expand your written vocabulary. Use the thesaurus to add variety to your writing, but use it cautiously. Many words only approximate the meaning you may be looking for. Because approximations are not good enough, don't be misguided into thinking that any word listed in the thesaurus will be as good as any other word. In the previous sentence, take the word *misguided,* for example. The thesaurus in Microsoft Word lists the following as synonyms: *mistaken, foolish, ill-advised, unwise, erroneous, injudicious, imprudent,* and *wrong.* All these words come close to the key word *misguided,* but not one of these so-called synonyms can properly serve as a substitute in the given sentence—not at least without making another revision to eliminate an awkward use of the word. Keep this caution in mind whenever you call up the thesaurus for help.

2. LEARN THE ROOTS OF WORDS

The second part of vocabulary improvement is to learn how to examine the parts of words. Many of the words in the English language have three parts: a prefix, a root, and a suffix. If you learn some prefixes, some roots, and a few suffixes, you can multiply your vocabulary rather than merely add to it word by word.

You would benefit more from memorizing a hundred roots and how to use them than from memorizing five thousand individual words. Of the more than six hundred thousand words in our language, almost half come from about eight hundred roots.

The word *root* is apt, for as the root of a tree supplies the means of growth, so does a knowledge of word roots enable your vocabulary to grow. Not only will you improve your knowledge of meaning but also of spelling. So, take the shortcut to word power—learn roots, and how to use them.

All of the words of English have individual histories, all have origins deep in the past and deep in other languages. The two ancient languages that provide the roots for many of our words are Latin and Greek. Ten Latin verbs provide roots for more than two thousand of our own words.

Latin Verb	Meaning	Roots for English Words
capio	take, seize	cap- (cip-) capt- (cept-)
duco	lead	duct- duc-
facio	do, make	fac- (fic-) fact- (fect-)
fero	carry, bear	fer- lat-
mitto	send	mit- mitt- miss-
plico	fold	-plica- plicat- (plect-) (plex-)
pono	place, put	pon- posit-
tendo	stretch	tend- tent-
teneo	have, hold	tene- tent-
specio	observe, see	spec- (spic-) speci- spect-

Notice that the root *tent-* may come from either of two of the Latin verbs. You will need to remember that as you examine words. For example, from which root does re*ten*tion come, and from which root does con*ten*tion come? The difference in the origin of the roots alters the meaning significantly.

As a beginning to your study of roots, try to find three English words that come from each of the ten Latin verbs.

3. LEARN PREFIXES AND SUFFIXES

The third part of vocabulary building is to learn prefixes and suffixes. These are the parts added to the beginning (prefix) or to the end (suffix) of the root. They will alter the meaning of the word and so are very important. For example *pre*tend and *in*tend mean rather different things, even though they come from the same root. The prefix has made all the difference.

The following list is of common prefixes and their meanings. How many are you familiar with?

Prefix	Meaning	Example
a, ab	from, away	avert, abstain
a, an	without, not	atheist, anarchist
ad, af, at, ag	to	adhere, affix, attain, aggressive
ambi	both	ambidextrous
amphi	around	amphitheater
ant, anti	against	antonym, antipathy
ante	before	antedate
cata	down	cataract, catacomb
con, cor, com	with, together	convene, correlate, compare
contra	against	contradict
de	from, down	descend, debase
di	apart	divert, divorce
dia	through	diameter, diagonal
dis	not	disagree, disappear
e, ex	out of, over	evaluate, exponent
em	out	emanate
em	in	embark
en	in	enclose
hyper	above, over	hypercritical
hypo	under	hypodermic
il	not	illegal, illegible
im	in, not	import, impossible
in	not	inactive
ir	not	irresponsible
per	through	permeate
peri	around	perimeter
post	after	postpone, posterity
pre	before	predict, precede
pro	for, forth	pronoun, procession

re	back, again, down	recall, revive, retreat
sub, sup	under	subordinate, suppose
super	over, above	supervise
trans	across	transport, transmit

Now use the prefixes and the roots to create some words. Check your accuracy with your dictionary. For example, check out: *complicate, emit,* or *reception.* How many words can you create?

Suffixes usually tell us how the word is to be used rather than telling us something about its meaning. They tell us whether the word is a noun, an adjective, or a verb, or the comparative degree of an adjective: small*er*, small*est*. Two suffixes may be added to a root to create a word, as in aggress*ively*. You should have a working knowledge of at least the following suffixes.

Suffix	How Word Will Be Used	Meaning	Example
-able, -ible	adjective	capable of	digestible, reliable
-ac, -al, -ial	adjective	pertaining to	cardiac, natural, facial
-acy	noun	pertaining to	legacy
-ance, -ence	noun	state of being	abundance, obedience
-ant, -ent	noun	one who does	servant, student

-er, -or	noun	one who does	actor
-ive	adjective or noun	state of being	aggressive, executive
-ish	adjective	the quality of	mannish
-ity	noun	the quality of	humility
-less	adjective	without	sleepless
-ly	adjective or adverb	like	cheerfully, lovely
-ness	noun	state of	goodness
-ry	noun	state of	rivalry
-ion	noun	act of	tension

This list is by no means exhaustive. At best, it merely suggests what kinds of changes suffixes can make in words.

Now use your knowledge of roots, prefixes, and suffixes to define these words: *missive, permissive, permission, conduct, conductor.*

4. USE NEW WORDS

The fourth and final part of vocabulary building is to use the new words you have learned. Incorporate them into your writing for class and into your everyday speech. Without use you will lose the words you have worked to learn.

To make the words familiar friends, strive to memorize them and their meanings. Use new word lists or, far better, new word cards. Keep a list of new words along with their meanings; especially a list of basic vocabulary words that apply to a particular subject, such as biology, chemistry, history, or geometry. The word should be written with the definition that is directed toward the subject. If there are synonyms that help fix the meaning in your mind, they should be written in a column to the right of the definition as here shown:

NEW WORD   DEFINITION   SYNONYM

The card system for new words is, however, greatly recommended. Most students find it more workable and, adaptable. Vocabulary builder cards can be bought. (Try Barron's *SAT I Wordmaster* cards as a start. They contain 600 words you should know, especially if you're preparing for SAT I.) Or, if you want to build your own set, equip yourself with the smallest index cards you can buy—$1\frac{1}{2} \times 3$ or 3×5. Keep them handy as you read or study. When you come upon a new word, write it on the front of the card. On the back write the definition or definitions, and a synonym or two. Carry half a dozen or more cards with you, or display them on your desk, until you have put them in your working vocabulary; that is, until you are using them in conversation and in your writing. This will seldom take more than three or four days. The cards may then be filed alphabetically or by subject vocabulary. Just a few weeks of practice and the new word cards become second nature. They can be studied while riding or walking to and from classes, waiting for a bus, and at myriad other odd moments. Put the new word card system to work to expand your vocabulary.

VOCABULARY BUILDING

Use Your Dictionary

When you come upon a new word, a new use for an old word, a word that you think you know but are not sure of, reach for your dictionary. Always keep it within easy reach. Also, install a web site containing a dictionary in one of your favorite places on your computer. *Refdesk.com* is a popular source that puts a dictionary, a thesaurus, and many other useful reference books at your fingertips. Some of your more technical textbooks may have a glossary at the front or back. The glossary will provide the meanings of technical words pertaining to the particular subject, and may also supply meanings for new scientific words—so new they are not in your dictionary. The most comprehensive dictionary in the world is the *Oxford English Dictionary*, affectionately called the OED, a multi-volume set that can be found in most libraries. For use at home, you can buy a one-volume OED, which comes with a high-powered magnifying glass, or purchase a CD of the OED. For everyday use, though, nothing beats a good desktop dictionary, such as the *American College Dictionary* published by Merriam Webster, or the *American Heritage Dictionary of the English Language*. And so that you'll never be out of touch, why not invest in an inexpensive paperback dictionary to stuff in your backpack with your hacky sack and other indispensible gear.

Your dictionary study may lead you to other helpful books: A *Dictionary of Modern English Usage,* H. W. Fowler; Fernald's *Synonyms and Antonyms*; and Roget's *Thesaurus of English Words and Phrases.*

The word *thesaurus* comes from the Greek word meaning treasury. Indeed, all dictionaries are treasuries; storehouses not for money but for information.

Become a Word Surgeon

Learn to dissect words into their parts—prefix, root, and suffix. Study word parts until a glance reveals the pattern of the word—whether it is single root, built upon prefix, root, suffix, two roots, or some other combinations. Divide *autobiography, bibliography, pandemonium,* and *transmutation* into word parts. A working knowledge of a few fundamental parts, keen powers of observation, and conscientious practice, is the fast way to add new words to your vocabulary.

Collect New Words

Keep a record of new words. You might write them and their definitions in a notebook or on index cards to keep in your pocket. Or, whenever you're reading a newspaper or magazine and you encounter an unfamiliar word, snip out the sentence or paragraph in which the word appears and add it to your collection. Students often report that once they have met a new word, they keep running into it again and again, as if the word has been planted in the material just for them. Of course, the word has been lying in wait for them all along, but the students' new awareness of the word has suddenly made it rather common.

A word becomes part of your working vocabulary when you can pronounce it, spell it, and use it effortlessly in speech and writing. New words will fade unless you sustain them with everyday use.

Use the Unlimited Word-World of Fascination That Surrounds You on All Sides

John Ruskin defined genius as "a superior power of seeing." Why not use this definition to give yourself the quality of genius in word study? Exercise that "superior power of seeing" to enjoy for the first time place names, your own names, words derived from people's names, trade names, words that name our foods, our days, our weeks, our months, our seasons, and how about your own last name? Make a game of improving your vocabulary and the ability to use that vocabulary. "To carry the feelings of childhood into the powers of manhood," said Coleridge, "to combine the child's sense of wonder and novelty with the appearance which every day for years has rendered familiar, that is the character and privilege of genius. . . ." Keep "the child's sense of wonder and novelty" for your word study.

LOOKING BACK

1. One of the best ways to broaden your vocabulary is to consult a dictionary frequently in order to find the meaning of unfamiliar words. But wordsmiths with the biggest and richest vocabulary say they owe their achievement to a lifelong habit of reading. Are there any words in your vocabulary that you remember acquiring specifically while reading for school or for pleasure?

2. The meaning of many words can be figured out using roots, prefixes, and suffixes.
   What answers would you give if you were tested on the words *biped, retrogress, matriarchy*?

3. "Some of the earth's benefactors came to greatness through their ability to give color, simplicity, enduring strength, and nobility to words."

The above quotation comes from Chapter 10 and will, no doubt, remind you of Churchill, Lincoln, and other great wordsmiths who have been mentioned in this book. Can you name three contemporaries who use language skillfully? Think of newspaper columnists, TV personalities, lyricists for rock groups, your friends and teachers. Can you quote some of their most memorable lines?

Chapter 10

Written Work: The Product and Its Package

TRUE CONFESSIONS

1. When your teacher returns a graded paper or essay to you and it's filled with corrections and bears a low grade, what do you do? Examine it carefully, tear it up, hide it and read it later when no one is around? Do you try to take advantage of the comments on your papers, or do you view them as a sadistic form of harrassment?

2. At the start of English class, Mr. Snyder distributed paper for a brief writing assignment on a short story in Raymond Carver's *Cathedral*. Several students asked, "Does this count?"

   Would you have been likely to ask that question? How do experienced teachers usually respond to the question?

3. "I know that the paper I handed in was sloppy looking, but I think that teachers ought to be more concerned with content than with looks. Anyway, my printer is all messed up, so that's why my paper looks bad. If I get a failing grade because of that, I'm going to complain."

   Tell why you would or would not support such a protest.

THE NATURE OF THE PRODUCT

Of the several skills you will develop in educating yourself—listening, reading, speaking, thinking, and writing—the one that will give your teachers the widest range for measuring your ability and achievements will be your writing. While preparing a piece of written work for a course, you may talk over your idea with others, you may write a draft or two that your classmates may scrutinize, you may even ask for help in resolving a sticky problem of usage or meaning. Nevertheless, the product you ultimately hand in to your teacher for a grade is yours alone and reflects solely on you. When reading your piece, the teacher will not be judging your friends, your classmates, the librarian who gave you help, but you and you alone.

Your skill in writing will, fortunately or unfortunately, affect what your teachers in every subject think of your work because it is largely in writing that you demonstrate what you have learned. Writing, to some extent, also reveals more of your character and motivation than perhaps any other type of schoolwork.

Virtually all your writing adds to your teachers' impressions of you. These impressions are formed not from the quality of your term paper or your performance on big exams. Rather, they begin to take shape on the first day of the term and continue to grow with each day's work, whether it be a paragraph in response to a poem, a list of ten sentences containing new vocabulary words, answers to questions in a history textbook, or even five math problems. In fact, any written work you hand in adds another dimension to your portrait as a student—not only in English class but also in science, health, art, and any other course you happen to be taking.

The primary purpose of all written work is to impart information and to develop thought. Ideally, whatever you submit for evaluation should be (1) clear, (2) interesting, (3) enlightening, (4) correct, and (5) attractive. To be sure, not all your assignments can be judged by all five criteria. A group of math problems or a list of vocabulary words will be measured largely by their degree of correctness. Appearance counts, too, but not as much. A list of ten words haphazardly strung across a page torn from a notebook and illegibly written in pencil, however, says something about you quite different from a list numbered down the page in a straight column, neat and legible. Similarly, five math problems arranged on clean paper for symmetry and neatness, each problem distinctly numbered, each answer marked for easy identification, impresses more favorably than an indifferent, messy presentation, even though both papers show the correct answers.

Ideally, every assignment ought to reflect your best. That means the work you submit should demonstrate that you have studied, that you know the material, and that you have taken pains to make it presentable. A written assignment should display information clearly and effectively. It should be coherent, well organized, made up of fully developed paragraphs, and mechanically correct. Above all, it should show evidence that you have given the assignment a decent effort. Teachers respect effort and are generally unenthusiastic about capable students whose work is no more than passable. Nothing disappoints a teacher more than receiving mediocre papers from a student who has the potential to shine. Believe it or not, you have the means to give your teachers a lift by giving each assignment all you've got.

All effective written composition presupposes having something to say. Yet, unfortunately, some students, in spite of having nothing in particular on their minds, fill up pages with what in polite circles might be called oatmeal and in more earthy places a substance that can't be printed here. Granted, few students start out trying to write papers filled with unsubstantiated generalities and meaningless rubbish, but because they really have nothing to say, they say nothing—nothing of significance, at any rate. In contrast, students who understand the importance of clear thinking and writing will submit papers that have been so carefully and refreshingly prepared that teachers will actually look forward to the experience of reading them. If your written work is not clearly understandable, and in the form of which you are capable, your teacher will detect it in the first paper you write.

WRITING ESSAYS

Many students love to write—stories, personal remembrances, letters, poems, editorials, diary and journal entries—but not essays.

Essay writing for school has probably earned its reputation as a least favorite kind of writing because it is hard work, especially when the writer has little to say about the assigned subject. It also creates anxiety. There seem to be so many things that can go wrong, from faulty grammar to false logic. It's often hard to tell whether an essay is good or whether it's garbage, and at times you may have thought you've handed in a respectable essay only to have it returned full of symbols and notations indicating what was wrong with it. Small wonder, then, that essay writing ranks with giving a speech and taking grammar tests as one of the things students like to resist.

Of course, not everyone is vexed by essay writing. Innumerable students consistently write exemplary essays that are read aloud in class, printed in the school magazine, or come back with As and a happy face. Yet even the most enthusiastic essay writers rarely choose to write essays in their spare time.

There is no danger that this chapter will transform essay writing into your favorite pastime. But it can clear the air about essay writing by tearing away its mystique. To be sure, every kind of writing is pitted with traps into which unwary students may stumble, but with these pages as your trap detector, you may begin to avoid the most prominent hazards.

Unless you are a natural-born writer—in which case go on to the next chapter—keep this book by your side. Let it nag you into seeking the three most basic and most desirable writing goals: clarity, interest, and correctness.

1. *Clarity* because your ideas need to be clear to you before you can make them clear to readers.

2. *Interest* because readers will abandon your essay if you bore them.

3. *Correctness* because, whether it's fair or not, readers will judge you and your work according to how well you demonstrate the conventions of writing.

Clarity, interest, and correctness! After you've achieved them, you'll have found the secret of life. Well, maybe not life, but at least the essay writing part of it. The English language is rich with adjectives that describe good writing: *effective, eloquent, well-written, lively, stylish, polished, descriptive, honest, vivid, engaging,* and countless more. But in one way or other they all refer to clarity, interest, and correctness.

Composing an Essay

Just as most people follow a ritual when they get up in the morning, most writers adhere to a routine that helps them do their best work. Think about how you normally write an essay for school. Do you talk to others about the topic? Do you seek ideas or do they just come to you out of the blue? Do you preplan exactly what to say, or do you usually discover your point once the essay is underway? Before writing a draft, do you make notes or prepare an outline? Are you preoccupied with spelling and grammar as you write, or do you write freely? Do you reread as you go along or only at the end? How much do you actually write before revising anything? Do you habitually write in pencil, in pen, or on a computer?

Whatever your answers to these questions, you use some sort of process for writing essays. Through trial and error, you have probably found a process that works for you, but one that may change from time to time depending on the importance of the assignment and the amount of time you have to write it. Regardless of the details of your process, writing an essay generally comes in three stages. The first, *prewriting,* consists of all you do before you actually begin writing the text of your essay. During the second stage, *composing*, you choose words and form sentences that express your thoughts. And finally, during the *revising and proofreading* stage, you polish and refine the text of your essay word by word, making it true, clear, and graceful. Actually, the lines between the stages are not at all distinct, but in spite of blurry boundaries, it pays to keep the functions of each stage in mind.

Although every essay topic offers a different challenge, the basic principles of writing remain constant. Success in essay writing depends in large measure on how honestly you can respond *yes* to these twelve questions about good essay writing.[1] Use the questions as a checklist after you have composed your essay and before you turn in your final draft for a grade.

1. Have you studied the topic closely or answered the specific question being asked?
2. Have you narrowed the topic sufficiently to write about it within the permissible number of words?
3. Have you clearly articulated the main point(s) you intended to make about the topic?
4. Have you collected ideas and arranged them in a sensible sequence?
5. Have you written an appealing and informative introduction?
6. Have you developed your ideas with specific examples and details?
7. Have you guided your readers with transitions between sentences and paragraphs?
8. Have you used plain, precise, lively, and fresh words?

---

[1]Adapted from George Ehrenhaft, *How to Prepare for SAT II: Writing* (Hauppauge, NY: Barron's, 1994), 170.

9. Have you omitted needless words?
10. Have you varied your sentences to create interest?
11. Have you ended your essay unforgettably?
12. Have you followed the conventions of standard English and proofread your paper?

The topic you choose for an essay plays a big part in the results you get. In general, there are five types of topics that should be avoided, if possible:

1. One that is too broad—*The Roaring Twenties* rather than *Using Metal Detectors in High Schools.*
2. A topic that is too trite—*My Summer Vacation* rather than *Windsurfing on Long Island Sound.*
3. A topic that is too personal and in questionable taste—*My Two-Timing Father* rather than *Computer Nerds.*
4. A topic that may be too controversial for the reader to maintain objectivity—*Why Teacher Tenure Doesn't Work* rather than *The Zen of Lawn Mowing.*
5. A topic that requires too much background research—*Airline Safety* rather than *Shopping at The Gap.*

One trouble with an excessively broad topic is that it's very difficult to condense into five hundred or even a thousand words of material that would ordinarily require a whole book or more. A short essay on a broad topic often ends up as a series of vague generalizations. Or it covers the material superficially and is too bereft of substance to show your readers that you can think deeply. Therefore, it is crucial to limit the topic mercilessly. A well-focused essay on a limited topic is always preferable to an essay that tries to cover too much ground in just a few paragraphs. That's why narrowing the topic is one of the crucial steps in planning an essay. If the topic is sufficiently narrow, you stand a far better chance of saying something sensible, scintillating, meaningful, provocative . . . yes, interesting! And never doubt that an interesting essay will work in your behalf. That doesn't mean you must titillate your readers or write something quirky just to attract attention. Rather, to demonstrate that you know what you are talking about, a thoughtful discussion on a narrow topic will serve you best.

Childish topics such as "What I Did Last Summer" or "What I Think About Getting My Driver's License" may be cute and timely, but unless such topics are handled in a fresh and unique way, they are apt to be clichés. To write your thoughts about a highly personal topic may be good therapy, but it may show poor judgment. While every topic has its time and place, is an essay for English class an appropriate place for airing your thoughts on a drug problem or your parents' divorce? An apt personal experience, however, can be used effectively for illustration or for an example to prove a point. But it should be well thought out and simply presented.

Controversial topics can quickly lose all objectivity and become subject to personal feelings. Other people do not necessarily share your feelings and prejudices. Teachers grading your paper would not consciously give a lower grade for ideas with which they were not in agreement, but it is wise to remember that judgment is not immune to the weaknesses of human nature.

If you are like most students, your time is precious. Choosing a topic that requires a great deal of back-ground research can be worthwhile but very time consuming. Rather than write an essay that rings hollow and superficial because you haven't had time to learn about it in depth, choose a topic with which you are familiar. Dip into your well of experience and present data that you already know. Without consulting a book or computer, you are an expert on many topics pertaining to the life of the teenagers in your school, for example.

If the topic is assigned, you have no problems; if not, there are intelligent approaches to selecting one. An excellent approach is to consult general sources of information, such as an encyclopedia, to find out about a subject that interests you. Suppose you are interested in black holes in space. By checking the encyclopedia, you might find information about them and also references to other sources of information. You would need to narrow your topic, perhaps by choosing to concentrate on one of the noted astronomers or the methods used in the search for black holes. If either of these topics appeared too broad, further reading would help you to narrow the topic. The encyclopedia, however, is always a good place to start, as are Internet web sites, especially those that will link you to other appropriate sites.

In selecting a topic, pick one from the world you know. Chances are you'll write more vividly and interestingly about, say, the gnarled and ancient sycamore tree outside your bedroom window than about a storm at sea that you've never experienced.

Choosing a Main Idea

Once you've narrowed the topic sufficiently, it's time to decide what to say about the topic. That is, search for an idea that will become the purpose, or point, of the essay. An essay may not simply be "about" something—about the law, about art, or about field hockey, free will, the Grammy Awards, or any other subject in the universe. What counts is the statement your essay makes about the law, art, field hockey, free will, the Grammys, and so on—in other words, your main idea.

Nothing will disappoint a reader more than arriving at the end of an essay only to discover that it lacks a point. Essays may be written with beautiful words, contain profound thoughts, and make readers laugh or weep. But without a thoughtful main idea an essay remains just words in search of a meaning. After they've finished, readers may scratch their heads and ask, "Huh? What's the point?"

The point, or main idea (also called the thesis), is the thought to lock onto as you write. Every piece of the essay from its opening sentence to the conclusion should contribute to its development. It lays out a well-defined path for the reader. Any material that wanders from the main idea should be discarded. It not only wastes words but dilutes the impact of your essay.

It stands to reason that the main idea of an essay will depend on the topic. If you are asked to agree or disagree with a particular point of view, the essay's main idea will be a statement of your opinion. For example, if the topic happened to relate to required dress codes in high school, a main idea might be any one of the following:

1. Yes, high schools should impose dress codes on students.
2. No, high schools should not impose dress codes on students.
3. High schools should impose dress codes on freshmen and sophomores but not on juniors and seniors.

Using one of these main ideas as your starting point, the essay would then go on to prove the validity of your opinion.

Another topic may give you a chance to use your imagination, say, to invent a solution to a hypothetical problem. For example: If the world were to end one year from today, how would you spend your time? Or, If you won $100,000,000 tax free, what would you do with the money? The answer to either of these questions would be your essay's main idea.

Or the topic may be rather open-ended. For instance, you may be given a word or phrase and invited to take off in a direction of your choice. Let's say, for instance, that the topic asked you to write about seat belts. You might choose to enumerate the uses of seat belts or describe how they work. Or you could discuss their history and development, perhaps compare different types, or comment on the state laws that require occupants of a car to buckle up—all grist for an essayist's mill. Although the topic of such an essay may be self-evident, the essay still needs a point. An essay about seat belt laws must lead to some sort of conclusion about those laws. It could make the point that seat belt laws infringe on a driver's freedom of choice. Or its point might be that safety laws supercede a person's right to choose whether to wear a seat belt. Or you might use the essay to prove that driving without seat belts is dangerous and stupid.

When choosing a main idea, if possible, pick one that matters to you personally, one that truly reflects your thinking. Teachers won't fault you for stating opinions with which they disagree, so there's no good reason for choosing a main idea that makes you sound politically correct or one that you think will please or flatter the teacher. If you give readers only what you think they might want, you're being dishonest, posing as someone you are not. Likewise, because you don't want to sound pompous or pretentious, avoid picking main ideas solely to demonstrate your intellectual superiority. An essay that is truthful and comes from the heart will serve you best.

At the same time, however, steer clear of main ideas that are clichés and platitudes. Consider your reader. As teachers plod through scores of essays, they'll appreciate and reward those that contain fresh ideas. If possible, therefore, try to develop a main idea that will set you apart from other students. However, don't consider that piece of advice as a license to be quirky or weird just for the sake of attracting attention. Unusual creativity is not essential. You'll never be penalized for a clearly written, sober essay that accurately reflects your thinking and beliefs. Nevertheless, try to make your main idea as insightful as possible. If you begin with a tired, worn-out idea, the rest of the essay is not likely to be provocative or interesting.

Gathering and Arranging Ideas

Unless you are blessed with a digital mind that can instantly process an issue and draw insightful conclusions, you could do yourself a big favor by spending a few moments to gather and arrange specific ideas, arguments, anecdotes, examples—whatever you can think of to support and develop the thesis of your essay. Search your knowledge and experience. List your thoughts on paper as they occur to you—just a word or two for each idea. These jottings, in effect, will become the working outline of your essay. Once the flow of ideas has slowed to a trickle, sort through your notes by drawing circles around key words, connect related ideas with arrows, cross out the rejects, or just underline the thoughts you'll definitely use in your essay.

No one technique for gathering ideas excels over any other, provided it helps you identify what you're going to write. As you plan the essay, who knows—a new, irresistible thesis may jump out at you, or one idea may trigger a flood of others. In the end, you may end up with more brilliant ideas than you can use. (Everyone should have such a problem!) Your task then would be to make choices, to pick out and develop only the best of the best.

With materials assembled, put them in some kind of order. Decide what should come first. Second. Third. In most essays, the best order is the clearest, the order your reader can follow with the least effort. But, just as a highway map may show several routes from one place to another, there is no single way to get from the beginning to the end of an essay. The route you plan depends on the purpose of the trip.

Each purpose will have its own best order. In storytelling, the events are often placed in the sequence in which they occur. To explain a childhood memory or define an abstract term takes another organization. An essay that compares and contrasts two books or two people may deal with each subject separately or discuss point by point the features of each. No plan is necessarily superior to another provided there's a valid reason for using it.

The plan that fails is the aimless one, the one in which ideas are presented solely according to how they popped into your head. To guard against aimlessness, rank your ideas in order of importance. You may want to begin the essay with your strongest point, thus starting off with a punch. On the other hand, it sometimes is preferable to work toward your best point, not away from it. Giving away your *pièce de résistance* at the start is self-defeating. Therefore, if you have, say, three good ideas in support of your thesis, you might save the strongest for last. Launch the essay with your second best, and sandwich your least favorite between the other two. A solid opening draws readers into the essay and creates that all-important first impression, but a memorable ending is even more important. Coming last, it is what readers have fresh in their minds when they assign the essay a grade.

Although the following guideline may not apply to every essay, a body consisting of three sections is just about right. Why three? Mainly because three is a number that works. When you can support your main idea with three pieces of solid evidence, you appear to know what you are talking about. One is insufficient and two only slightly better. But three indicates thoughtfulness. Psychologically, three also creates a sense of rhetorical wholeness, such as "blood, sweat, and tears," and "of the people, by the people, and for the people."

It shouldn't be difficult to divide a main idea into three secondary ideas. A narrative essay, for instance, naturally breaks into a beginning, middle, and end. A process is likely to have at least three steps, some of which may be broken into sub-steps. In an essay of comparison and contrast, you should be able to find at least three similarities and differences to write about. A similar division into thirds applies to essays of cause and effect, definition, and description, and certainly to essays of argumentation.

Each of three ideas may not require an equal amount of emphasis, however. You might dispose of the weakest idea in just a couple of sentences, while each of the others gets a whole paragraph. But whatever you emphasize, be sure that each idea is separate and distinct. That is, the third idea mustn't simply rehash the first or second in the guise of something new.

Hooking Your Reader with a Gripping Introduction

Introductions let readers know what they're in for. Don't make a formal announcement of your plan: "This discussion will show the significance of television as an influence on the learning of children from age 3 to 12. Distinctions will be made between early childhood (age 3–7) and middle childhood (8–12)." Such announcements should be reserved for long expository essays or for subsections of monographs and textbooks. They may help keep readers focused on the purpose of the piece, but in an ordinary essay written for a class, they would be out of place.

Rather, just state your point. The reader will recognize the topic soon enough, even without a separate statement of your intention.

Terry F, for example, began an essay on the rights of high school students this way:

> On Monday morning, October 20th, I arrived in school to find every locker door in my corridor standing ajar. Over the weekend, school officials had searched through students' lockers for drugs and alcohol. I believe that this illegal action was a violation of both my civil rights and the civil rights of every other student in the school.

This opening promises the reader a discussion of students' rights. It also sets the essay's boundaries. Terry can't include everything about students' rights or about the duties and responsibilities of school authorities. Instead, she'll concentrate on one issue raised by her personal experience on that Monday morning.

The best essays usually begin with something catchy, something to lure the reader into the piece. Think of the opening as a hook—a phrase, a sentence, or an idea that will grab your readers so completely that they'll want to keep reading. Once you've hooked your readers, you can lead them almost anywhere. Hooks must be very sharp and very clean. They also must surprise, inform, or tickle the reader in an instant. Terry's hook is effective because it tells an informative anecdote that leads directly to the main subject of her essay.

Here are some common techniques for hooking readers:

1. Start with brief account of an incident—real or invented—that leads the reader gracefully to the point of the essay.
2. State a provocative idea in an ordinary way or an ordinary idea in a provocative way. Either one will ignite reader interest.
3. Use a quotation—not necessarily a famous one. Take it from Shakespeare, a popular song, or your grandmother. Whatever the source, be sure the sentiment relates to the topic of the essay.
4. Refute a commonly held assumption or define a word in a new and surprising way.
5. Ask an interesting question or two that you will answer in your essay.

It isn't always necessary to devise a catchy opening. A direct, clearly worded statement of the essay's main idea could serve just as well. But if a sharp hook occurs to you, use it. Work hard to get it right, but not too hard, because an opening that seems forced may sound phony. Beware also of an introduction that's too cute, too shocking, or too coarse. Be thoughtful and clever, yes, but not obnoxious. Also, keep it short. An opening that comprises, say, more than a quarter of your essay reflects on your sense of proportion.

Developing Ideas Fully

Paragraphs

Because essays consist of a series of paragraphs, pay attention to the structure and function of each paragraph you write. Each paragraph is, in effect, an essay in miniature. It has a purpose, an organizational plan, and a progression of ideas. You can scrutinize a paragraph just as you would scrutinize a complete essay.

The person who invented paragraphs was a trailblazer, a genius who figured out a simple way to mark a reader's path through a piece of writing. The paragraph indentation alerts readers to get ready for a shift of some kind, somewhat like a car's directional blinker that tells other drivers that you're about to turn.

Yet, not every new paragraph signals a drastic change. The writer may simply want to nudge the discussion ahead to the next step. Using paragraphs facilitates that progression. Some paragraphs spring directly from those that preceded them. The paragraph you are now reading, for instance, is linked to the one before by the connecting word *Yet*. The connection was meant to alert you to a change in thought, but it was also intended to remind you that the two paragraphs are related.

Abrupt starts are useful from time to time because sudden turns keep readers on their toes. But writers must guard against a whole string of surprises. By shifting too often, they may lose readers and transform surprise to annoyance or boredom. Connecting words, on the other hand, while diluting the impact of the surprise, integrate paragraphs into the essay. They create a sense of belonging.

Another function of paragraphs is that they permit readers to skip rapidly through your work, particularly when each first or last sentence summarizes the rest of the paragraph, as they often do in textbooks. Readers may then focus on paragraph openings and closings and skip what's in between. Readers in a hurry will appreciate that, but you can force readers to linger a while by varying the location of the most important idea in each paragraph.

In an essay, most paragraphs play a primary role and one or more secondary roles. An *introductory paragraph*, for instance, launches the essay and makes the intent of the essay clear to the reader. The *concluding paragraph* leaves the reader with a thought to remember and provides a sense of closure. Most paragraphs, however, are *developmental*. That is, they are used to carry forward the main point of the essay. In one way or another, developmental paragraphs perform any number of functions, including:

- Add new ideas to the preceding discussion
- Continue or explain in more detail an idea presented earlier
- Reiterate a previously stated idea
- Cite an example of a previously stated idea

- Evaluate an opinion stated earlier
- Refute previously stated ideas
- Turn the essay in a new direction
- Provide a new or contrasting point of view
- Describe the relationship between ideas presented earlier
- Provide background material
- Ask a hypothetical or rhetorical question about the topic
- Serve as a transition between sections of the essay
- Summarize an argument presented earlier

Whatever its functions, a paragraph should contribute to the essay's overall growth. A paragraph that fails to amplify the main idea of the essay should be revised or deleted. Similarly, any idea within a paragraph that doesn't contribute to the development of the paragraph's topic needs to be changed or eliminated.

Topic and Supporting Sentences

Whether readers skim your paragraphs or slog doggedly through every word, they need to find sentences now and then that, like landmarks, help them to know where they are. Such guiding sentences differ from others because they define the paragraph's main topic, hence the name *topic sentence*.

Most, but not all, paragraphs contain topic sentences. The topic of some paragraphs is so obvious that to state it would be redundant. Then, too, groups of paragraphs can be so closely knit that one topic sentence states the most important idea for all of them.

Topic sentences come in a variety of forms. What they all have in common is their helpfulness. Consider them landmarks. To drive from your home to school, for example, you turn left at Blockbuster, take a half right under the railroad trestle, and a left at the gas station. Each landmark tells you where to turn. Similarly, in a piece of writing, a topic sentence often marks a turning point that tells readers the direction they'll be going for a while.

No rule governs every possible use of a topic sentence. A sense of what readers need in order to understand the essay must be your guide. Consider your readers absent-minded wanderers who need frequent reminders of where they are and where they are going. If in doubt, grasp their hands too firmly rather than too loosely. Follow the principle that if there is a way to misunderstand or misinterpret your words, readers will most certainly find it.

Of the second kind, the *supporting sentences*, there are likely to be several. Supporting sentences provide the particulars needed to develop topic sentences. Some supporting sentences themselves need support, provided by minor supporting sentences. The following paragraph contains examples of each kind:

> [1] The Industrial Revolution changed to the manner in which products were manufactured. [2] Before the revolution, most manufacturing was done by skilled workers very knowledgeable about every aspect of the product they made. [3] A barrel-maker, for example, had the ability to construct a barrel from start to finish. [4] He knew his materials, had the tools, and understood the entire process. [5] With the growth of factories, assembly lines began to produce the same goods with less skilled workers, each of whom may have mastered only one step in the process. [6] One worker may have become an expert stave cutter, another a specialist in manufacturing the metal hoops that hold barrels together.

Sentence 1 is the topic sentence of the paragraph. Each supporting sentence adds evidence to prove its validity—that the Industrial Revolution caused change in manufacturing practices. Sentence 2 is a supporting sentence that requires additional support, provided by sentence 3. Similarly, sentence 6 supports sentence 5, and taken altogether, sentences 2–6 support sentence 1.

Most topic sentences come first in a paragraph, but in truth they can be anywhere. Nor are topic sentences always separate and independent grammatical units. Rather, they may be woven into a supporting sentence as a clause or a phrase. (In the paragraph you are now reading, for instance, the topic of the paragraph is stated in the second clause of the first sentence.) Writers frequently vary the location of topic sentences to avoid monotony. A topic sentence saved for the end of a paragraph may stand out boldly as the climax to which the supporting sentences lead.

In some kinds of writing—particularly narrative and descriptive—the topic sentence is often left out. Instead, the paragraph's main idea is implied by accumulated details and ideas. For instance, the writer who sets down several observations of a fast-food restaurant, including the crowd, the noise, the overflowing garbage cans, the smell of cooking oil, the lines of people, the crumb-strewn formica tables, and so on, creates the impression of a frenetic place. It would have been superfluous to state explicitly "It was a busy day at Burger King."

The key to unlocking a paragraph's purpose usually lies in the topic sentence. If a reader fails to catch the main idea, the meaning of the entire paragraph could fall apart. Instead of a coherent unit of meaning, the paragraph may seem to be a diffuse collection of unrelated sentences. The overall effectiveness of a paragraph, therefore, is tied to its supporting details. A loose or ambiguous connection erodes the effectiveness of both the paragraph and the entire essay.

Some paragraphs also contain what is called *transitional sentences* that link the thoughts in one paragraph to those of the previous or subsequent paragraphs. Transitional sentences, in other words, serve as bridges. For example:

> Now that the symptoms of asthma have been described, let us turn to methods of treatment.

Such a transitional sentence may be appropriate in a lengthy report, but not in a short essay. Rather, bridges in a short piece should be built more simply, with transitional words and phrases.

Like the essay of which they are the building blocks, paragraphs should have a discernible organization. Ideas may be arranged from general to specific or vice versa. Chronological and spatial arrangements make sense for narrative and descriptive paragraphs. In a cause-and-effect paragraph, logic dictates that the cause precede the effect, but the converse may sometimes be preferable. As always, clarity and intent should govern the sequence of ideas. In a coherent paragraph each sentence has its place and purpose. Disjointed paragraphs, on the other hand, consist of sentences arranged in random order. Or they contain ideas only vaguely related or irrelevant to the development of the main idea.

Writers shun formulas in creating paragraphs but concur that a paragraph consisting of one or two sentences is skimpy. To develop an idea thoroughly calls for several sentences. Not always; journalists, for example, often rely on paragraphs consisting of only one or two sentences. Most modern writers of nonfiction, however, customarily include four to eight sentences in a paragraph. But recognizing that readers need frequent breaks, they rarely write paragraphs of a dozen or more sentences. In a coherently written paragraph, sentences often contain clues that bind them to each other. Although meaning serves as the primary indication of relationships, transitional words and phrases such as *for example, also, but, on the other hand*, and others create strong links.

Including Transitions for Coherence

Writers, like music makers, strive for harmony in their art. Every chamber ensemble, barbershop quartet, and reggae, rap, and rock group works hard to achieve a pleasing and unified sound, and as a listener you can tell almost instantly whether they've done it. Likewise, when you write an essay you have to work at blending the parts harmoniously. A discordant essay—one in which the pieces seem disconnected—will leave your readers befuddled.

Fortunately, the English language is brimming with transitional words and phrases for tying sentences and ideas together. What follows is a collection of common transitional words and phrases grouped according to their customary use. With a bit of thought, you could probably add to the list.

➤ When you **ADD** ideas: *moreover, in addition, further, besides, also, and then, then too, again, next, secondly, equally important* . . .

➤ *When you make a* **CONTRAST**: *however, conversely, in contrast, on the other hand, on the contrary, but, nevertheless, and yet, still, even so* . . .

➤ When you **COMPARE** or draw a **PARALLEL**: *similarly, likewise, in comparison, in like manner, at the same time, in the same vein . . .*

➤ When you cite an **EXAMPLE**: *for example, for instance, as when, as illustrated by . . .*

➤ When you show **RESULTS**: *as a result, in consequence, consequently, accordingly, therefore, thus, hence . . .*

➤ When you **REINFORCE** an idea: *indeed, in fact, as a matter of fact, to be sure, of course, in any event, by all means . . .*

➤ When you express **SEQUENCE** or the passing of **TIME**: *soon after, then, previously, not long after, meanwhile, in the meantime, later, simultaneously, at the same time, immediately, next, at length, thereafter . . .*

➤ When you show **PLACES**: *here, nearby, at this spot, near at hand, in proximity, on the opposite side, across from, adjacent to, underneath . . .*

➤ When you **CONCLUDE**: *finally, in short, in other words, in a word, to sum up, in conclusion, in the end, when all is said and done . . .*

It's not always necessary to tie every sentence together with a specific transitional expression. Sometimes the ideas themselves create a link. For example, in the following pairs of sentences, notice how the underlined words of the second sentence echo an idea expressed in the first.

> (1) As a kind of universal language, music unites people from age eight to eighty. (2) <u>No matter how old they are</u>, people can lose themselves in melodies, rhythms, tempos, and endless varieties of sound.

(1) At the heart of *Romeo and Juliet* is a long-standing feud between the Capulets and the Montagues. (2) <u>As enemies</u>, the two families always fight in the streets of Verona.

(1) To drive nails into very hard wood without bending them, first dip the points into grease or soap. (2) <u>You can accomplish the same end</u> by moistening the points of the nails in your mouth or in a can of water.

Whenever you use a transition, you do your readers a favor. You assure them a smooth trip through your writing. Without such help, or when every sentence stands unconnected to the next, readers find themselves lurching from one idea to another. Before long, they'll either give up or be hopelessly lost, like travelers on a road without signposts or markers. Although many sentences won't contain transitions, three or four sentences in succession without a link of some kind may leave readers doubting that their trip is worth taking.

Links between sentences lend a hand to writers, too. They help them stick to the topic and avoid inadvertent detours that may disorient even the most careful readers. Ideas that fail to connect with others around them or are unrelated to the paragraph's main idea should be revised, moved, or discarded.

Varying the Sentences

Monotony kills interest. A steady diet of oatmeal dulls the taste buds. Two hundred miles on a straight road takes the kick out of driving. Day after day of routine slows the brain. Listening too often to the same song depletes its charm. Yes, monotony kills interest.

So it is with writing. It's easy to fall into a rut by using the same sentence pattern over and over and over.

Repetition makes readers yawn. To avoid boring your readers, serve them a variety of sentences. Because English is a malleable language, sentences can be endlessly twisted and turned. A mix of sentences can enliven prose and cause readers to twitter in delight.

Variety for its own sake, however, is hardly preferable to assembly-line writing—writing in which every sentence has been cut from the same pattern. But variety that clarifies meaning or gives emphasis to a particular idea is something else again.

As you probably know, most simple declarative sentences start with the subject, followed by the verb. A string of sentences with this subject-verb pattern resembles the prose in a grade-school primer. Make your move to a more mature style by analyzing one of your recent essays. Do several sentences begin with grammatical subjects? If so, try shifting the subject elsewhere. Try leading off with a prepositional phrase, or with an adverb, adjective, or some other grammatical unit. By varying sentence openings, you'll write more boldly and vibrantly.

No rule of thumb governs the proportion of sentences in an essay that should depart from the usual subject-verb word order. It all depends on the purpose and style of the essay. But if you use any sentence pattern repeatedly, be sure you know why you are doing so. If the repetition is accidental, revise for greater sentence variety.

Our language offers writers a rich menu of sentence types. Declarative sentences predominate in most essay writing. (Just to refresh your memory, a *declarative* sentence, such as the one you are now reading, simply makes a statement.) But using other types of sentences, you can create all sorts of fascinating effects. Take interrogative sentences, for example. (Do you remember that *interrogative* sentences ask questions?) An interrogative sentence appropriately placed in a passage consisting of declarative sentences changes the pace and rhythm of the prose, can underscore an idea, and promote the reader's involvement in the essay.

Don't forget about *imperative* sentences (remember that they make requests or give commands), and *exclamatory* sentences (what strong emotion they can express!). Furthermore, you can write sentences interrupted at some point by a dash—although some editors and teachers claim that it's not proper to do so in formal prose. And you can use direct and indirect quotations. Once in a while, you may wish to drive home a point with a single emphatic word. Excellent!

Another technique for fighting monotony in essay writing is to vary the length of sentences. The shortest sentence in the English language is probably the pronoun "I," which stands as a complete sentence when it is used as a response to such questions as, "Who drank the last Pepsi in the fridge?" or "Who'd like to take out a canoe?" You could also make a case for any other letter, too, as when someone asks, "Do you spell *xylophone* with an *x* or a *z*?"

The longest English sentence has not yet been written, but rest assured that it will be far longer than any essay you have ever written. In fact, it will go on infinitely. Long sentences that stretch on and on can still be grammatically correct. (Don't confuse long sentences with "run-ons," which contain structural errors.) But they demand greater effort from readers because, while stepping from one part of the sentence to the next, they must keep track of more words, modifiers, phrases (not to speak of parenthetical asides), and clauses without losing the writer's main thought, which may be buried amid any number of secondary, or less important, thoughts.

Short sentences are easier to grasp—but not always. (Remember Descartes' famous five-word assertion: "I think; therefore, I am"?) But generally, a brief sentence makes its point quickly, sometimes with astonishing intensity, since all the words concentrate on a single point. Take, for example, the last sentence in this passage:

> For three days, my parents and I sat in our S.U.V. and drove from college to college to college, in search of the perfect place for me to spend the next four years. For seventy-two hours we lived as one person, sharing thoughts and dreams, stating opinions about each campus we visited, taking guided tours, interviewing students and admissions officials, asking directions a hundred times, eating together in town after town, and even sleeping in the same motel rooms. But mostly, we fought.

A terse closing sentence following a windy, forty-six-word sentence produces a mild jolt. Indeed, it has been planted in that spot deliberately to startle the reader. The technique is easily mastered but should be used sparingly. Overuse dilutes its impact. A sequence of short sentences can be no less tiresome than a long, lumbering sentence. If you find that your essay contains a string of four or five sentences of almost equal length, create a better balance by sentence combining—that is, grammatically splice two sentences into one.

Balancing short and long sentences creates a rhythm in prose. Because readers usually pause, albeit subconsciously, at every period, short sentences slow the tempo. Long sentences speed it up, but the pace depends mostly on the placement of clauses, the amount of parenthetical matter, and choice of words. Although essays are usually meant for silent reading, writers can slow the pace by carefully choosing difficult-to-pronounce words or selecting words containing many hard consonants. *The squad plodded agonizingly across the ugly swamp* is an example. Similarly, speed increases with sentences with softer, more flowing sounds, as in *While shaving and dressing Sam perused his face in the mirror.*

Varying Sentences—A Summary

➤ Start sentences with:

1. A prepositional phrase: *From the start, In the first place, At the outset*
2. Adverbs and adverbial phrases: *Originally, At first, Initially*
3. Dependent clauses: *When you start with this, Because the opening is*
4. Conjunctions: *And, But, Not only, Either, So, Yet*
5. Adjectives and adjective phrases: *Fresh from, Introduced with, Headed by*
6. Verbal infinitives: *To launch, To take the first step, To get going*
7. Participles: *Leading off, Starting up, Commencing with*
8. Inversions: *Unique is the writer who embarks . . .*

➤ Use a variety of sentence types.

➤ Balance long and short sentences.

➤ Combine series of very short sentences.

➤ Dismember very long sentences.

Ending an Essay Memorably

At the end of your an essay you can lift your pen off the paper and be done with it. Or you can present your readers with a little gift to remember you by—perhaps a surprising insight, a bit of wisdom, a catchy phrase—something likely to tease readers' brains, tickle their funny bones, or make them feel smart.

Choose the gift carefully. It should fit the content, style, and mood of your essay and spring naturally from its contents. A good essay can easily be spoiled by a grating conclusion. A serious essay shouldn't end with a joke. Steer clear of endings that are too common or too cute, such as: *that's it; a good time was had by all; tune in next time—same time, same station; it was a dream come true; good night and God bless,* and many other equally trite expressions. Such banal endings leave readers thinking that the writer either lacks imagination or may be too lazy to choose a more thoughtful gift. In short, don't spoil a fresh essay with a stale conclusion.

Because it comes last, the final paragraph leaves an enduring impression. A weak, apologetic, or irrelevant conclusion may dilute or even obliterate the effect that you tried hard to create. Above all, stay away from summary endings. When an essay is short to begin with, it's insulting to review for readers what is evident on the page in front of them. Readers are intelligent people. Trust them to remember what your essay says.

A catchy conclusion isn't always necessary, but even a short ending may be preferable to none at all. Effective endings leave readers fulfilled, satisfied that they have arrived somewhere. A judiciously chosen ending may sway readers to judge your essay somewhat more leniently than otherwise. There are no guarantees, of course, but readers are bound to be touched by a memento of your thinking, your sense of humor, or your vision. Even an ordinary thought, uniquely expressed, will leave an agreeable afterglow.

Here are several techniques for writing conclusions:

1. Have a little fun with your conclusion; try to put a smile on your reader's face.
2. End with an apt quotation drawn from the essay itself or from some other source.
3. Finish by clearly restating your essay's main point but using new words. If appropriate, add a short tag line, a brief sentence that creates a dramatic effect.
4. Bring your readers up to date or project them into the future. Say something about the months or years ahead.

IMPROVING YOUR WRITING

Grades are important, but they are not the main purpose of writing essays. Rather, your teachers want to assess the quality and depth of your knowledge, your ability to think, and of course, your writing proficiency. If you are not satisfied with the grades you customarily earn on essays, there is something you can do about it.

When an essay is returned to you, look it over carefully, examining every symbol and comment that your teacher has written. If in doubt about the meaning of anything, ask your teacher to explain. If possible, do it right after class, or set up an individual writing conference. Keep the essay in a writing folder or portfolio. When your next essay is assigned, check your weaknesses from the last one before you start to write. A list of types of mistakes and shortcomings and the frequency with which they occurred on successive themes offers graphic incentive for improvement.

By studying the mistakes you make frequently on two or three essays, you can make yourself an improvement chart or "rubric" to fit your needs. It might appear as follows, although its categories would be tailored to your needs:

SAMPLE RUBRIC FOR EVALUATING AN ESSAY

Types of Errors & Weaknesses Noted	Number of Times Occurring					
	1st Week	2nd Week	3rd Week	4th Week	5th Week	6th Week
Whole essay 　Clarity of main idea 　Focus/Unity/Purpose 　Overall organization 　Economy of expres- 　　sion						
Paragraphs 　Topic sentences 　Development of 　　ideas 　Use of transitions 　Arrangement of 　　ideas						
Sentences 　Variety 　Sentence errors 　　Run-ons 　　Fragments 　　Comma splices						
Word choice 　Appropriateness 　Interest						
Usage and Grammar						
Mechanics 　Spelling 　Punctuation						
Mark received						

Overall Criticism Teacher's Comments	First Week
	Second Week
	Third Week
	Fourth Week
	Fifth Week
	Sixth Week

Certainly, there are few among us who do not enjoy evidence of self-improvement. The improvement chart, listing your particular shortcomings, can be used to encourage and record your improvement. If your particular faults can be pinpointed, it will be wise to include them specifically rather than under a general entry. For example, if you make apostrophe and semicolon mistakes more often than others, make individual entries for these under punctuation. Your teachers could probably give valuable help in preparing your chart.

You will certainly profit if you go to your teacher after class with a paper in hand and ask for extra help. Ask the teacher to show you how to express more clearly or economically what you have tried to say in your paper. In this way you will see how to better arrange your topic or express yourself about your topic. If you do not go with paper in hand, your teacher will be glad to help you, but may supply personal examples. It is more helpful to have the examples come from your own paper; you will understand them better and be better able to apply the lessons you learn to your other writing. Going to ask for help from your teacher with your work in hand also will show that you honestly wish to improve and are not asking in order to make a good impression.

GUIDELINES FOR WRITTEN WORK

➤ Written work reveals your ability and motivation; therefore, always give it all you've got.

➤ The main purposes of written work are:
1. to impart information to a reader
2. to develop habits of clear thinking

➤ To demonstrate writing ability, your work should be
1. clear
2. interesting to read
3. correct
4. presented attractively and in the proper form

➤ Students use many different approaches to written work. Try various processes, and stick to the one that produces the best results.

➤ Excellence often comes from taking pride in one's work.

LOOKING BACK

1. In deciding on an essay for your health class, four titles come to mind:
   a. Maintaining Good Health
   b. Why Smoking Is Bad for You

    c. My Fight Against Depression

    d. Teenagers' Sleeping Disorders

      Which one would you select? Why? Which is the poorest choice you could have made? Why?

2. In this chapter, several principles of good writing have been discussed. Which of them did you find the most worthwhile? Are there any that you would like to talk over with a teacher or other writing instructor?

3. The opening sentence of this chapter is: "Of the several skills you will develop in educating yourself—listening, reading, speaking, thinking, and writing—the one that will give your teachers the widest range for measuring your ability and achievements will be your writing."

      Tell whether you agree with the statement. Why?

      Select one of the other skills and explain why that one is the most significant for the career you are planning.

Chapter 11
Written Work: Style and Usage

TRUE CONFESSIONS

1. Do you remember Winston Churchill's famous reference to "wounds, unrelenting labor, perspiration, and weeping"? Of course you don't, because Churchill used "blood, toil, sweat, and tears" in his stirring speech to his countrymen.

   Why all the fuss over Churchill's choice of words? Did they really matter? Why? What makes one slogan more memorable than another?

2. Some years ago an advertising copywriter was preparing an ad for Ivory soap. In two hundred words he told about the "unique saponification" of Ivory, and how it was engineered to stay atop the water "during one's ablutions." His boss studied the results, then drew a red line through the whole article and replaced it with two words: "It floats!"

   Was the boss' revision an improvement? Tell why?

3. Have you ever uttered sentences similar to those below?
   a. They say it will rain today.
   b. He's very fickle, they say, and won't go out with the same girl for more than a few weeks.
   c. They say she's a terrible mother who actually neglects her children.

Do you see anything wrong with such statements? If so, why do people use them?

MODELS OF STYLE

Written work is critical to your success in school. You cannot escape it—you must write not only in English class, but also in history, science, math, and foreign language classes. Now that we have examined essay writing in some detail, let us turn to the examination of style and usage.

First, let's examine what some of the world's great thinkers have written to see how their prose works. Thucydides, the Greek historian, writing a history of the Peloponnesian War, wrote in "such a way," said Plutarch, "as to make his hearer a spectator." Here is the beginning paragraph of Thucydides' description of the deadly plague that ravaged Athens in 429 B.C., carrying away half the population of the city, among whom was the city's foremost leader—Pericles. Note the simplicity of the words used. Not a single technical or medical term appears in the whole three-page description of the disease, yet doctors are able to diagnose the epidemic from symptoms so clearly described. Here follows a single paragraph:

> Words indeed fail one when one tries to give a general picture of this disease; and as for the sufferings of individuals, they seemed almost beyond the capacity of human nature to endure. Here in particular is a point where this plague showed itself to be something quite different from ordinary diseases: though there were many dead bodies lying about unburied, the birds and animals that eat human

flesh either did not come near them or, if they did taste the flesh, died of it afterwards. Evidence for this may be found in the fact that there was a complete disappearance of all birds of prey: they were not to be seen either round the bodies or anywhere else. But dogs, being domestic animals, provided the best opportunity of observing this effect of the plague.[1]

Sophocles, listed always among the world's greatest dramatists, has the following description of man at the end of the first scene in his play, *Antigone:*

There are many wonderful things, but none more wonderful than man. Over the whitecaps of the sea he goes, driven by the stormy winds, topped by the towering waves; and the Earth, oldest of the gods, eternal and tireless, he wears away, turning furrows with his plow year after year. He snares the lighthearted birds and the wild beasts of the fields, and he catches in his nets the fish of the sea, man forever resourceful. He tames the animals that roam the meadows and mountains, yoking the shaggy horses and the powerful bulls. And he has learned the use of language to express wind-swift thought, and he has mastered the art of living with other men in addition to the conquest of nature. Skillfully he meets the future; although he has found no escape from death, he has discovered release from painful diseases. His ingenuity results in evil as well as good; when he respects his country's laws and justice he deserves honor; but may the arrogant

---

[1]Thucydides, Book 2, 50. As translated by Rex Warner, *Thucydides, The Peloponnesian War* (Baltimore: Penguin, 1954), 125.

man, untrue to his city, never come to my hearth or share my thoughts.[2]

In the corridor of the library of Cambridge University hangs a small frame, enclosing a short speech of two hundred eighty-seven words. Under the frame is a placard with the inscription: THE NOBLEST PROSE EVER WRITTEN. The speech is:

> Fourscore and seven years ago our fathers brought forth on this continent a new nation, conceived in liberty, and dedicated to the proposition that all men are created equal.
>
> Now we are engaged in a great civil war, testing whether that nation, or any nation so conceived and so dedicated, can long endure. We are met on a great battle-field of that war. We have come to dedicate a portion of that field as a final resting-place for those who here gave their lives that that nation might live. It is altogether fitting and proper that we should do this.
>
> But, in a larger sense, we cannot dedicate—we cannot consecrate—we cannot hallow—this ground. The brave men, living and dead, who struggled here, have consecrated it far above our poor power to add or detract. The world will little note nor long remember what we say here, but it can never forget what they did here. It is for us, the living, rather, to be dedicated here to the unfinished work which they who fought here have thus far so nobly advanced. It is rather for us to be here dedicated to the great task remaining before us—that from these

---

[2]Sophocles, *Antigone*, II. 333–373. As translated by Walter R. Agard, *The Greek Mind* (Princeton: D. Van Nostrand Co. Inc., 1957), 143.

honored dead we take increased devotion to that
cause for which they gave the last full measure of
devotion; that we here highly resolve that these
dead shall not have died in vain; that this nation,
under God, shall have new birth of freedom; and
that government of the people, by the people, for
the people, shall not perish from the earth.[3]

On November 19, 1863, a national cemetery was
being dedicated at Gettysburg, Pennsylvania, where
during the first three days of the previous July,
thousands of soldiers had died. Senator Edward Everett
was the principal speaker at the dedication. He dealt
with concepts of government, the evolution of democracy, and many other profound abstractions for an hour
and fifty-five minutes. The world has forgotten what
he said, but it remembers 265 words of Lincoln's
Gettysburg Address. Why? Because seldom in history
have words been guided by the mind to produce such
clarity, simplicity, sincerity, and ordered beauty.

As we turn to look at the uses to which words can
be put, the attributes they take on, and how you can
make them work best for you, keep constantly in mind
the four qualities found in the models just observed:
(1) clarity, (2) simplicity, (3) sincerity, and (4) order—
which by arrangement produce beauty. These should
stand guard over whatever you speak or write, and
should be the primary elements of your style. These are
the qualities that your teachers, your readers, and your
listeners hope to find as you express your thoughts.

---

[3]Abraham Lincoln, *The Collected Writings of Abraham Lincoln*, ed.
Ray P. Baslen, 9 vols. (New Brunswick: Rutgers Univ. Press, 1953),
7:23.

CLARITY

To put it simply, clarity is saying exactly what you mean to say. Denotations are the primary, explicit definitions that a dictionary gives. Connotations are meanings that, through custom and use, have come to be associated to a word. When you use a word, all its denotations and connotations will be evoked in a reader's mind. For example, as a reader of this book, you are probably one of those persons described as a *teenager,* an *adolescent,* a *young adult,* a *youth,* a *minor,* a *juvenile,* a *postpubescent,* a *preadult.* Do you see any differences among these labels? How would you clarify the differences among them to a foreigner just learning to speak English? Do you like or dislike any of them? Are there any other words that are missing from this list?

Now, try a little practice at examining connotations. Examine the word *mark.*

MEANING	USE
Denoted:	Mark your notebook for
to make a mark (verb)	easy identification.
a line, dot, etc. (noun)	Who put the mark on
	the desk?
Connoted:	He will mark time until
to wait	summer.
a sign or indication	The ability to listen is the
	mark of a civilized man.
to listen, heed	Mark my words, he will not
	return.
a sign of evil	He is cursed with the mark
	of Cain.

a standard of quality	This paper is not up to the mark.
importance, distinction	The chairman is a man of mark.
impression	He left his mark on his students.
a guide or point of reference	The harbor lights were a mark for fliers.
a target	He did not hit the mark.
an aim, goal	The mark of the campaign was to raise six thousand dollars.
a nautical term	Bits of leather indicated the marks on the sounding line. Samuel Clemens adopted the riverboat call "mark twain" as his pen name.
to show plainly	Her smile marked her happiness.
to be ready	I am on my mark.

See how many connoted meanings you can find for the following familiar words:

   term, take, tag, table, tack, sweep, snap, spread, train, and pick

Now try the simple word *run,* it has more than a dozen connoted meanings. Write your own meaning for each use as shown in the sentences that follow:

1. The boys have the *run* of the club.
   Meaning:

2. The bus *runs* past the store,
   Meaning:

3. The depression caused a *run* on the banks.
   Meaning:

4. She got a *run* in her stocking from kneeling.
   Meaning:

5. He *runs* the assembly with an iron hand.
   Meaning:

6. The dog *run* in our backyard provided exercise for
   our terrier.
   Meaning:

7. The musical, *Cats,* had one of the longest *runs* in
   theatrical history.
   Meaning:

8. Derek Jeter hit another home *run* last night.
   Meaning:

9. The mayor had a close *run* in the election.
   Meaning:

10. The fishermen had a *run* of good luck on trout.
    Meaning:

11. The broker *runs* up a big telephone bill.
    Meaning:

12. Anton *ran* the spear through the door.
    Meaning:

13. Cleveland *ran* for president twice.
    Meaning:

14. Pasteur *ran* down the cause of the silkworms
    dying in Provençal.
    Meaning:

Distinctive use lifts the common and familiar out of
the realm of the ordinary. Great improvement in ability
to handle words can be derived by practice in replacing

many overused and tired words with more pointed and graphic connotative substitutes. Read with a keen eye for finding new uses for the many words which heretofore have had only one or two meanings for you.

Meanings can be made clear by examining the use of the word in the sentence. A word may have meanings that are almost opposite, as shown by the uses of *fast* in this sentence: The torpedo was *fast* approaching its target; seconds before it had been *fast* in its tube. The first connotes great speed, and the second implies being held motionless. As with new words, new meanings must be put to work if you expect to keep them in your vocabulary.

SIMPLICITY

Simplicity is the using of ordinary words and ordinary structures of grammar. Some people appear fond of words of many syllables and use them even when short, memorable ones are more suitable. In your writing prefer simple, concrete words to vague, complex ones: *run* or *walk* instead of *move, group* instead of *assemblage, then* instead of *at that point in time.*

Plain and Precise Words

To write clearly, use plain words. Never use a complex word because it sounds good or makes you seem more sophisticated. Use an elegant word only when necessary—that is, when it's the only word that will let you add something to the essay that you can't achieve in any other way. Why? Because an elegant word used merely to use an elegant word is bombastic . . . er . . . big-sounding and artificial.

Besides, simple ideas dressed up in ornate words

often obscure meaning. Worse, they make writers sound phony, if not downright foolish. For instance, under ordinary circumstances you'd never utter the words, "Let's go to our domiciles" at the end of a day at school. Nor would you call your teachers *pedagogues* or your dog a *canine*. Yet, the following overblown sentence appeared in a student essay:

> Although my history pedagogue insisted that I labor in my domicile immediately upon arrival, I was obliged to air my canine before commencing.

How much clearer and direct it would have been to write:

> I had to walk the dog before starting my history homework.

Fortunately, English is loaded with simple words that can express the most profound ideas. A sign that says STOP! conveys its message more clearly than CEASE AND DESIST. When a dentist pokes at your teeth, it *hurts,* even if dentists call it "experiencing discomfort." Descartes, the famous French philosopher, said, "I think. Therefore, I am," a statement that forever afterward shaped the way we think about existence. Descartes might have used more exotic words, of course, words more in keeping with the florid writing style of his time, but the very simplicity of his words endows his statement with great power. In fact, a sign of true intelligence is the ability to convey deep meanings with simple words.

Perhaps you've heard of Wee Willie Keeler, a hard-hitting outfielder for the New York Giants about a hundred years ago. When asked the secret of his success as a batter, thank goodness Willie didn't say, "I swing my bat and launch the spheroidal projectile to

areas of the playing field devoid of defensive players."
No, Willie knew the power of keeping it simple and
said, "I hit 'em where they ain't."

Once you have chosen simple, direct words, use a
simple grammatical structure to combine those words
in sentences. Avoid piling clause upon clause—if you
find yourself writing a sentence which is too long or
complex, break it up into two or more shorter and
simpler sentences. At the same time, do not use such a
multitude of short declarative sentences that you bore
your reader.

In addition to care in word choice and sentence
structure, choose carefully the voice of your verbs. The
most important characteristic of life is action, and
speaking and writing that reflect the thoughts of life
most effectively do so through action. For that reason,
it is always better to use the active rather than passive
voice of verbs. To say "Fishing is enjoyed by John"
(passive voice), leaves John motionless; but to say
"John enjoys fishing" (active voice), starts him on his
way, making the subject act upon something.

After the subject, which is the reason for the
thought being expressed, the *verb* is *the important
word.* It carries the weight, contains the vigor, and, if
carefully chosen, is capable of sound and color. Note
the verbs in the sentences that follow:

1. The USSR *declined* rapidly after the failed coup of
   1991; both political and economic strength were
   gone.
2. The USSR was *doomed* after the failed coup of
   1991; disorder, debility, and despair prevailed.

> Even though the verb *declined* is given a
> modifier to speed the action, it does not bring the
> USSR crashing with the resounding sense and

sound of *doom.* And what of *were gone* as compared with *prevailed*? The tense of *were gone*
removes the action of political and economic
strength, but there remained action—disorder,
debility, and despair *prevailed.*

CHOOSING ACTIVE WORDS

One of the glorious achievements of man, said
Sophocles, was that "he has learned the use of
language to express windswift thought."[4] Another
translation puts it in slightly different word:

> Words also, and thought as rapid as air,
> He fashions to his good use.[5]

Which words impress us most when we hear or read
them? Surely, those that produce action and bring a
thought to life. Words, which, as Sophocles puts it, are
active enough to express thoughts as swift as wind.

Of all the parts of speech, verbs carry more action
than the others. Active verbs stimulate reader interest.
They perform, stir up, get up and move around. They
excel in their power to pump vitality into your writing.
They add energy and variety to sentences. As a bonus,
active verbs often help you trim needless words from
your writing.

In contrast, being verbs are stagnant. They don't do
anything. Notice the lifelessness in all the most
common forms of the verb *to be: is, are, was, were,
am, has been, had been, will be.* When used in a
sentence, each of these being verbs joins the subject to
the predicate—and that's all. In fact, the verb *to be* acts

[4]Sophocles, *Antigone*, trans. Agard, 143.
[5]Sophocles, *Antigone*, 1. 353. As translated by Dudley Fitts, *Greek
Plays in Modern Translation* (New York: Dial Press, 1947), 470.

much like an equal sign in an equation, as in "Four minus three *is* one" $(4 - 3 = 1)$, "Harold *is* smart" (Harold = smart), or "Coke *is* the real thing" (Coke = RT). Because equal signs (and being verbs) show no action, use active verbs whenever you can.

Of course, being verbs are perfectly acceptable in speech and writing. You can't get along without them, but use them sparingly. If more than twenty-five percent of your sentences use a being verb, you may be relying on them too heavily.

Substitute active verbs for being verbs by extracting them from other words in the sentence:

BEING VERB: Linda *was* the winner of the raffle.
ACTIVE VERB: Linda *won* the raffle.

Here the verb *won* has been extracted from the noun *winner*.

Active verbs may also be extracted from adjectives, as in:

BEING VERB: My summer at the New Jersey shore *was* enjoyable.
ACTIVE VERB: I *enjoyed* my summer at the New Jersey shore.

Sometimes it pays to substitute an altogether fresh verb:

BEING VERB: It *is* not easy for me to express my feelings.
ACTIVE VERB: I *find* it difficult to express my feelings.

Practice will help you purge being verbs from your sentences and thereby add vitality to whatever you write.

SINCERITY

You must choose a style and words that are appropriate to the occasion. You must never be condescending or supercilious or you will turn off your readers to anything you wish to say.

Viewpoint is an important consideration, too. Choose words for the person or persons to whom you wish to convey your thoughts. When Abraham Lincoln spoke at Gettysburg, the words he chose were not for himself or the dignitaries who were present. He selected words that had meaning for the veterans of the battle who leaned on their crutches or dangled empty uniform sleeves in the November wind. He knew that among his listeners there would be mothers who had lost sons, wives who had lost husbands, and brothers who had lost brothers. These people would remember what he said because he spoke for them.

Churchill, in his famous "Blood, Sweat, and Tears" speech, did not choose his words for the members of Parliament. He chose them for the thousands of Britishers who would bleed and sweat, and bleed and sweat some more, in the impending holocaust.

There are a number of questions you should ask yourself in order to show sensitivity to the audience with whom you wish to communicate.

1. What words will they clearly understand?
2. What would they really like to hear?
3. What are their interests?
   But far more significant,
4. What are their needs?

Having answered these questions adopt an appropriate point of view that respects your audience.

SELECTING THE BEST WORDS

Diction, the name given to choice of words, demands a special concern for concreteness in words. We might have many favorite abstract words—*decadence, prosperity, patience, charity, temptation.* But if solid nouns and verbs can make an exact word picture, naming the subject and action of decay, or of prosperity, or of patience, then pleasant generalizations and abstractions must be passed over for the sake of clarity.

Precise words are memorable, while hazy, hard-to-grasp words fade as quickly as last night's dream. Tell your garage mechanic vaguely, "This car is a lemon," and he'll ask for more information. Say precisely "My car won't start in freezing weather," and he'll raise the engine hood and go to work. If a patient in the E.R. says, "I feel pain," a surgeon might at least like to know exactly where it hurts before pulling out her scalpels. In other words, precise language is more informative, more functional, and thus more desirable.

In the first draft of a personal essay about a day he'd like to forget, Jeff S wrote this paragraph:

> It was an awful day outside. Everything was going wrong. I felt terrible. Things weren't going well in school. I got a below-par grade on a paper, and I was sure that I had failed my science quiz. I also had lots of things to do at home and no time to do them. My mother was in a bad mood, too. She yelled at me for all kinds of things. Then Penny called, and we got into a disagreement. I had trouble with my DVD player, and I couldn't pay for repairs. I went to bed early, hoping that tomorrow would be better.

Reviewing the essay a few days later, Jeff realized the paragraph begged for more precise writing. Yes, the day had been dreadful, but his account needed details to prove it. The next draft took care of that:

> It had been a cold and rainy November day, and my life was as miserable as the weather. I felt chills all day, and my throat was sore. In school I got a D on a history paper about the Bubonic Plague, and I was sure that I had failed the chemistry quiz. The homework was piling up—two lab reports, over 150 pages to read in *Wuthering Heights,* a chapter in the history text, and about a hundred new vocabulary words in Spanish. I didn't have time or energy to do it all, especially when my mother started to pick at me about my messy room, the thank you letters I'm supposed to write to my grandparents, and sending in my registration for the ACT. Then Penny called to tell me that she wouldn't be coming over for Thanksgiving after all, and we argued about loyalty and trust and keeping promises. When I put on a DVD to watch *Lord of the Rings* again, the DVD player kept skipping scenes. The repairman said he would charge $100 just to look at the damn thing, but I don't have that kind of money. By 9:00 P.M. I was in bed, hoping that tomorrow would be better.

In this version Jeff included many precise details that vividly illustrate the wretchedness of that miserable day. And he's made clear why he picked that day as the subject of his essay.

Of course, not every essay topic calls for such detail. Some topics invite you to write more vaguely, more abstractly, perhaps more philosophically. For example, concepts such as *loyalty, trust, and keeping promises,* as well as *love, freedom, spirit, fairness, conformity, satisfaction,* and countless others stand for ideas that exist in our hearts and minds. The power to express principles, concepts, and feelings is unique to humans, and such a gift shouldn't go untapped, but an essay consisting solely of abstractions will leave readers at sea. However amorphous the topic, therefore, an essay's success depends on precise, hard-edged, concrete words.

Undoubtedly, vague, shadowy words are easier to think of. But they are often meant to cover up a lack of clear and rigorous thinking. It's a cinch to pass judgment on a book, for example, by calling it "good" or "interesting." But what readers want to know is precisely why you thought so. How simple it is to call someone an "old man" without bothering to show the reader a "stooped white-haired gentleman shuffling along the sidewalk." A writer who says her teacher is "ugly" sends a different image of ugliness to each reader. If the teacher is a "shifty-eyed tyrant who spits when she talks," then, by golly, say it. Or if the teacher's personality is ugly, show her ill temper, arrogance, and cruelty as she scolds her hapless students.

Good writers often experience the world more intensely than other people. Like artists, they think visually. They also listen hard to the sounds and voices around them and are extra-sensitive to smells, to tastes, and to the feel of things. They keep their senses at full throttle in order, as the writer James Baldwin once said, "to describe things which other people are too busy to describe." They understand that much good writing must appeal to their readers' senses. To write precisely, then, is to write with pictures, sounds, and actions that are as vivid on paper as they are in reality. Exact words leave distinct marks; abstract ones, blurry impressions. It can't hurt to anticipate your readers' reactions to every word you write. Ask yourself, "Might readers understand this word in any other way than how I meant it?" If so, strike it out and find another.

Obviously, the precisely worded sentences are richer in meaning than the hazy ones. But they are also much longer. In fact, it's not always desirable or necessary to define every abstraction with precise details. Each time you mention *dinner,* for instance, you don't have to recite the menu. When you use an abstract word in an essay, ask yourself what is more important—to give readers a more detailed account of your idea or to push on to other, more important, matters. The context, as well as your judgment of the readers' intelligence, will have to determine how abstract your essay can be. Remember, though, that no one wants to read an essay that never deals concretely with anything.

Concrete words need few modifiers. Care should be taken to avoid the use of overworked adjectives. If an adjective is used at all, it should be tested for efficiency: Is it the right adjective, or is there a brighter, better one? The same judgment must be made of adverbs, for nothing can muddle a word picture as quickly as "excess baggage" adverbs. If the verb is strong, the contribution of the adverb must be studied carefully before it is added. If the horse *galloped* over the pasture, to add that it galloped *rapidly* is questionable. The adverb modifying the adjective must also be studied with a critical eye. If the adjective had already put the icing on the cake, further icing or decoration would be redundant. It would be preferable to form the habit of choosing among several synonyms to provide more exact modifiers when modifiers are necessary.

COMMON USAGE ERRORS

There is a subtle distinction between conversation and writing. When you speak, you are present and can clarify any errors of misunderstanding by explaining further. Consequently, speech need not be as precise as written work. When you write, your words must bear the burden of conveying meaning all by themselves and so must be clear and follow accepted usage.

The onslaught of television, sports announcing, and advertising, because they emphasize immediacy at the expense of depth of understanding and clarity, have helped to blur the lines between standard and non-standard English usage.

Many usage errors arise from lack of precision.

What follows is a list of common usage errors that most educated people generally avoid.

Errors of Grammar

➤ Use verbal nouns (gerunds) with the possessive case rather than the participle with the obective case.

> INCORRECT: I knew about *him taking* first place.
> CORRECT: I knew about *his taking* first place.

➤ Avoid using nouns as direct modifiers.

> INCORRECT: an aggressive-type man
> CORRECT: an aggressive man

To modify one noun by another, put the modifier in a prepositional phrase.

> INCORRECT: an I.R.S. tax audit
> CORRECT: an audit *of taxes by the I.R.S.*

➤ Avoid using a negative with the word *hardly*.
Hardly means barely able, or not able. Thus, if you use a negative with it, you'll be using a double negative and saying the opposite of what you mean.
  To say, "The boy can't hardly climb the tree," doesn't mean that the boy is barely able to climb the tree. It means that he can climb it easily. Look at it this way: The boy cannot (hardly, not able to) climb the tree. The two negatives in a row cancel one another out.

➤ Do not use the intensive pronoun as a substitute for the pronoun. Any intensive pronoun should only be used to make a noun or another pronoun stand out in the sentence, as in: St. Paul himself wrote these words. (The word *himself* is intensifying the use of St. Paul.)

> INCORRECT: Martha, Mary, and myself went to Washington for the inaugural celebration. (The word *myself* has nothing to intensify.)
> CORRECT: Martha, Mary, and I went to Washington.

➤ Do not use the word *that* after the word *but*.

> INCORRECT: I do not doubt *but that* Henry will become a great teacher.
> CORRECT: I do not doubt *that* Henry will become a great teacher.
> INCORRECT: He would have been on time *but that* he got stuck in traffic.
> CORRECT: He would have been on time, *but* he got stuck in traffic.

➤ Do not use the pronoun *they* without clearly indicating the antecedent. To use *they* in a nonspecific way is to betray fuzzy thinking; and certainly, it is not clear speaking.

> INCORRECT: I went to the infirmary, and *they* said I had the flu.
>
> INCORRECT: *They* say that the Infiniti is the finest car on the road today.

Who are they? The antecedents in these sentences are not expressed. No one knows who *they* are, and no one has any way of finding out.

> CORRECT: I went to the infirmary, and *the nurse* said I had the flu.
>
> CORRECT: *All my friends* say that the Infiniti is the finest car on the road today.

Never, never use *they,* alone. Always make sure there are nouns in your sentence or paragraph to explain who *they* refers to.

Errors of Weakness

➤ Do not make nouns into verbs.

> WEAK: The President will deplane in a half an hour.
> STRONG: The President will leave the plane in half an hour.

➤ Avoid redundancies which, although correct grammatically, add nothing new to the sentence.

> WEAK: He is a *man who is* too fat.
> STRONG: He is too fat.

➤ Avoid tautologies, the needless repetition of ideas.

> *reiterate again*

Reiterate means *repeat and repeat and repeat some more*. To use the word *again* after reiterate is to write a tautology.

> *true facts*

Facts can only be true, otherwise they are not facts at all.

> *In my mind I think Michael Jordan was a great basketball player.*

Where else but in one's mind does one think?

➤ Do not modify the word *unique*.
Unique means *singular, one of a kind*. So to say that someone is *very unique* is to say that he or she is *very one-of-a-kind*. How can anyone be *very one*, or *more one*, or *less one*? One can only be one. Use *unique* without any modifier.

Misuse of Words

➤ can, may
Can means *be able to*.

> He *can* climb the mountain.

May means *be permitted to*.

> He *may* keep the book if he likes it.

➤ disinterested, uninterested
Disinterested means *impartial*.

> Lawyers strive to find *disinterested* jurors.

Uninterested means *lacking in interest*.

> Television commercials try to persuade *uninterested* viewers to buy new cars.

➤ effect, affect
The prefixes give the clue here. *Ef* means *from*, *af* means *toward*; so *effect* describes something that comes out of a situation, and *affect* describes something that comes to a situation.

Effect, as a noun, is the result (what came out) of an action; and as a verb, it means to produce the result.

> The elements of careful design combined for a stunning *effect* when the curtain rose on the first act.

Affect is a verb meaning to influence.

> How did your training *affect* your playing?

➤ farther, further
Both declare that something has advanced. Nonetheless, they are not interchangeable.
   – *Farther* is used for distance in air, on land, or at sea.

> The sloop is *farther* out in the bay than the launch.

   – *Further* is used for distance in time.

> The scientist engaged in *further* study.

➤ imply, infer
Imply means *to express indirectly*.

> The reporter *implied* that the mayor was corrupt.

Infer means *to draw a conclusion*.

> What can you *infer* from her choice of words?

➤ like, as
These two words are misused more often than any others. Never use them interchangeably. To keep them straight, remember how they are used.

– *Like* is a preposition and will modify nouns and is never used in verbal expressions. It means *similar to*.

  She is *like* my sister.

– *As* is a conjunction or adverb and should be used with verbs or phrases. It means, when used as an adverb, *equally, when*, or *where*.

  He is *as* tall *as* my brother.

When used as a conjunction the word *as* means *because, since*, or *in the way or manner that*.

> *As* you are going to town anyway, will you post this letter for me?
> Do *as* I say, not *as* I do.

➤ less, fewer
Both declare that something has been reduced in quantity. Nonetheless, they should not be used interchangeably.

- *Less* should only be used with abstractions or singular nouns of quantity.

  Because of my illness, I have *less* time to complete my research paper.
  Put *less* milk on my cereal next time.

- *Fewer* should only be used with numbers or concrete nouns.

  This flock has *fewer* sheep than that flock.

➤ loan, lend

- *Loan* is a noun.

  One goes to a bank to seek a *loan*.

- *Lend* is a verb.

  It is improper to say Please *loan* me some money.
  It is proper to say, Please *lend* me some money.

➤ there, their

- *There* is an adverb or is an expletive.

  (adverb) Look over *there*.
  (expletive) There are many errors of usage.
- *Their* is a possessive.

  The boys said that *their* brother had won
  the bicycle race.

➤ *Transpire* is used incorrectly as a substitute for *occurred*. It means to *become known*, not *to happen*.

  INCORRECT: The lawyer asked the witness what had *transpired*.
  CORRECT: The lawyer asked the witness what had *occurred*.

➤ two, to, too

- *Two* is a number.

  There are *two* books on the table.

- *To* is a preposition or a particle indicating an infinitive.

  (preposition) Mary ran *to* the car.
  (particle) It is difficult *to* run twenty-six miles without stopping.

- *Too* is an adverb.

  The boy was *too* large to sit on the high chair.

Misuse of Prepositions

➤ Avoid the phrase *kind of* when you mean *rather*.

  INCORRECT: She was *kind of* pretty.
  CORRECT: She was *rather* pretty.

➤ Remember that *of* is a preposition, while *have* is a verb.

  INCORRECT: He would *of* been on time, had he started earlier.
  CORRECT: He would *have* been on time, had he started earlier.

➤ *Due to* has come to mean *because* rather than an expression to indicate something owed. When you mean to say *because,* say so, by using *because.*

  Homage is *due* a king.
  The game was cancelled *because* the field was muddy.

➤ *Inside of*—do not use *of*. *Inside* is complete by itself.

➤ *Later on*—do not use *on*. *Later* is complete by itself.

➤ *Off of*—do not use *of*. *Off* is complete by itself.

➤ *Plan on*—do not use *on*. *Plan* is complete by itself.

➤ *Subsequent to*—why use two words when one will do? When you mean *after,* use the word itself; say *after,* not *subsequent to.*

➤ *Prior to*—again, why use two words? When you mean *before,* say so; use *before,* do not use *prior to.*

➤ *Words with prefixes.* When using words that have prefixes, use the English preposition that has a meaning similar to the prefix.
  According to (*ac* = to) is much more concise than *in accordance with* and so is preferable.

➤ different than, different from
  Different from (*dif* = from) is the only proper construction. *Different than* is simply wrong; *than* is not a preposition; it is used to indicate the second of two parts in a comparison and must follow an adjective in the comparative degree.

> Suzy is *different from* Cathy.
> Suzy is *taller than* Cathy. (Note the adjective in the comparative degree, *taller,* and that Cathy is the second of two parts of a comparison.)

Barbarisms

Barbarisms are those words that have crept into our language and insidiously eaten away at clarity and forceful speech. Excise them from your everyday language and from your prose.

➤ Irregardless
Irregardless is a redundancy.

Regardless means *without concern*. Adding the prefix *ir*, which means *not* or *without*, makes the word mean *not without concern*—the opposite of what you are trying to say.

➤ Enthuse
Enthuse is a verb that has sprung from a noun. Such creation of verbs is weak and imprecise.

Do not say: Edith was *enthused* about her recent trip to Europe.

Say instead: Edith was *pleased*, or Edith was *happy*, or Edith was *enthusiastic*, about her trip.

➤ -ize or -ness words
Avoid turning words into nouns by adding the suffixes *-ize* or *-ness*.

Examples: (*-ness*) His directions to the mall lacked *specificness*.
(*-ize*) *Finalize* your plans, at this point in time, to rid yourself vocabularywise of such barbarisms.

Almost any word that contains these suffixes can be replaced by a much stronger word.

Do not use *prioritize*, use instead *assign priorities*.
Do not use *finalize*, use instead *finish*.

Do not use *humbleness,* use instead *humility.*
Do not use *speediness,* use instead *speed.*

➤ -wise words
Also avoid turning adjectives into adverbs by adding
the suffix *-wise.* In general, you can better express your
idea by a prepositional phrase.

Do not use *contrarywise;* instead use *on the contrary.*
Do not use *likewise;* instead use *in a similar way.*

LOOKING BACK

1. Good writing style is clear, interesting, and correct.
   Of the three qualities, which one could you
   neglect and still be considered a good writer?

2. You should know the difference between *denotation*
   and *connotation.*
   How many connotations can you list for the
   words *home, motherhood,* and *America?*

3. Which of the following sentences contain usage
   errors?
   a. Sylvia can't hardly play the piano.
   b. I would of passed the test if I had been present.
   c. We returned back to the beach after lunch.
   d. How will the election affect the stock market?
   e. Alyse has less subjects than her twin sister, Gail.
   If any sentences are wrong, how would you
   correct them?

Chapter 12

Spelling and Punctuation

TRUE CONFESSIONS

1. Albert Einstein and Alexander Graham Bell are reputed to have been terrible spellers. Based on this fact, what conclusion can you draw about the correlation between native intelligence and the ability to spell?

2 "I think it's foolish to waste so much time on spelling. Today we have spell checkers and electronic gadgets of all kinds that can correct our mistakes for us."

   What is your opinion of this student's statement?

3. "Marge," said Joan, "is a meathead."
   "Marge said Joan is a meathead."

   Who is the meathead? What important observation regarding punctuation can we make from examining these two short sentences?

DOES SPELLING COUNT? YOU BET IT DOES!

Face it, spelling counts. Whether it's fair or not, the quality of your writing will be judged by how accurately you can spell. In class as well as on standardized essay tests like the SAT II: Writing, poor spelling will adversely affect your grade. Good spellers don't earn extra credit for avoiding errors but poor spellers lose credit for making them.

Similarly, poor punctuation leaves a negative impression on readers, particularly when erratic punctuation interferes with the clarity of the writing. A mere comma can make the difference. Notice what the absence of commas does to the clarity of these two sentences.

> While Karen was riding her bike got a flat tire.

> Jeff left alone for the weekend invited his friends to a party.

A great deal of hard work and effort may fall to pieces if you fail to spell and punctuate properly.

SOLVING SPELLING PROBLEMS

Many people make most of their mistakes by misspelling the same few words over and over. If this describes you, remedies are at hand if you are willing to try them:

➤ Help yourself with careful pronunciation and by dividing words into syllables, thereby spelling words part by part. Another method that helps is studying word parts, namely *prefixes, suffixes, roots,* and *stems.*

A prefix is the name of a group of letters at the beginning of some words that help convey the meaning of the word. You can't speak English without using words that contain prefixes, such as

> *re,* meaning *again,* as in *re*peat, *re*read, and *re*visit
> *co,* meaning *together,* as in *co*operate and *co*captain
> *mis,* meaning *bad* or *improper,* as in *mis*take and *mis*demeanor

Suffixes, like prefixes, also convey meaning, but suffixes are found at the ends of words, such as

ism, meaning *belief,* as in extrem*ism,* liberal*ism,* monothe*ism*

er or *eer* or *or,* meaning *a person who,* as in mountain*eer* (a person who climbs mountains) and sail*or* (a person who sails)

A great many words also contain roots or stems. Roots are word parts that originated in other languages, mostly Latin and Greek, that have been absorbed by English. Stems are a variety of roots that have evolved into new forms. Both roots and stems convey meaning—just as though they were prefixes or suffixes. For example:

tempor, meaning *time,* as in temporary (for a short time) and contemporary (at the same time)

terr, meaning *land,* as in terrestrial (of the earth) and subterranean (underground)

There are literally hundreds of prefixes, suffixes, roots, and stems. Knowing many of them can help you figure out how to spell unfamiliar words.

➤ Another technique is to keep a list of words you misspell most often. When you add a word to the list, illuminate the part of the word you misspell by capitalizing the letters you miss most often.

apitude	apTitude
seperate	sepArate
privelege	privIlege
litrature	litErature
Febuary	FebRuary
boundry	boundAry
ocassionaly	oCCaSionaLLy

Second, go over this list orally from time to time. Then close your eyes, and visualize the trouble spots in capital letters. Open your eyes, and repeat the list; then close them, and visualize the word in small letters, as they would appear on the printed page. Then write the list correctly several times.

➤ One of the most common spelling problems is transposing letters, as in *villian* (villain) and *pyschology* (psychology). If you can recognize errors such as these when you reread what you have written, you will improve your spelling by merely paying closer attention to each word. When you have completed a paper or essay, proofread slowly and carefully. But read it backwards. By reading right to left, your eye will pause on each word, enabling you to catch errors that you might miss reading the words in normal order. You might also correct this kind of error by keeping a list of words you commonly misspell. Head the list *Personal Spelling Demons* and review it frequently. After a while, the demons may vanish from your writing.

➤ Some spelling errors spring from mispronouncing words. Many educated people, for example, say *jewler-y* instead of *jew-el-ry* and *real-a-tor* instead of *re-al-tor*. Even former President Jimmy Carter, at one time the skipper of an atomic submarine, has been heard to say *nuc-u-lar* instead of *nuc-le-ar*. Dropping and adding syllables to the spoken word may also lead to spelling mistakes.

You will find that pronouncing words carefully and correctly will help your spelling, even though many English words are not spelled phonetically (according to sound). You may find it helpful to underline the syllables you add or omit.

labratory	laboratory
practicly	practically
disasterous	disastrous
rememberance	remembrance
hinderance	hindrance
enterance	entrance
intrest	interest

➤ Some people have difficulty with homonyms. "Homonym" comes from the Greek words *homos*, meaning same, and *onoma*, meaning name—thus, "homonym" means same name. Homonyms are words that have the same name (sound) but different meaning and spelling, such as *to, too, two—right, write, rite, wright—you, yew, ewe*—and *pair, pare, pear.*

Some of the most commonly misused homonyms are:

aloud	berth	coarse
allowed	birth	course
altogether	born	corps
all together	borne	corpse
all ready	bough	compliment
already	bow	complement
alter	brake	council
altar	break	counsel
assent	by	decent
ascent	buy	descent
advice	canon	dual
advise	cannon	duel
bare	capitol	desert
bear	capital	dessert

dear
deer

fair
fare

forth
fourth

goal
gold

grown
groan

hear
here

heir
air

heal
heel

him
hymn

hole
whole

herd
heard

knew
new

lesson
lessen

led
lead (metal)

meat
meet

made
maid

mist
missed

pail
pale

peace
piece

peal
peel

plain
plane

pour
pore

principal
principle

profit
prophet

seam
seem

shown
shone

steal
steel

steak
stake

stationary
stationery

son
sun

tale
tail

there
their
they're

to
too
two

threw
through

write
right
rite

weather
whether

SPELL CHECKERS

Because of the advent of spell checkers in most word processing programs, some people claim that accurate spelling has become an obsolete art. Don't believe it. Computer spell checkers do a wonderful job, but they have severe limitations. For one, they don't contain every word you are likely to use in your writing. A built-in dictionary of, say, 50,000 words may sound like an ample selection, but your mind is capable of devising perfectly acceptable variations of words that dictionary writers never thought to include in spelling programs. A more serious limitation, however, is the inability of spell checkers to single out misused words. For example, in this sentence—*The angel is ninety degrees*—every word is correctly spelled, but still the sentence contains a spelling error: *angel* should be *angle*. In other words, you can't depend on spell checkers to identify properly spelled words that are incorrect in a particular context. You, as the writer, still have to know when to use *there, they're* and *their*, as well as *through* and *threw,* and scores of other homonyms. In short, when it comes to spelling, you are smarter than your computer.

SPELLING RULES

At some time in your schooling you may have been taught the basic spelling rules of English. If you haven't used them regularly, you may have forgotten them, or perhaps you were absent on the day they were taught. Here, to refresh your memory, are several helpful rules that happen not to be "rules" in the strict sense of the word. Because English spelling grew haphazardly, the rules are merely observations of patterns that developed over time.

To improve your spelling, study and use the following guidelines:

1. Use *i* before *e* except after *c*, if the sound is *ee*.

➤ If the sound is *ee*, use *i-e*, as in *achieve, believe, siege, field, relief,* and *niece,* except after *c,* as in *ceiling, receive, deceit, perceive,* and *conceit.*

Exceptions: *either, leisure, caffeine, protein, seize, weird, counterfeit, plebeian, species, financier*

➤ If the sound is NOT *ee*, use *e-i*, as in *neighbor, height, weigh, weight, foreign,* and *heir.*

Exceptions: *friend, sieve, mischief,* and *handkerchief*

2. When adding a prefix to a word, the spelling of the base word remains unchanged.

For example: dis   +   appear   =   disappear
           mis   +   spell   =   misspell
           un   +   natural   =   unnatural
           over   +   rule   =   overrule
           with   +   hold   =   withhold

➤ When a prefix adapts to the first letter of the base word or root, use a double letter, as in ad+tract (draw) = *attract*; in+regular = *irregular*, and in such words as *appoint, announce, correspond, collect, illegal, immortal, occur, oppose, suffer,* and *suppose.*

3. When adding a suffix that begins with a consonant, the spelling of the base word remains the same.

For example: sad   +   ness   =   sadness
           hope   +   less   =   hopeless
           care   +   ful   =   careful

Also: excitement, meanness, drunkenness, government

➤ With base words ending in *y*, the *y* is usually changed to *i* before the suffix is added, as in *happiness, loneliness, beautifully*, and *happily*.

Exception: one-syllable words ending in *y*, such as *dryness* and *shyly*.

➤ When adding an *-ly* ending to turn an adjective into an adverb, normally just add *-ly*, as in *extreme + ly = extremely, definite + ly = definitely, careful + ly = carefully, beautiful + ly = beautifully*, and *accidental + ly = accidentally*.

➤ Words ending in *-ic* form adverbs by adding *-ally*, as in *basically, terrifically*, and *fantastically*. Exception: *publicly*.

➤ Words ending in *y* preceded by a consonant change the *y* to *i*, as in *happy-happily* and *necessary-necessarily*.

➤ Words ending in *-ble* and *-ple* drop the *e*, as in *probable-probably* and *simple-simply*.

➤ Words ending in *-ue* drop the *e* and add *-ly*, as in *true-truly* and *due-duly*.

　4. In words of one syllable ending in a single vowel followed by a single consonant, double the final letter of the base word.

For example: *tap-tapping, hop-hopping, scar-scarred, spar-sparring*

➤ Words ending in a silent *e* drop the *e*, as in *stare-staring, spare-sparing, come-coming, excite-exciting, argue-arguing*

Exceptions: Words ending in *-oe: canoeing, hoeing*
　　　　　　Words ending in *-ce* and *-ge: notice-noticeable, manage-manageable,*

courage-courageous (The *e* keeps the sound "soft," like *j* and *s*.)

Words ending in *-ic* or *-ac* insert a *k* before the *-ing*: *picnic-picknicking, panic-panicked, traffic-trafficker*

5. In words of more than one syllable that end in one vowel and one consonant (such as *happen, occur, prefer, commit*) double the consonant before adding *-ing, -ed, -able, -er* **only** when the emphasis falls on the last vowel.

For example: *begin-beginning, refer-referring, occur-occurring, regret-regrettable, forget-forgettable*

➤ Do not double the consonant if the emphasis shifts, as in *prefer-preference*, and not before the suffixes *-ity* and *-ize*, as in *equality-equalize*.

➤ Do not double the consonant if the emphasis is anywhere but on the last syllable before the suffix, as in *happen-happening, offer-offered, travel-traveler*.

Exceptions: *handicapped, kidnapped*

6. To turn singular nouns into plurals, add *s*, as in *dog-dogs* and *picture-pictures*. After *s, x, ch, sh*, and *z*, add *-es*, as in *dress-dresses,* and *sex-sexes*.

➤ If the noun ends in a consonant followed by *y*, drop the *y* and add *-ies*, as in *liberty-liberties, monastery-monasteries, lady-ladies, story-stories, ally-allies*.

➤ If the noun ends in a vowel followed by *y*, simply add *s*, as in *donkey-donkeys, valley-valleys, chimney-chimneys, boy-boys, tray-trays*.

➤ For nouns ending in *i*, add *s*, as in *alibis* and *rabbis*.

➤ For nouns ending in *o*, add *s*, as in *pianos, dynamos, photos*.

Exceptions*: tomatoes, potatoes, heroes, mosquitoes, echoes, mottoes, torpedoes, cargoes, volcanoes, vetoes, embargoes, tornadoes, dominoes, buffaloes, desperadoes, haloes, noes*

➤ Some nouns ending in *f* and *fe* are made plural by turning the *f* to *v* before adding *s*, as in *calf-calves, wife-wives, knife-knives, half-halves, shelf-shelves, thief-thieves, loaf-loaves*. Some such words may be spelled either way: *hoofs-hooves, wharfs-wharves*.

➤ Some English nouns of foreign origin keep their original plurals, as in *crisis-crises, oasis-oases, criterion-criteria, phenomenon-phenomena, alumnus-alumni, larva-larvae, medium-media, ox-oxen*.

➤ Plurals of hyphenated compound nouns usually add the *s* to the main noun part, as in *passers-by* and *mothers-in-law*.

➤ Some nouns have the same form in both singular and plural, as in *sheep, aircraft, moose, deer, fish,* and *swine*.

➤ For some nouns, the difference between the singular and plural form lies in their vowels, as in *foot-feet, goose-geese, man-men, tooth-teeth*, and *woman-women*.

There are other rules and other exceptions, but this half dozen will help you form better habits of spelling.

SPELLING DEMONS

Because there are literally millions of ways to err in spelling, if you slip up now and then, you can still take pride in being a near-perfect speller. Many unusual words offer spelling challenges. You won't be faulted for spelling *hemmorhoids* or *silhouette* with a misplaced letter or two, but beware of the numerous ordinary words that are often misspelled. The list that follows contains a few dozen of them. Skip the list if you are a pretty good speller, but if you tend to make mistakes on occasion, review the words. You may find a surprise or two among them.

a lot

A lot is two words, not one. *A lot* of people make this mistake. *A lot* of writers frown on using *a lot* in formal prose.

acquaintance

The *ance* ending gives some people trouble, but more people stumble over the *c* after the initial *a*. The rule is that only words referring to water, as in *aqueduct* and *aquatic*, begin with *a-q*. All others include *c* between the *a* and the *q*, as in *acquaint* and *acquiesce*.

allies, alleys

The plurals of *ally* and *alley* illustrate the basic rule that nouns ending in *-y* become plural by adding *-ies,* and that nouns ending in *-ey* are simply given an *-s* to make them plural. Thus, *liberty/liberties* and *monkey/ monkeys*, and so forth.

affect, effect

Affect is a verb, *effect* is a noun (with one exception). Spelling *affect* (verb) when you mean *effect* (noun) will *affect* your reputation as a proficient speller. The *effect* on the ACT may be a lower score. Then again, your score may not be appreciably *affected*. The exception: when *effect* means to bring to pass or to accomplish, as in: Study hard to *effect* a change in your spelling performance.

all right, already, altogether

All right is two words; it's never one. It's different from *already* and *altogether*, which may be either one word or two, depending on their meaning. Remember that, and you'll be *all right*.

Already is one word unless used in the sense of: We are *all ready* to take the spelling quiz.

Altogether is also one word except when referring to a group as in: The senior class met *all together* for the first time in four years. Otherwise, altogether means thoroughly or completely, as in: Spelling is altogether too complicated.

athlete

Because *athlete* is often mistakenly pronounced *ath-a-lete*, as though the word contains three syllables, some people spell it "athelete."

conscience, conscious, conscientious

Conscience, made up of *con* and *science*, means a sense of moral righteousness.

Conscious, the opposite of *unconscious*, means being mentally awake.

Conscientious looks like a blend of *conscience* and *conscious*. It means hard-working, an attribute of a *conscientious* speller.

could've (could of), could have

Could've is a marriage of two verbs, *could* and *have*. The phrase *could of* is sometimes mistaken for *could have*. But *could of* is not standard English. Don't use it or its cousins: *should of, might of, would of*. Instead, write *should have, might have*, and *would have*.

desert, dessert

This spelling demon may remind you of your third-grade teacher, who probably told you that, because kids like two helpings of *dessert*, spell the word with two *s*'s.

doesn't

Doesn't combines *does* and *not*. The apostrophe takes the place of the *o* in *not*. Because that's the only difference between spelling *does not* and *doesn't*, it makes little sense to write *dosen't* or *doesnt*.

etc.

Etc. is the abbreviation for *etcetera*. People use it when they can't think of what else to say or when subsequent items on a list are too obvious to spell out, as in 1, 2, 3, 4, *etc*. Notice that because *etc.* is an abbreviation, it is always followed by a period, even in mid-sentence. Why so many people write *ect.* is a puzzle. In general, avoid using *etc.* in your essays. Instead, use "and so on" or "and so forth."

its, it's

It's combines *it* and *is*. That's the only way *it's* correct. *Its* (without the apostrophe) indicates possession. One would never write *his's* or *her's*, so don't write *it's* unless it means *it is*.

jewelry

Mispronunciation lies at the core of why *jewelry* is often misspelled *jewlery* or *jewelery*.

judgment, judgement

This word is a gift from the spelling god. Both versions are perfectly acceptable.

loneliness

Anyone who writes *lonliness* doesn't know the spelling rule that says keep the final *-e* before a suffix beginning with a consonant. Therefore, write *ninety, careful*, and *effectively*, and so forth.

lose, loose

One *o* makes a difference. Don't confuse *lose*, which you can do when you make a bet, with *loose*, which rhymes with *goose*. Be careful with *loose* change in your pocket, or you might *lose* it.

lovable

Lovable exemplifies the rule that says drop the final *-e* before a suffix beginning with a vowel. Therefore, write *lovable* instead of *loveable* and *arguing* instead of *argueing*. There are exceptions, however, such as *mileage* and most words in which a suffix with an initial vowel is added to a word ending in *-ce* and *-ge*, as in *noticeable* and *knowledgeable*.

misspell

Misspell has two *-s*'s because the prefix *-mis* is added to the verb *spell*. The rule says that prefixes must be kept intact even when their final letter is the same as the initial letter of the word that follows. Thus, write *unnecessary, de-emphasize, re-enter, cooperate, sub-basement*, and so on.

nuclear

Because so many prominent people, including Presidents, say *nuc-u-lar*, when they mean *nuc-le-ar*, the word has become troublesome. Think of *nucleus*, and you won't go wrong.

occasion, occasionally

Both *occasion* and *occasionally* have two *c*'s and only one *s*. Don't sneak in a double *s*. One is enough.

perform

Because *pre-* is a common prefix, it precedes many words, as *predict, prevent, prejudice. Pre* means before, as in *prewar* (before the war). *Perform* is unrelated. Why the word is often spelled *preform* remains a mystery worth pondering.

precede

Three words in English end with the letters *-eed: exceed, succeed,* and *proceed.* Obviously, *precede* is not one of them. Therefore, don't write *preceed.*

preferred

This word exemplifies the following long-winded spelling rule: Double the final consonant when adding a suffix that starts with a vowel, such as *-ed* or *-ing*, but only if the word has one syllable (like *run* or *plan*), or if it is a two-syllable word with the accent on the second syllable (*prefer* and *occur*). Keep this rule in mind the next time you write *occurred, preferred, deferred,* and *propelling*, among other words.

prejudice, prejudiced

Prejudice is a noun. Its derivative *prejudiced* is an adjective. The two words are not interchangeable. A *prejudiced* person suffers from *prejudice*, which is not spelled *predjudice*.

principal, principle

In grade school you may have been told that the *principal* is your pal. That's why you spell the word *principal.* One might hope that principals have noble *principles*, but that is not always the case. As an adjective, *principal* means most important or highest in rank.

professor, profession
Professors, are sometimes called "Prof," a title with one **f**, which is also the grade one deserves for spelling *professor* and *profession* with two.

psychology
The *p* in *psychology* throws some people. Also, because of the *h* some people confuse the word with *physiology*, which relates to the body, not the mind. When pumped up, you are *psyched*, not *psysed*.

receive
This word exemplifies the familiar rule "*i* before *e* except after *c*, except as in words like *neighbor* and *weigh*." Add to those exceptions other words like *weird, foreign, seizes, either,* and *neither*.

rhythm, rhyme
Note that the *y* in *rhythm* and *rhyme* sounds like *i*. But it's the unnecessary *h* in both words that can lead you astray.

schedule
Schedule is a two-syllable word sometimes given a third by those who pronounce it *sched-u-al* and spell it as they hear it—*schedual*. If pronounced *sched-yule*, it will probably be spelled as it should.

separate
Look for *a rat* in *separate*, and you'll never go wrong.

similar
Because *similar* resembles familiar, people often write *similiar*. Don't let the similarity between the two words confuse you.

supposed to, used to
Supposed is the past tense of the verb *suppose*.
Because the past tense of many verbs end with the
letter *d*, don't write *suppose to* or *use to*, as in "Tanya
use to live in Texas."

than, then
When making a comparison (Phil eats faster *than*
Fido), use *than* instead of *then*. *Then* is a time word,
like *when*. Both contain the letter *e*.

there, their, they're
Don't confuse these three words. Each has its own
separate use and meaning. *There* is the opposite of
here. Both are places. *There* are many places to use this
word. *Their* indicates possession: *Their* spelling is
getting better all the time. *They're* combines *they* and
are. *They're* words that can easily be combined.

through
Because this word resembles *though* and *thorough*,
some people misspell it. They often take the easy way
out and write *thru*, as in *thruway*. But *thru* is
commercial jargon like *lite* for *light* and *e-z* for *easy*,
and should not be used in essays.

tragedy
Isn't it sad that writers sometimes add an extra *d* to
tragedy? If you write *tradgedy*, it's no *tragedy*, but it
is dead wrong.

villain
Villain is a treacherous word to spell because people
mistakenly use the *i-a* combination found in such
words as *brilliant* and *Machiavellian* instead of the *a-i*
found in *pain* and *gain*.

Wednesday
The first *d* in *Wednesday* causes problems because it is silent. Most people have no trouble abbreviating the third day of the week, *Wed.*, but when it comes to spelling the whole word, the third letter, *d*, falls into fourth place or is left out altogether.

who's, whose
Like every contraction, *who's* combines two words, *who* and *is*, as in *Who's* not going to misspell *who's* anymore? *Whose*, on the other hand, is a pronoun indicating possession, as in You're the person *whose* spelling is bound to improve.

woman, women
It's odd that few people err when it comes to spelling *man* and *men*, but when the gender changes, they make a mess of spelling *woman* and *women*.

➤ Make a list of your own, starting with spelling demons from the preceding selection. Add words you commonly misspell until you have reached three hundred. If you master your troublesome list of three hundred, you will probably be a better than average speller for the rest of your life. You will have evaluated your faults and developed habits to correct them.

SUMMARY: HOW TO IMPROVE YOUR SPELLING

1. By self-examination find the few words you misspell again and again. Make a list of them, and check it until you can recognize each troublemaker at a glance.
2. Scrutinize each word you write in order to avoid the omission, addition, and transposition of letters.

Practice pronouncing the words syllable by syllable. Stay alert to the prefixes, suffixes, and roots to be found in countless words.

3. Keep a handy list of the most confusing homonyms. Use it to avoid incorrect usage. Know the basic rules of spelling, and keep one or two examples in mind.

4. Keep your own list of spelling demons. Study the list of simple words most often misspelled. Compare your own list of troublesome words with other lists. Note any weaknesses by checking the type of mistake you make: is it the *ei—ie* word, is it the *ly* suffix, is it the dropped *e*? Conscious awareness is often more than half the remedy.

5. Prolific reading may be a long-term solution to spelling problems. Read as much and as often as you can.

WHY PUNCTUATE?

The function of punctuation is to "slow down" or "stop." The word *punctuation* comes from the Latin word *punctus,* meaning a point. Thus, the differently shaped points (marks) of punctuation keep words from running away. In the "slowing" and "stopping" process, marks of punctuation replace gesture, changes of voice, pauses, and changes of thought.

Punctuation usage has changed over the centuries. People used to read everything aloud, so punctuation maintained a closer control than is necessary for rapid, silent reading. As people learned to read silently, punctuation did not need to control as strictly. Modern writers use less punctuation than was the custom a hundred years ago. At the same time punctuation usage is flexible enough to be personal to a degree. Whether you use close or loose punctuation is not of first importance. Rather, you should know the basics of punctuation in order to convey your thoughts clearly to a reader. If you violate the rules, as sometimes you might for the sake of clarity or to avoid saying something barbaric, you should at least know that you are doing so.

THE MARKS OF PUNCTUATION

The character of the *period* is to indicate a full stop. It implies a pause at the end of a unit of thought standing alone.

Related to the period is the *semicolon,* whose nature is to indicate a "slowing down" between coordinate elements within a sentence—two clauses (related or parallel thoughts). The "slowing down" indicated by the semicolon may be compared to the slowing down of a car for the yellow traffic signal between the red and the green.

The *comma* is related to the semicolon in that it is a pause. However, it is much weaker, resembling in many respects a blinking caution light, which demands less "slowing down." *Parentheses* and the *dash* sometimes replace the comma in setting off added words or ideas (called parenthetical material). The writer is given certain freedoms in the use of each to achieve emphasis, variety, and to suit different conditions.

The nature of the *colon* is to indicate that something important is being introduced: (1) a significant explanation, (2) a long quotation, or (3) a list which may be words or groups of words.

One of the simplest of all the marks of punctuation is the apostrophe. It has three main uses: (1) to show *possession* (John, John's; somebody, somebody's; Caesar, Caesar's); (2) the *omission of letters* in words (doesn't, can't, won't, couldn't); and (3) the *plural* of letters or words when simply adding an *s* might cause confusion (k's, a's, too's, but's). Sometimes apostrophes are used for the plural of numbers (1960's, 6's).

With a knowledge of rules and an understanding of the nature of punctuation, you should have no difficulty choosing, where choice is allowed, to suit your own style of writing and distinctive conditions. In an essay entitled *Guide to Usage,* Harrison Platt, Jr., gives a wonderful bit of advice: "If a sentence is very difficult to punctuate," he writes, "so as to make the meaning clear, the chances are that the arrangement of words and ideas is at fault. The writer will do better if he rearranges his word order instead of wrestling with his punctuation."[1] This advice is worth remembering the next time you are faced with a stubborn sentence that won't say what you want it to say.

SUMMARY: HOW TO PUNCTUATE

1. Appreciate the basic function of punctuation—to give your written word its final clarification.
2. Know the rules that govern the use of punctuation marks.
3. Know the nature and general character of the several punctuation marks, particularly those that perform related functions.
4. Use the freedom allowed the writer, within the rules, in order that punctuation may be personal and a part of the individual style in writing.

---

[1] Harrison Platt, Jr., "Guide to Usage, *The American College Dictionary* (New York: Random House, 1969), 1455.

5. And remember always—if punctuation cannot clarify, change the word arrangement.

LOOKING BACK

1. The foregoing chapter contains a number of suggestions for improving your spelling. Which suggestions are you willing to try? Which are you likely to ignore?

2. Did this chapter tell you anything about spelling that you hadn't heard or didn't know beforehand?

3. Most people remember the *ie, ei* rule by saying "*i* before *e*, except after *c*, or when as pronounced *ay*, as in neighbor or weigh."

   Make up a similar jingle for any of the other spelling rules in this chapter.

4. Insert the five punctuation marks referred to in this chapter (period, semicolon, colon, comma, apostrophe) where they belong in the following sentence:

   The store detectives boss gave him the following orders mingle with the crowds keep your eyes open for people with large bags be alert he promised he would do his best.

Chapter 13
Research Papers

TRUE CONFESSIONS

1. You are asked to do a research paper (about ten pages, or 3,500 to 4,000 words) for your English class on some phase of Shakespeare's life or his works. How does the assignment grab you? How will you proceed to select your topic and begin the research?

2. The assignment for the paper on Shakespeare is given to you the third week in September. The final draft of the paper, submitted typed and in accord with the guidelines of the Modern Language Association (MLA), is due the first week of December. What kind of schedule would you prepare to enable you to get the work done on time?

3. To do research, you go to a fully equipped library in your school or town. Do you know the resources you'll find there for information on your topic? If not, do you know how to find out what's available?

WHAT IS A RESEARCH PAPER?

A research paper is an opportunity for you to show several things:

1. that you have thought and read about a topic on which you have become something of an authority
2. that you can use tools and methods of research

3. that you can find and use a variety of resources
4. that you can organize a bulk of information in a clear and logical way
5. that you can write in a way that makes your text interesting, informative and correct.

The skills you develop while preparing and writing a research paper will serve you well in college, in graduate school, and, depending on the career path you choose, for your entire working life.

THE PROBLEM OF PLAGIARISM

Let's get this sticky problem out of the way first: Don't plagiarize! It's dishonest, immoral, and it can get you into a whole mess of trouble.

Plagiarism is the theft of someone else's words or ideas and passing them off as your own—a transgression for which there is no legitimate excuse.

It is inevitable in a research paper on almost any topic, however, to rely on the ideas of others. The way to do so honestly, to avoid plagiarism, is to keep readers informed of your sources of information. Simply, give credit to authors, books, web sites, articles, interviews— to whatever you used and wherever you gathered material.

Later in this chapter you'll find information on the form to use in acknowledging sources.

STEPS IN WRITING A RESEARCH PAPER

Writing a research paper can be broken down into several steps. What follows is an organizational plan, not meant as the last word on how to do the job correctly but rather as a guide to follow while you write your paper. Thousands of students have used this plan successfully. It isn't the only plan that exists, but experience shows that it is assuredly one that works. Although the steps are listed in the order that they logically occur, the lines between them are often blurry. It's often hard to tell where one step ends and the next begins because in a complex process such as this one several steps may be occurring simultaneously.

1. The first step is to read general literature about the subject area you have chosen. It may seem strange to begin reading before you have chosen a topic, but you will find that by reading in general literature, you will be able to choose a specific topic that interests you and for which there is sufficient information to do a paper.

   In order to read in general literature, you must have an idea about your topic. For example, if you have received an assignment in history to write a paper on something that happened in the years from 1609 to 1865, you should think about what era you want to examine. Would it be the Puritans, the Revolution, the War of 1812, or the writing of the Constitution? Then, once you have chosen the general area, you would go to the reference section of your library and read articles in the encyclopedias and specialized reference works dealing with U.S. history, such as *Dictionary of American Biography*. You could also read sections of a standard textbook of U.S. history, and check your library's collection of books, tapes, and periodicals that may contain information on the era you are thinking about as a focus for your paper. Also log onto the Internet where you are apt to find numerous additional sources.

2. As you do your reading in general literature, you should be looking for a suitable topic. Finding your topic is the second step in writing a paper.

   After you have chosen your topic, limit it. Think about what particular aspect of it you are going to examine. For example, if you decided to do research on the writing of the U.S. Constitution, you could limit your topic to "the role of James Madison in the writing of the Constitution," or "the seventeenth century political philosophers who influenced the writers of the Constitution," or perhaps "the role of Benjamin Franklin in the writing of the Constitution." By limiting your topic, you are making it specific. You will be able to guide your research and avoid reading works that pertain to your general area of research, but not to your specific topic. This limiting of your topic will become a great time saver.

3. Once you have narrowed your topic, you should begin thinking about a tentative thesis for your paper. That is, ask yourself what point you want to make about your topic. What is it that you hope to demonstrate or conclude about your topic? Say, for instance that you have discovered in your reading that James Madison not only worked hard on writing the Constitution, but that many of his personal interests and biases are clearly reflected in its wording and substance. In other words, Madison may well be regarded as the architect of the Constitution. That idea is perfect for a thesis, for it's an idea that can be proven or demonstrated in a relatively

short research paper. With a tentative thesis in mind, you can focus your reading and research directly on matters that pertain to what you are going to write in your paper. Since you know just what you are looking for, you can avoid considerable reading that is unrelated or only marginally relevant to your paper.

4. Now is the time to begin creating bibliography cards on the books, articles, and other sources you find. Use 3 × 5 index cards, one source per card.

To find book titles, use all the resources your library has to offer. Turn first to the card catalogue (if your library still has one), or to the computerized catalogue, which will list and probably print out the names of many books that are related to your topic. Encyclopedia articles will recommend books to read for further study; indexes, such as the *Reader's Guide to Periodical Literature,* will also provide help. Even if your school or town library doesn't own a particular title that looks promising, inter-library loans can be arranged. In other words, your library is likely to be connected electronically to a central catalogue of books available in school, public, and college libraries in your area. This service enables you to borrow books from any library on the network, either by going directly to the library that owns the book or by requesting the title to be sent to your own library. Obviously, the latter method is easier, but it takes considerably more time—a reason to get started on your research long before the paper is due.

You may also wish to log onto Internet web sites that offer the full or partial texts of articles and documents on many different topics. In fact, you may find much more than you can use, in which case you will need to discriminate between information that is valid and information of questionable worth. Be very skeptical of material that has been posted by individuals rather than, say, universities, foundations, and professional organizations. Because any crackpot with a computer can create a web site, much of what you find on-line may be biased and full of untruths, regardless of how convincing it sounds.

However you obtain sources for your paper, whenever you have found a likely book, article or other resource, write down complete information on your index card. For a book put the full name of the author, the full title (including subtitle), the name of the publisher, the place of publication, and the copyright date. For articles, write the name of the author (if given), title of the article (if given), the name of the magazine or encyclopedia, the date of issue of the particular magazine or encyclopedia, and the page numbers of the article. If you are reading an encyclopedia article, include all the publishing information that you would include for any book. Information from a web site should contain the complete address.

Bibliography cards should contain all the information you'll need when writing footnotes in your paper or when you prepare a list of the works you cited. Having complete information at your fingertips could also be helpful in the event you need to refer to the book or resource again once you have returned it to the library. If you have gathered material with a computer and need to retrieve it,

you will be greatly aided by having a record of the
commands you used and the path you followed to
access it the first time.

5. The next step in the process of writing a research
paper is to write a working outline. A working
outline is a preliminary organizer for your research.
You will make your thesis statement, saying what it
is that you will try to prove, and then divide your
topic into its natural, general divisions. You will not
need to make this outline detailed—merely a
statement of what the major areas of the topic are.
For example, to continue, let's see what a preliminary outline might be for the topic, "The role of
James Madison in writing the Constitution."

I. Thesis: Madison the "architect" of our Constitution

II. Early Life
   A. Childhood, adolescence, things Madison
       studied
   B. What Madison did during the Revolution

III. How the Constitution was written
   A. Nature of government under "Articles of
       Confederation"; failure of that government
   B. Convening of the Constitutional Convention
   C. How the convention operated
       1. Factions
           a. Supporters of "Articles"
           b. "Federalists"
       2. Major ideas that were proposed

IV. Role of Madison
   A. His faction
   B. Importance to that faction

    C. His accomplishments
        1. When Convention opened
        2. As the Federalists' proposals came forth
    D. Madison's proposals

  V. Final form of Constitution.
    A. Brief survey of theoretical model of U.S. Government
    B. Madison's contribution

 VI. Conclusion showing that thesis statement is proved

6. The sixth step is to read the works and take notes. Take your notes on 5×8 or 4×6 cards, one note to a card. Write only on one side of the card. If your note runs over one card, write on a second card rather than on the back of the first card. That way, when you lay the cards on your desk as you write, you won't have to turn them over to see what is on the back, and you will save time.

    At the top of each card write an abbreviation of the title of the work cited and the pages in the work from which the note came. Write down direct quotations if you must, but it is better to put the notes in your own words. Keep your cards in a box or packet.

7. After you have taken your notes, write a detailed outline of your paper. Because this outline serves as a guide for writing your paper, make it as detailed as you can. Arrange your ideas clearly and logically.

8. Then assemble your note cards, putting them in the order of your final outline, and begin to write your first draft.

    Although each topic requires a different paper, the following plan, or map, explains the order of material and roughly how much space to devote to each major segment of your paper. Again, these are guidelines only, not to be followed religiously. Your topic and good common sense should determine the proportions to use in your own paper.

A. **Introduction** (approximately ten percent of the total paper) contains material that
   1) engages the reader's interest in the topic. Use an interesting fact or two, an unusual story, a startling statistic, an appealing anecdote—anything that will grab your reader.
   2) introduces the topic, perhaps by stating its importance or implications, its timeliness, its impact, a controversy surrounding it, or anything else that may explain why the topic is worth reading about.
   3) summarizes or states the thesis that you are trying to prove or demonstrate.

B. **Background** (approximately twenty percent), if appropriate for your topic, contains material that
   1) provides a concise history of the topic.
   2) explains key events, key people, terminology, unusual or ambiguous words or phrases in your thesis.
   3) defines the limits of time, place, scope of your paper.

C. **Main body** (approximately forty to sixty percent) contains material that
   1) states important information and key evidence in support of your thesis. Use your own words. Use quotations from your sources only to support or illustrate ideas you have stated in your own words first.
   2) is organized in a sensible way. Present your arguments in order from strongest to weakest,

from least controversial to most controversial, or in 2, 3, 1 order (that is, second best argument, third best argument, best argument). Think out the best order for your particular topic and thesis.

D. **Refutation of opposition and/or reinforcement of your position** (ten to twenty percent) contains material that
   1) states other theories or opposing viewpoints, if any.
   2) assesses the strength of opposing arguments and finds their flaws.
   3) shows the strength of your ideas in comparison to the ideas of others.

E. **Conclusion** (ten percent) contains material that
   1) reviews your thesis, if appropriate, and your best reasons for its validity. Try not to rehash everything you've already written. Hit the highlights, using different wording than you used earlier, although you might use some of the same key words to remind the reader of what you stated before.
   2) avoids introducing new ideas that might need more development than you can provide in the conclusion.
   3) suggests that your discussion has significance or interest or implications beyond itself. In other words, indicate that there's more to be said and thought about your topic. Or tell the reader that this paper sheds light or raises questions about related areas of inquiry.

F. **List of works cited** (about a page) that contains complete information about each source.

9. After you have completed a rough draft, let it cool for several days, if possible. Then return to it and reread it with an eye toward making plenty of revisions. Let others—a trusted friend, a teacher, a parent—critique your paper too. Don't be offended if they criticize; they are only trying to help. But don't immediately accept or reject what they tell you. Just ponder it, and if you think their comments are valid, make the changes they suggest. As the author of your paper, you must have the final say. Don't be pressured to make changes unless you fully agree that the changes are for the better.

10. Finally, put your paper in the form required by your teacher or school. Use a recommended system of footnoting and bibliography. If no guidelines are given, use the system suggested by the MLA (Modern Language Association) that appears later in this chapter.

DOING RESEARCH

The first thing you should do when assigned a research paper is to write down a schedule. Allot time to each of the ten steps, allowing about $^1/_3$ of the total time for Steps 1–4, about $^1/_3$ for reading and taking notes, and the remaining third for composing the paper, Steps 7–10.

To allot time for the steps, start your estimates from the date the paper is due and work backward. For example, you have received an assignment from your history teacher and have been told that the paper must be turned in on the last day of the term, nine weeks later.

Write a schedule like the one below, and put the date the paper is due next to Step 10. Then, next to Step 6, put the date of the day that is three weeks before the end of the term. Then, next to Step 5, put the date of the day that is six weeks before the end of the term.

After you have divided the available time into the major parts, subdivide the major areas. In our example you were given nine weeks to complete the assignment. Your division would be something like this: Of the three weeks for Steps 1–4, allow yourself about five days for general reading, about two days for selecting and limiting your topic, and about two weeks for deciding on a tentative thesis, and collecting your working bibliography; of the three weeks you allow yourself for writing, estimate that your outline will take five days, composing the rough draft about five days, revising about six days, and preparing the final copy about five days.

Once your schedule is in place, you are ready to begin. As you search through general literature, be systematic in your efforts. Being systematic is perhaps the key to success in doing research. Look carefully at all available general literature. and then when you begin to collect your bibliography, be systematic in the writing of the cards. When you are writing your notes, be systematic again. Make sure every notation is *clear,* especially the page numbers, so that you will not have to retrace your steps and redo some research because you couldn't remember from which source a good idea came.

Date Due	Step Number	Description of Step	Check Mark to Show Step Done
	1	Read in general lit.	
	2	Select & limit topic	
	3	Decide on a tentative thesis	
	4	Collect working bibliography	
	5	Write a working outline	
	6	Read and take notes	
	7	Write detailed outline	
	8	Write rough draft	
	9	Revise, revise, and revise	
	10	Put final draft in required form	

DOCUMENTING YOUR SOURCES

You must cite the source of quotations that you use in your paper. You must also give the source of ideas and opinions that you have borrowed, paraphrased, or adapted from others. Otherwise you are being academically dishonest. Basic factual material that is commonly known or is easily found in a reference book or other source does not require a citation.

Give the sources for quotations and the ideas you use in proper form. Footnotes or endnotes have been the standard for a long time, but current practice calls for sources to be documented within the text of the paper by a brief parenthetical reference, like this: (Trimmer 1), which means that the quote or idea comes from page 1 of a work by someone named Trimmer. To find more details, you would turn to the List of Works Cited at the end of the paper, where complete bibliographical information should be given.[1]

Citations should always be as concise and clear as possible. How to document every type of source is beyond the scope of this book, but here are a few examples of common citations:

➤ In parentheses, cite the author's last name and page number:

> One writer argues that "some children may be better off if they escape their parents' grip, healthier if they grow up wild and free and sort things out on their own" (Denby 56).

Notice that there is no punctuation needed between the author's name and the page number.

➤ If you name the author in your text, there is no need to repeat the name in the citation:

> Commentator David Denby argues that "some children may be better off if they escape their parents' grip, healthier if they grow up wild and free and sort things out on their own" (56).

➤ If you are citing the entire work, give the author's name in your text, but do not cite a page number:

> In a *New Yorker* article, Denby argues that parents cannot control their childrens' TV viewing habits, with or without the V-chip, so why bother to try?

---

[1]This material on documentation is adapted from Joseph F. Trimmer, *A Guide to MLA Documentation* (Boston: Houghton Mifflin, 1996).

➤ If the work you are citing was written by more than one author, use only the first author's name and add *et al.,* meaning "and others." For example: (Wood, et al. 150).

➤ If the author has more than one work in your List of Works Cited, add a shortened version of the title you are referring to: For example: (Toffler, *Greening* 35*).*

➤ If no author is given, cite the work by the first word or words of the title: ("Living with Deer" 12).

All your citations should refer to items listed alphabetically in your List of Works Cited at the end of your research paper. By turning to your list readers should readily find complete information about the book, article, pamphlet or other source that you used. This gives readers a chance to pursue the topic in greater depth, if they are so inclined, and it also allows them to judge the validity of the information in your paper. If, for example, you claimed in your paper that Great Britain's royal family is free of marital strife, the copyright date of the book—say, 1980—would instantly show that the assertion is out of date.

Therefore, you should take pains to prepare an accurate and thorough List of Works Cited. As the title suggests, the list contains only those works you have actually made reference to in your paper. Your teacher may prefer that you prepare a list of works consulted, however, in which case you need to keep track of every work that you used, whether or not you referred to it. The term *bibliography,* meaning list of books, is no longer applicable in many research papers because modern students often use films, CD-ROMS, interviews, newspaper articles and other non-book sources.

Use the following guidelines, recommended by the MLA, to set up your list.

1. The list should come immediately after the last page of your paper. Number the page accordingly.
2. Double space all items on the list. Use indentations as illustrated in the examples shown below.
3. List items in alphabetical order according to the last name of the author. If the work has more than one author, use the name of the first one listed. If no author is indicated, alphabetize according to the title of the work, excluding words like *a, an,* and *the.*
4. Underline or *italicize* the titles of books, plays, films, CD's, videos, magazines, and pamphlets.
5. Put quotation marks around the names of short stories, essays, articles, editorials, poems, chapter titles, songs, lectures, and any unpublished material.
6. Use a period and a space to separate the author (last name first), the title, and the publication information.

Examples of items frequently found in a list of works:

➤ If a book has one author:

> Morgan, Edmund S. <u>Benjamin Franklin</u>. New Haven: Yale University Press, 2003.

➤ If you are citing two different works by the same author:

> Abbey, Edward. <u>Confessions of a Barbarian</u>. Boston: Little Brown, 1994.
> _____ <u>Fire on the Mountain</u>. Albuquerque: University of New Mexico Press, 1962.

➤ If a book has more than one author:

> Edwards, Paul, and Arthur Pap. <u>Modern Introduc-tion to Philosophy</u>. New York: The Free Press, 1965.

➤ If no author is given:

> Town of Harrison Tricentennial. Charles Dawson
> History Center, 1996.

➤ If an editor but no author is given:

> Zinsser, William, ed. Inventing the Truth: The Art
> and Craft of Memoir. Boston: Houghton Mifflin,
> 1987.

➤ If an article with author's name appears in a periodical
or newspaper:

> DeKorne, Clayton. "Crown Molding Fundamentals."
> Fine Homebuilding January 2003: 58–63.

➤ If an unsigned article appears in a periodical or newspaper:

> "Teenagers Meet the Elderly," Practice Digest 3:1
> (June 2000): 23-24.

➤ If you use a CD-ROM:

> Picture Atlas of the World. CD-ROM. National
> Geographic, 1994.

➤ If you use a source from a computer network:

> Altman, Gary. "Olympic Madness." AOL. World
> Wide Web. 8 July 1996.

➤ If you use a film:

> Courage Under Fire. Dir. Edward Zwick. With
> Denzel Washington and Meg Ryan. 20th
> Century Fox, 1996.

Preparing a list of works can sometimes be frustrat-
ing and time consuming. Doing it perfectly, though, is
a signal to your reader (presumably your teacher) that
you respect the established practices of academic

scholarship. You are bound to be rewarded for the effort, both in the pride you'll feel about doing it right and in the grade you earn for the paper.

If you look on the research paper as a challenge and a chance for discovery and creative work, the product will be what you'd expect—a well-written piece of work, reflecting wide reading and a firm grasp of material. Your teacher will be intellectually stimulated while reading it and will reward you with the grade you deserve.

Originality in the term paper is always of great value, but your grade probably is derived more from the scope of the paper—scope referring to the extent of your reading on the subject before you start to write. Remember, too, that the medium is the message. A handsome, easy-to-read paper is bound to receive a warmer reception than a paper that looks as though it had been tossed together at the last minute.

RESEARCH PAPER SUMMARY

➤ Make a schedule of the ten steps in research and assign a date for completion of each step. Put the schedule in your work place.

➤ Allow $^1/_3$ of your allotted time for writing.

➤ Use all of the resources of your library, including the librarian.

➤ If you find you have chosen a topic for which you can't gain ready access to information, *change your topic,* and revise your work schedule. You should be able to tell whether you need to change when you try to compile your working bibliography. If you can't find many books and articles, take the hint—you will have a difficult time gathering notes and writing your paper.

➤ Be systematic in taking your notes. Make sure that every page number is accurate and that you will be able to find the passage cited if you are asked to do so.

LOOKING BACK

1. Why is it important for a footnote to contain the publication date of a book? Why the place of publication?

   CLUES: Suppose it were a book on physics or one on economics.

2. "The ten research steps are very comprehensive," said Josh, "but as I see it, unless you pick the right topic, you are in deep trouble."

   What's your reaction to Josh's statement? Is selection of the right topic the most important of all the steps? Why?

3. Let us suppose that you selected "Shakespeare and Religion" as your topic. You scour the public library and your school's library, but find only two brief references to the topic. *The Encyclopedia Britannica* provides you with a few additional notes.

   You have four weeks left to complete and submit the research paper. What would you do?

Chapter 14
The Library: How to Use It

TRUE CONFESSIONS

1. What is the most important space in your school? The locker room? The guidance office? The library? The cafeteria? Although all those places play a role in the life of a school, this chapter will try to convince you that the library lies at the core of an academic institution. Can you speculate why?

2. How well do you know your school's library? First off, do you know the name of the head librarian? If you wanted to look up something in the *Reader's Guide,* do you know where to find it? Does your library use the Dewey Decimal System to categorize books, or does it use the Library of Congress system? When you walk through the entrance to the library, which way would you turn to find shelves holding collections of short stories?

3. Does your school library fine students who don't return borrowed materials on time? If not, is there another penalty? Have you ever failed to return library materials on time? If so, did you have a reasonable excuse? Did you resent whatever penalty was imposed on you?

THE CONTEMPORARY LIBRARY

A cutting-edge library contains an awesome array of print and nonprint materials. It has books on tape, videos, slides, microfilm, microfiche, computer workstations, DVDs, VCRs, photocopiers, scanners, printers, projectors, and a well-informed staff eager to assist anyone who needs a helping hand. Indeed, there is no end of resources that a contemporary library can offer its patrons.

However well stocked and technologically savvy a library may be, though, the meat and potatoes of any library still remains the trusty, old-fashioned book— that thing consisting of pages bound inside a cover.

Finding Books

To find a book that your library owns, it helps to know the name of the author, a key word in the title, or the main subject matter. With this information you are prepared to search for the book, either in the card catalogue or in the computer catalogue of the library's holdings.

The card catalogue, if your library still happens to use one, is contained in a series of drawers labeled with the letters of the alphabet. The cards inside really make up an alphabetical index to the library and are filed alphabetically by author's last name, by book title (beginning with the first important word—not *A, An,* or *The*)—and by subject. The *title card* is probably the quickest one to find if you know what book you want.

EXAMPLE OF TITLE CARD

	Surviving an eating disorder	(Title)
	Seigel, Michele	(Author)
616.85Se	Oxford University Press, 1995	(Call # and publication data)

Suppose you read the book and would like to read some more of the author's work. Return to the card catalogue and look up Seigel, Michele. If the library owns any additional books by Michele Seigel, the *author cards* will tell you their titles, dates of publication, and so forth. There will be an author card for each separate work by the author.

If you wish to pursue your study of eating disorders, but don't know the authors or titles, a third card is available to help you. It is called the *subject card,* and will be indexed under a general subject (EATING) or under any number of more specific or related subjects, such as EATING DISORDERS, ANOREXIA, BULIMIA, OBESITY, PSYCHOLOGY, and so on. Subject cards are usually not included for works of fiction, however, so you won't find a Stephen King novel by looking up HORROR, MURDER, GHOSTS, DEVIL WORSHIP, CULTS, and other such goodies.

More than likely your library has replaced its card catalogue with a computerized system. To use the computer catalogue, it helps to know something about the material for which you are searching, usually title, author, key words, date of publication, or subject matter. The more information you have, the more quickly you are apt to find what you want. Computer catalogues are user-friendly and will instruct you every step of the way. To locate a book, you simply type in answers to the questions you see on the monitor, hit ENTER on the keyboard, and in a moment you will know whether the library owns the book you are looking for.

If you use the computer to search for books on a certain subject, you type in a key word, and the computer will quickly give you a list of titles containing that key word. If the word you typed is fairly general, you will probably find numerous titles that contain the key word but have nothing to do with the subject you have in mind. For instance, if your interest is eating disorders, and you typed EATING in the subject box, you would end up with a list of hundreds of titles that include cook books, diet books, books about nutrition, books on cuisines of the world, books on the history of food, and even a play called *Eating People is Wrong.* To narrow the search, type in EATING DISORDERS, a more specific subject that will generate a far shorter list. After perusing the list, which may contain a brief description of each book, you may wish to know more details about a particular title. In that case, the computer screen will display more information about the book than you need to know. Because you might need the information later, though, it may pay to copy it, either by hand or by a printer that is connected to the computer.

Title:	Straight talk about eating disorders
Author:	Maloney, Michael, 1944 -
Publisher:	New York, NY: Dell Publ., 1993, c. 1991
Collation:	138 pages; 18 cm paperback
Note:	Includes bibliographical references and index

616.85M (PBK)

In many libraries, the computer will also tell you whether the book is available or has been checked out. Should the book be out, the computer may search the collections of other libraries on the network and tell you where another copy can be found.

No doubt you have noticed that library books are also identified by numbers. These numbers are symbols in a classification system that provides you with a *call number* by which you can search for the books you want. The same number tells the librarian in what section of the library, on what shelf, and in what specific order on the shelf each book is to be found. When you intend to seek a book from the library shelves, write down the call number, author, and title, and carry that information with you. In some college and university libraries access to the shelves, or stack as they are sometimes called, is limited to members of the staff or to researchers. To obtain a book in such libraries, you will fill out a request form and wait for a library runner to bring the book to you.

SYSTEMS OF CLASSIFICATION

There are two widely used systems of classification: the Dewey Decimal System and the Library of Congress System. The Dewey Decimal System is the one you will probably see in small public and school libraries. It was developed at Amherst College in 1873 and catalogues all knowledge under *ten divisions,* each division being assigned a group of numbers.

DEWEY DECIMAL SYSTEM

Numbers	Main Divisions	Subdivisions
000-099	General Works	Almanacs, encyclopedias, bibliographies, magazines, news-papers. Materials that cannot be narrowed to a single subject.

DEWEY DECIMAL SYSTEM (*Continued*)

Numbers	Main Divisions	Subdivisions
100-199	Philosophy	Logic, history of philosophy, systems of philosophy, ethics, and psychology.
200-299	Religion	Sacred writings (the Bible), mythology, history of religions, all religions and theologies.
300-399	Sociology (Social Sciences)	Group dynamics, law, government, education, economics.
400-499	Philology (Study of Lingustics)	Dictionaries dealing with words (not of biographies), grammars and technical studies of all languages.
500-599	Science (Subject and Theoretical)	Astronomy, biology, botany, chemistry, mathematics, physics, etc.
600-699	Applied Science (Useful Arts)	Agriculture, all types of engineering, business, home economics, medicine, nursing, etc.
700-799	Fine Arts (Professional and Recreative)	Architecture, painting, music, performing arts, sports, etc.

DEWEY DECIMAL SYSTEM (*Continued*)

Numbers	Main Divisions	Subdivisions
800-899	Literature	All types of literature—drama, essays, novels, poetry, etc.—in all languages of all countries.
900-999	History	All history, biography, geography, travel, etc.

If you go to the section of the library shelving Applied Science, 600-699, you will see immediately that each division is further divided. For example, 600-610 will have general books or collections dealing with applied science. Medicine will be classified under 610. Books on engineering will begin with 620 and be further broken down by smaller decimals. A glance at the history shelves will reveal that 900-909 are general works of history; 910 is geography; and so on by decimal subdivision. English is subdivided into literature of nations, then further catalogued. For example, English literature is 820; English poetry 821; English drama 822; and so on to 829.99. English poetry, 821, is further subdivided; 821.1 is Early English poetry; and so on to 821.9, each subdivision designating a specific period. A little observation will make it easy for you to find the exact spot in a particular section of the library where the subject you are interested in can be pinpointed.

The Library of Congress System, used primarily in research libraries, such as those found in graduate schools and universities, but rarely in high school libraries, is an alternate system that designates the main divisions of knowledge by letters instead of numbers. Subdivisions in the Library of Congress System are made by the addition of a second letter and whole numbers. Within the main divisions, books relating to a specific topic are grouped together and within these topic subdivisions, books are shelved alphabetically according to the author's name.

LIBRARY OF CONGRESS SYSTEM

Letter	Main Divisions
A	General Works
B	Philosophy and Religion
C	History—Auxiliary Sciences
D	History—Topography (except American)
E–F	American History—Topography
G	Geography—Anthropology
H	Social Sciences
J	Political Sciences
K	Law
L	Education
M	Music
N	Fine Arts
P	Language—Literature (nonfiction)
Q	Sciences
R	Medicine
S	Agriculture
T	Technology
U	Military Science
V	Naval Science
Z	Bibliography and Library Science
P–Z	Literature (fiction)

Fiction and Biography

In libraries using the Dewey Decimal System fiction and biographies are housed in separate sections.

Fiction books are arranged alphabetically by the author's last name. In case of two or more books by the same author, they are shelved alphabetically by title. Some libraries use the classification symbol *F* or *Fic* plus the first letter of the author's last name.

Biographies (including autobiographies) are designated with the letter *B* and are arranged alphabetically according to the last names of the subject. Those libraries that use the Library of Congress classification will shelve biographies with other works best reflecting the occupation of the person whose life is being told.

REFERENCE BOOKS

The chief function of the reference section in the library is to make facts of every conceivable variety available to you. As you prepare reports, essays, or research papers, you can get a good start by using reference books. They not only will give you general information about a topic, but will name other works that cover your topic in greater depth.

In addition to providing access to general information, the reference section of a library is also a microcosm of the whole library. By walking through it, you will learn how the whole library is arranged, since the reference books will be organized according to the classification system used throughout the library.

Reference sections of libraries will contain many different kinds of works, and what follows here is merely a guide to some basic kinds of reference books.

Perhaps the first book to catch your eye in the reference section of the library will be an unabridged dictionary, a book so voluminous that it has its own special rack. An unabridged dictionary contains nearly all the words in the language, giving definitions, showing pronunciation, and presenting information about the origin and history of each word. As well as entries about words, such a dictionary contains biographical and geographical information, abbreviations, tables of weights and measures, and commonly used foreign phrases. Two unabridged dictionaries often found are Merriam-Webster's unabridged dictionary and the Random House unabridged dictionary of the English language. The most comprehensive of all the dictionaries is the *Oxford English Dictionary.* It is many volumes long, and because of the exhaustive length and the high quality of its scholarship, it is the most respected authority on words.

When using these massive books, you will encounter abbreviations, the meaning of which will be listed, either in the front or back. Consult this list whenever you don't know the meaning of an entry.

The reference section also carries Roget's *Thesaurus* as well as other books of synonyms, all of great value to anyone doing any kind of writing.

Another source of good information about words is *The New Century Cyclopedia of Names,* which provides an abundance of information about the origins, history, and meaning of names used in English. Two sources of information about English as spoken and written in the United States are H. L. Mencken's *The American Language* and Bergen Evans' *Dictionary of Contemporary American Usage.*

In your English class you may be asked to write essays about works of literature. The reference section of the library contains many examples of literary criticism and much information about authors. *Contemporary Literary Criticism* is a collection of reviews of books by living authors. *Twentieth Century Literary Criticism* contains biographical essays about authors, as well as collections of reviews and essays about them. *Contemporary Authors* has few reviews of works, but is filled with biographical information about living authors, including lists of titles of their written works. *Book Review Digest* is perhaps the standard reference of literary criticism, for it contains excerpts from reviews of almost all published nonfiction and fiction. Any work of nonfiction that receives two reviews in periodicals or journals will be listed and so will any work of fiction that receives four reviews.

Whenever you are asked to do a research paper, one place to look for a topic is in general encyclopedias. Encyclopedias, their very name derived from the Greek *enkyklios* (encircle) and *paideia* (education), enclose in one volume or set of volumes masses of information on nearly any conceivable topic.

Every reference section of libraries will contain encyclopedias, some libraries will have several. Most common are *World Book*, especially written for younger people, *Americana, Britannica,* and *Colliers,* but there are others as well. Most encyclopedias update their information by adding a volume, called an annual or a yearbook, each year for a decade or so after publication.

All encyclopedias are arranged alphabetically by subject, and most contain indexes both to topics and contributing authors. The essays in encyclopedias are written by experts; give information in a clear, compact form; and will often contain a brief bibliography of other works that pertain to the essay's topic.

In addition to these encyclopedias of many volumes, there is an excellent single volume work, *The Columbia Encyclopedia.* It covers the vast array of human knowledge, but necessarily devotes less space to topics than a multiple-volumed work does.

There are also specialized encyclopedias that deal with particular subjects and are limited to particular fields of knowledge such as art, science, technology, music, or history. Libraries sometimes have encyclopedias that limit their scope to particular religions and ethnic groups, such as the *Catholic Encyclopedia* or the *Jewish Encyclopedia.*

For information on contemporary events you can turn to one or another of the yearbooks that you might find in the reference section. *Facts on File* is an annual collection of digests of news articles on current events, and all subjects are indexed for easy use. Annuals, such as the *World Almanac,* contain up-to-date statistics, some valuable facts about government agencies and personnel, sports, scientific developments, and information on many other topics. Both national and state governments produce yearbooks of various kinds. You will find all of these works to be of great assistance if you have to prepare a paper on contemporary developments.

Most reference sections also contain numerous biographical dictionaries. Some volumes will be specifically devoted, for example, to musicians, writers, or statesmen. Others will give sketches of noteworthy persons from every walk of life. *Who's Who in America, Dictionary of American Biography, Webster's Biographical Dictionary,* and *Chambers's Biographical*

Dictionary are general works. *Dictionary of National Biography* is devoted to noteworthy citizens of Great Britain. *Current Biography*, published in magazine form several times a year, and put in book form by years, is a place to gather facts on someone who has become prominent in the immediate present.

In addition to contemporary material afforded by yearbooks, there are many interesting and valuable articles in magazines and newspapers. *The Reader's Guide to Periodical Literature* is the standard reference to magazine articles. The *Reader's Guide* is published twice a month and lists alphabetically, by author and subject, the significant articles from more than a hundred magazines. *The New York Times Index* is a guide to the articles found in that newspaper. The Index is published in two-week increments and lists alphabetically, by subject or author, articles, editorials, book reviews, and obituaries that appear in the paper. Each article is listed giving the date, sometimes the section, page, and column of the paper in which that article appears. If you find only a listing for a date, you are being referred to another subject. Turn to that subject in the index and you will find all articles listed chronologically. That is where that mysterious date will help you find the actual citation for your article. Because libraries can't store mountains of newspapers dating back over a hundred years, articles from the *New York Times* can be found on microfilm or microfiche, or in some libraries on CD-ROM or the Internet—if the library has paid the required fee to gain access to the *Times* archives.

You should know that many reference books are also available to you on the Internet. Although you won't find everything that libraries customarily stock on the shelves, many dictionaries, encyclopedias, and reference works related to specific topics can be accessed through *refdesk.com, accessplace.com, dogpile.com,* and many other sites.

TAPES, CDs, AND VIDEOS

Many school and public libraries have well-stocked audiovisual departments containing audio tapes of books, music, speeches, lectures, plays, poetry, and lots more.

Thousands of books, both fiction and non-fiction, have been recorded, some of them books that you may have been assigned to read by your English or social studies teacher. You can borrow the books on tape or CDs to listen in your car, on your Walkman, or wherever you go. In addition, your library's collection of tapes may include memoirs, true-life mysteries, self-help books, books on travel, comedy, adventure, science, sports—almost anything at all. As for current popular music, you are not likely to find much of a selection in the library, but there will be plenty of tapes and CDs of classical performances, Broadway show tunes, folk songs, and a variety of other music.

Most libraries also have a videotape collection, for both education and entertainment. Because libraries don't want to compete with Blockbuster, the selection of tapes will be different from that found in your local video store, and may include anything from how to improve your tennis game to the best way to apply makeup. You'll also find videos on travel, nature, health and fitness—virtually any topic of interest. Feature films are popular, too, but the selection is likely to be made up of older, often historically significant, and foreign films.

PERIODICALS AND MICROFILM

Typically, libraries subscribe to scores, if not hundreds, of periodicals. The periodical room of many libraries is often the most crowded space in the building, attracting readers of magazines on every conceivable subject. A glance at the periodical collection in your library will reveal that you can read about airplanes, basketball, crafts, fashions, nature, movies, rock climbing, foreign policy, furniture, teen life, music, and much more.

Because so much is published, even the biggest libraries have neither the space nor the resources to store everything worth reading. As a solution to the problem, vast quantities of information have been reduced in volume and in cost by microfilms and microfiche (sometimes called microcards). Most microfilm or microfiche holdings will be of newspapers (*The New York Times*), periodicals (*Time, U.S. News and World Report*), or rare books that would be too expensive to buy, such as an early manuscript of a play by Shakespeare. As you do research for history papers or perhaps for an English assignment, you may find that the material you want to read is on microfilm. Librarians will help you find the articles you want, show you how to use the microfilm and microfiche readers, and how to make photocopies of the pages you need.

COMPUTERS

Using a computer in the library or elsewhere, you can access the archives of scores of newspapers from around the world, hundreds of magazines both specialized and general, and TV and radio transcripts of news broadcasts. One source, among others, for this kind of information is the Electronic Library *(eLibrary.com)*.

Computers in the library not only help you locate material but connect you to the Internet, where you will have access to a wealth of data unavailable on the library's shelves. By logging on, you are multiplying a thousandfold the possible sources for doing your research. If, for example, you are preparing a report on water pollution for a science or social studies class, you might tap into OPAC (Online Public Access Catalogue) or the EBSCO Magazine Index, which would give you the names of numerous articles that contain the words WATER POLLUTION somewhere in their text. To be certain that the article is germane to your interest, you might tell the computer to restrict the search to articles that contain the phrase several times or to seek out articles that also mention the Hudson River. The more limits you place on the search, the more likely you will find material you can actually use for your schoolwork.

Once you have found some promising titles, you may be able to get ABSTRACTS, or brief summaries, of each article, or depending on the sources and databases you are using, printouts of the complete texts. You should know, however, that some sources of data, such as the Electronic Library, will charge you for sending you the full text of an article. To pay for it, you need a credit card number that you would type on the computer screen.

If you know the general topic you want to pursue, your librarian can advise you on which search engine is most likely to serve you best and most cheaply, and can help you interpret the mass of information that you may get in response to what may seem like a simple request.

Navigating the Internet

Some libraries will give you access to the Internet—
sometimes for a fee, sometimes for nothing. Once
online, you have the entire world at your disposal.
Navigating the Internet takes time and practice, but a
skillful surfer can tap the resources of universities,
libraries, museums, government agencies, and countless other repositories of information.

The Internet, or World Wide Web, has become an
increasingly large and complex place to do research.
As it grows, it adds PDF documents, movies and audio
files, product databases, and countless web pages that
change so quickly and often that it's impossible to keep
up. In fact, the most popular search engine, "Google,"
currently claims that it gives you access to between
three and four billion web pages. And others, such as
AlltheWeb, AltaVista, and Gigablast, make equally
mind-boggling claims. Therefore, it helps to know a
few tricks for navigating through the Internet labyrinth
and uncovering the information you want.

To become a more effective on-line searcher using
Google, AltaVista, Teoma, or any other search engine,
type in the topic you wish to find out about. If your
topic can be expressed in a phrase or other set of words
that always appear together, enclose it in quotation
marks. If, say, you entered the phrase *state of the art
handheld computers* (without quotation marks), you
would call up countless sites containing the word *state*
and an equally large number pertaining to *art,
handheld,* and *computers.* The quotation marks,
however, would limit the search to only those sites
containing the entire phrase, *state of the art handheld
computers.* Incidentally most search engines ignore
words such as "the" and "of" unless they occur in

phrases within quotation marks. Thus, if you typed in *of the people, by the people, and for the people,* you would get hundreds of thousands of sites containing the word *people,* only a few of which would relate to the quotation from the Gettysburg Address. If you enclosed the phrases in quotation marks, however, you'd more easily zero in on the words of Lincoln's famous speech.

Another time-saving trick is to limit searches by ruling out any pages containing a specific word. This is accomplished by putting a minus sign right in front of the word you want to eliminate. Were you interested in the construction of the ship *Titanic,* for example, a minus sign in front of *iceberg* would eliminate thousands of web sites that mention the accident that sunk the vessel on its maiden voyage. On the other hand, if you wanted to widen a search, type OR (in capital letters) between two words or phrases. A search with OR placed between *steamship* and *ocean liner,* for example, would double the number of responses.

Still another strategy is to use the asterisk in place of a word or word part. Entering *love* * will lead you not only to love but to all tenses of the verb, and also to love song, lovesick, lovebird, love nest, love potion, love triangle, love affair, and much, much more. The same is true if you can't think of the proper word to be inserted between two others. Thus, if you were to type *chocolate * cookies,* you would get your fill of chocolate-nut cookies, chocolate-marshmallow cookies, chocolate-chip cookies, and many others. Beware, however, that not all search engines provide these features.

Searching for current events? *News-google.com* and *altavista.com* provide access to news stories by the date and hour, whether yesterday, last week, or a month ago. AlltheWeb provides foreign newspaper articles, and *newsnow.com* links you to live feed, or the news that is currently breaking over the various news wire services.

Of course, there are hundreds of other tactics for effectively cruising the Internet. A book entitled *Google Hacks: 100 Industrial-Strength Tips and Tools,* written in 2003 by Tara Calishain and Rael Dornfest is a source of useful tips. Indeed, a short search on the Internet itself might uncover still more ways to enhance your cruising experiences.

It was stated at the beginning of this chapter that the library may be the most important space in your school, even the most important place in town. There is no better way to end this chapter than to state simply that tests given to both high school and college students reveal that those who make the highest marks are those who know how to use the library and use it regularly. It is a place for study, a place that provides the greatest storehouse of learning material. So learn to use it, use it to boost your grades, to widen your horizons, and enlarge your life.

PRACTICES FOR BETTER LIBRARY USE

1. Form the library habit. Get hooked.
2. Learn how to find material doing a search on the library's computer catalogue.
3. Save time by learning the locations of certain kinds of books in your library. Where, for instance, would you find a book of paintings by Winslow Homer? Where would you find the autobiography of

General Colin Powell? How about a book on edible plants and roots?

4. Know the methods of arranging fiction and biography used by your library. Arrangements vary from one library to another.

5. Study the reference section to learn generally what is available, its location, and the use to which the various materials may be put.

6. Learn to use a computer for research.

LOOKING BACK

1. Using the Dewey Decimal System, where would you look to find the following books?
   a. *Concepts in Modern Biology* by David Kraus
   b. *The Essential Shakespeare* by John Dover Wilson
   c. *Economics* by Paul A. Samuelson
   d. *The Autobiography of Malcolm X* by Malcolm X

2. What kind of information can we expect to find about words in the *Merriam Webster Unabridged Dictionary*?

   Use that dictionary or any other unabridged dictionary that is available to look up the following: *sleazy, cabal, Hobson's choice, narcissism, cyberspace.*

3. The personnel manager of a large corporation said, "I don't necessarily hire the most intelligent applicant, but I almost always go for the one who knows how to find the necessary information."

   Is your education preparing you for work in a field that requires information gathering?

Chapter 15
Computers for Learning

TRUE CONFESSIONS

The technological advances in computers are so rapid that books like this one cannot keep pace with the changes. A majority of jobs require the use of computers, and no one can remain immune from their influence. Bill Gates, the head of the giant Microsoft Corporation, boasts that "we caused a kind of revolution—peaceful, mainly—and now the computer has taken up residence in our offices and homes. Computers shrank in size and grew in power, as they dropped dramatically in price. And it all happened fairly quickly. Not as quickly as I once thought, but still pretty fast. Inexpensive computer chips now show up in engines, watches, antilock brakes, facsimile machines, elevators, gasoline pumps, cameras, thermostats, treadmills, vending machines, burglar alarms, and even talking greeting cards."[1]

Computers can be a great boon to anyone's education. How will you use this remarkable and powerful tool to your advantage as a student? The remainder of this chapter is meant to give you some ideas.

Regardless of the kind of computer you use in school or at home—Macintosh or PC—with a little patience and perseverance, you're soon apt to discover how computers can enrich your studies and add new dimensions to your life. In general, there are five areas

---

[1] *The Road Ahead* (New York: Viking, 1995), 2–3.

in which computers can be helpful: (1) writing and editing, (2) retrieving information, (3) communicating, (4) acquiring new skills and knowledge, and (5) presenting your work.

WRITING AND EDITING

Through a word-processing program a computer can help you become a better writer very quickly. Typing, or keyboarding, skills are very important. Those who type the fastest have learned to touch-type, either by taking a typing course or by teaching themselves, often using a software program that can easily be installed in most computers and offers effective typing instruction. Some people can type very rapidly using just a couple of fingers, but for the greatest efficiency, learn standard touch-typing. In either case, typing with fluency will enable you to quickly put your thoughts into writing, make changes and corrections easily, and rearrange your thoughts into the best sequence. Many students find that word processing unlocks their latent talents; reluctant writers become eager to compose papers, stories, and poetry. The key that a computer provides to unlock this talent is the ease of composition and editing. Through this one aspect alone, word processing may be your most valuable computer tool.

Almost every computer sold comes with an installed word processing program. Although great numbers of programs exist, they all resemble each other and work basically the same way. Once you have mastered, say, Macwrite on the Macintosh, or Microsoft Word on the PC, you will have little trouble switching between word processing programs. Some of the commands may be slightly different, and each may have features that another doesn't, but after a little while the differences become inconsequential. Most programs may check your spelling and grammar, enable you to write footnotes more easily, permit you to leave space in your text for pictures and graphics, let you type in two or more columns on a page, and so forth, but even the most rudimentary programs will undoubtedly enhance your writing performance in English and other classes.

Use of a computer also allows you to expand the audience for your writing. Teachers have customarily been the sole readers of students' writing. In fact, you may have had your teacher in mind as you composed an essay, story, or other piece of writing. But with a computer hooked up to the Internet or with special software installed, you can send your writing across the room to a classmate or to a reader almost anywhere in the world. In moments you may get rapid feedback on your drafts and make necessary changes before handing in the final paper to your teacher. Sites such as *www.scholastic.com,* which mainly serves students up to the ninth grade, and *www.teenwriting.about.com,* which caters to high schoolers, collect and publish writing so that students may see what others in their age group are writing. In short, your words can be read seriously by others, and, likewise, you can read and respond to what others have posted from their computers.

This sort of on-line peer review, as it is called, enables you to to practice critiquing others' work. As a by-product you may become a more incisive and objective evaluator of your own writing. Ideally, the feedback you get should help you improve, but frankly you may have to brace yourself for occasional tactless criticism that hurts more than it helps. Similarly, your comments to others should be as sensitively worded and constructive as you can make them.

Because web sites for peer review come and go constantly, search the Internet for functioning teenage e-zines, for Weblog diaries (or blogs), and Wikis (blogs with multiple authors). With a little patience and perseverance you will eventually find a congenial site. You might also consult your teacher who may have information about numerous networks, web sites, and software programs that were created with peer exchange in mind.

In addition to posting your own work for others to read, you can find an infinite variety of tips on writing well. Working on a short story? Sign onto *www.teenwriting.about.com* and get advice on how to build a better plot, how to develop characters, how to build interest and create tension in your story. Whatever help you may need with regard to fiction writing, you are likely to find it. The same holds true for essay writing, grammar and usage, and the study of literature. Hundreds of links to academic as well as commercial sites are available through the *teenwriting.about.com* web site.

FINDING AND EXCHANGING INFORMATION

It's small wonder that the present era is sometimes called the Information Age. With a computer, you have access to more information than you could ever want or need. The previous chapter in this book describes just a handful of possibilities for doing electronic searches for material on virtually every imaginable topic. Many libraries subscribe to information services whose sole function is to help you find whatever you may be looking for. The Internet expands still further the resources available to you. You could spend the rest of your life cruising on the Internet and never run out of places to contact for information. Not everything you find on your screen is worth the effort of the search, but very often the documents, databases, images, and even other computer software than you can load into your own computer make the time and effort very worthwhile. With a computer, a modem—the equivalent of a telephone—and a link to a search engine such as Google or AltaVista, you can literally explore the entire world for information.

Randy, a junior in a Washington State high school, writing about his telecommunications learning, said, "The best aspect of the I-Net is the ability to get information on any topic I want. You can join Listserv and find out about a topic from experts. Just e-mail the expert and ask a question. You'll get a response quickly. But the best way to get materials is through a regular search engine. I personally like Yahoo.com. The other day I needed information on Poland for a social studies paper. After I asked to search for articles on Poland I got nearly half a million responses. Obviously, I had to define what I wanted, which was Polish customs and traditions. Eventually, I boiled it down to how Poles celebrate Christmas, and I got lots of good material."

Impressed with the speed at which computers can transfer information, Jennifer, a senior in a Massachusetts high school, wrote, "My school has recently gained access to Internet2, which gives speedier data transfers than the old Internet, which is becoming jammed with huge quantities of traffic. The heart of Internet2 is called Abilene, which zips along at awesome speed. How fast is it? Well, the other day I transferred 6.7 gigabytes of data related to research in black holes, the equivalent of two feature-length DVD movies, to a guy I know in San Diego. It took less than a minute to do it—about 3,000 times faster than the broadband connection I used to have."

Literally at your fingertips, you have encyclopedias, everything printed in today's newspapers, weather information, the latest stock prices, databases on science, social studies, sports, business, and on and on and on. The U.S. Congress now gives access to the full text of all House and Senate bills, including summaries and chronologies of pending legislation, as well as the text of the *Congressional Record,* which reports every word uttered in Congress and is updated daily. If you are studying a foreign language you might make contact with a site in in the country where the language is spoken. A university in France, for example, maintains a site that features pointers about traveling throughout the country, provides information about places to visit, language, food, and culture. The Internet also offers SAT and ACT preparation, virtual tours of 3,500 colleges and universities, and so on.

Library computers will serve you well while you're in school, but after hours a computer will give you access to plenty of library materials—from reference books to literature related to every subject you are taking. In fact, the Web is filled with electronic libraries. At *memoware.com* and at *bartleby.com,* for instance, you'll find the complete works of nearly every author you may be studying in school, from Shakespeare to Orwell, from Hawthorne to Tolstoy. You'll also find a limited number of ebooks, but you won't find the writings of most serious contemporary authors because their copyrights have not yet expired.

The American Verse Project, run by the University of Michigan, offers an electronic archive of American poetry prior to 1920, and for more up-to-date poetry you can sign onto *ibiblio.org,* where you will find the text of many contemporary poems—along with oral readings by the poets themselves.

If your school hasn't already established a homework hotline, the Internet has countless sources of homework help in every subject: biology, Spanish, math, world history, and so on. Some homework sites will charge you a fee for help, but many others are free. *Kidinfo.com,* for example, has free links to over 2,500 sites that offer information about history, including links to specific eras, to historical documents, to time lines, and much more. For a charge of $40, Guru.net and other commercial sites offer help in all subjects. The quality of help varies from site to site, of course, so proceed with caution.

COMMUNICATING

Through e-mail and chat groups, both available via the Internet, you can make contact with people all over the world—other students, teachers, friends, experts in every field.

In short, people everywhere on the planet can participate in your education. Via e-mail, you can easily be a key pal with anyone, young or old, famous or ordinary. Rachel, a Washington, D.C. student, said, "Being on a network has expanded my circle of friends. . . . When I communicate with someone in Slovenia or England or Argentina I realize that the problems that they have are not very far away from me. So even though we are all far away from each other in miles, we are all part of the same global community."

Entire classes get involved in e-mail correspondence. A science class in Maine, for example, gathered and collected data on area wildlife to exchange for similar information with students in Hawaii. A New York high school class studying Russian literature became key pals with students in a school near Moscow. When it came time to write about the books they'd been reading, the American students asked their Russian counterparts to give them ideas about Tolstoy, Chekhov, and the other authors. The papers that were submitted, according to the teacher, were "the most interesting and varied" he had ever read. Through the Global Student Newswire, founded by journalism students at the University of Florida, you and the editors of your school newspaper can share ideas and content for publication. Occasionally, certain celebrities go on-line for a period of time to talk electronically with students. Recently students made personal contact with astronauts, former presidents, well-known scholars, authors, and poets.

The Internet also allows you to join chat groups composed of people with a common interest. To be sure, much of the electronic conversation may be insipid and a waste of time, but you never know when you might find a soulmate with whom to connect. Say, for instance, you participate in a group that is chatting about a passion of yours—movies. If one of the group seems particularly well-informed or engaging, you can exchange e-mail addresses and carry on a dialogue without the interference of other, less interested participants.

How these opportunities can make a difference to your performance in school is up to you. You may not earn extra credit for using e-mail, but think how the experience can add to your fund of knowledge and the pleasure you derive from learning. Although your grade-point average may not shoot up merely because you've gone on-line, you will ultimately be a more well-rounded person because of your greater aware-ness of the world and the broad perspectives you have gained.

ACQUIRING NEW SKILLS AND KNOWLEDGE

The amount of study material being published for students' use is overwhelming. In every subject, from art to tech-ed, the number of computer programs being sold suggests that CAI (computer-assisted instruction) is here to stay. Some of the programs are simple and easy to use. In fact, they are little more than textbooks transferred to computer disks. If you were to use a computer program to study for SAT I, for instance, the study material might come directly from a book. The computer makes the experience interactive, however, meaning that you'll see comments about your answers flashed on the screen, and your performance level will often determine which material you'll work on next. In all, such programs create the illusion that studying is less solitary than it really is and that someone (a com-puter chip, perhaps) is accompanying you as you work through the program.

Other programs are more varied and creative. CSILE (computer-supported intentional learning environment), for one, offers students in two different classes, two schools, even two different countries a chance to work together. Each class invents its own hypothetical ancient culture, produces, and buries artifacts used in that culture. Then each class does an archaeological dig at the other class' site, drawing inferences about the culture from the materials they uncover. A good deal of electronic conversation occurs between the classes as they explore the food, art, religion, language, values, and other aspects of each others culture.

This kind of simulation exposes students to the work of anthropologists, historians, sociologists, geographers, and archaeologists. But more than that, it shows how technology can be used to make students think. As you become adept at using computers, you may find yourself doing wonderfully inventive and enriching projects.

Spreadsheets play a major role in math and business. Using a computer, you can become familiar with accounting and bookkeeping, of course, but learning to use spreadsheets also exposes you to many crucial mathematical principles as well as to practical applications of math. If you were creating a budget for your future college expenses, for instance, an electronic spreadsheet would enable you to build several models of a budget, each one taking into account such variables as the cost of tuition, the distance from home, income from a part-time job, possibilities of financial aid, and so forth. If you were planning to buy a car, you would have to consider other variables such as the fluctuating cost of gasoline, expected driving mileage, cost of repairs and insurance premiums, and a host of other expenses. In other words, computer applications can be more than academic exercises; they can help you think in a mature way about some of life's major decisions.

CAD (computer-aided design) programs have awakened many students' interest in architecture, engineering, and design. Using such programs, students are drawing professional-looking plans for buildings and houses, machines, boats, automobiles and everyday objects found around the house. Adobe Illustrator is one of many computer programs for artists. Instead of pencil and paper, artists use the monitor screen and a mouse to draw and illustrate. If you aspire to work in any area of the visual arts, including advertising and filmmaking, you should most certainly acquaint yourself with computers and their special effects techniques and capabilities. Although your school is not likely to own the sophisticated, high-tech electronic equipment being used on TV or in Hollywood, your digital education should begin with an ordinary desktop computer.

PRESENTING YOUR WORK

Earlier in this book, you were encouraged to make your work look gorgeous before handing it in to your teacher. Although it may seem petty, the appearance of a paper or project often influences the grade you'll receive.

With a computer, there is no excuse for submitting anything that does not look sharp. With a desktop publishing program such as PageMaker or Ready, Set, Go (RSG), you can prepare pages that look as though a graphic designer had a hand in their creation. Word processors and color printers can give your work the appearance of a professionally printed manuscript.

With the right software, you have the potential to make displays and presentations that will impress your teacher and make your classmates envy your creative talent. PowerPoint, a popular Microsoft program, enables you to create any number of dramatic lettering and design effects. You have the capability of having words and letters dance, roll, rock and hop around on the screen. You can zoom in on an object and then zoom out. Shapes can blink on and off and be altered as you like. You can fade out of one display and fade into the next. Photographs and text can be incorporated in any configuration you choose, and if you would like to add background narration or musical accompaniment, that, too, can be done.

The next time you are assigned an oral report or a lengthy paper to write, ask your teacher for permission to do a multimedia presentation instead. There may be occasions when a PowerPoint show may be a welcome alternative to classroom business as usual.

GETTING STARTED

First, make yourself familiar with the equipment in your school. Learn how the different programs work, what their limitations and advantages are. Then use the computers at school regularly and frequently, so that you become adept and find them easy to use.

When it comes time to buy a personal computer, be sure to weigh the costs. Prices vary, of course, and depend largely on the speed, memory, and options. In college a computer may be a piece of standard equipment. You'll be expected to have one. Your dorm room will probably be outfitted with the wiring needed to connect your computer to the local campus network and to the Internet.

If you soon expect to be in the market for a computer, here is a list of suggestions to consider as you choose it.

1. What is the name of the computer? What are the name, address, and phone number of the manufacturer?

2. Does the manufacturer offer customer service on a hotline? Do you know anyone who has had experience using the hotline? Was the service good?

3. How big is the computer's memory? Is it possible to add more memory in the future? At what cost? To run complicated programs with sound and movement requires many GB (gigabytes) of memory. Is the computer you have in mind capable of doing what you want it to?

4. Will you need a desktop or a laptop? What about a printer? The cost of printers varies considerably. A scanner? A flash key for backing up files? Speakers? A surge protector? Do you have a desk or table on which to put your equipment? What will be the total cost for all the hardware?

5. Does the computer come with software installed? Is it software that you want, or will you be paying for programs that you'll never use?

6. Will all components be installed by the seller, or is installation up to you? How much does it cost to have your computer made ready to plug in and use?

7. Do you know anyone who owns the model you are considering? If so, can you try it out for a few hours? If not, can you rent one from the computer store for a trial run?

If you soon expect to be buying software, here is a list of suggestions to think about as you select it.

1. What is the name of the software? What are the publisher's name, address, and phone numbers?

2. Does the publisher offer help on a hotline? Do you know anyone who has had experience using the hotline? Was the service good?
3. Are the installation and operating manuals clearly written, easy to understand, and properly indexed?
4. What is the cost of the program? Are returns possible? Rebates? Updates?
5. Is the software for a Macintosh or for a PC? How much memory must the computer have to run the program?
6. For what subjects and in what ways can this program be used to help you in your schoolwork?
7. Do you know anyone who owns the program you are considering? If so, can you try it out for a few hours? If not, will the store sell you the program on approval (i.e., you may return the program if you are not satisfied)?

LOOKING BACK

1. Numerous web sites sell ready-made essays and term papers. Countless other sites contain more information than anyone can use about every conceivable subject. A recent survey conducted by the Center for Academic Integrity revealed that thirty-eight percent of high school and college students have at one time or other "cut and pasted" their way to a term paper or an essay without giving credit to their sources. In other words, plagiarism is a serious problem in academia. What do you think is the best way to prevent the dishonesty promoted by the vast amounts of information freely available on the Internet?

2. Thousands of students and teachers subscribe to Web-based systems that "read" and evaluate student writing. Skeptics say that the process dehumanizes students and their papers. Supporters like the immediate feedback and precise explanations of common grammar and usage errors, such as run-on sentences or disagreement between subject and verb. Can you think of other pros and cons regarding essays being read and judged electronically by computers?

3. In which course you are taking do you think computers are most profitably used? Are there any courses offered in your school in which a computer would probably not be helpful to students?

Chapter 16

Scoring High on Exams

TRUE CONFESSIONS

1. The ACT Assessment is being given next Saturday morning. How will you prepare for it? Is it possible to study for a test that measures what you have learned throughout your scholastic career?

    Your college counselor recommends that on the night before the exam you rent a DVD or relax with an enjoyable book, and then get a good night's sleep. What do you think of this advice?

2. Sir Walter Raleigh wrote, "In examinations, those who do not wish to know ask questions of those who cannot tell." Does that statement describe the dynamics that exist between your teachers and you? What are the real purposes of tests? Would the education system be improved if examinations were abolished?

3. Chris B. was fairly confident about her performance on both the verbal and math sections of the SAT I she took last Saturday. She had finished the test with time to spare, and on those questions about which she was unsure, she guessed. Imagine her shock, therefore, when she got a very low score. She didn't know that guessing on the SAT I works against you. Chris didn't know the strategies for doing well on the exam.

    Has something like this ever happened to you? How can such a disaster be avoided?

THE PURPOSE OF TESTING

Tests of various kinds will probably be a part of your life from now on. As you must know, tests have long been part of going to school. But they also play a significant role in business, industry, government, and even the armed forces. They are used to measure fitness for jobs, for entrance into professional schools and training programs, for the licensing of physicians, lawyers, fire fighters, social workers, teachers, building contractors, and numerous other positions. Tests often determine promotions in business, industry, and the military. Most of these tests measure aptitude, thinking skills, and knowledge of specific topics. Obviously, doing well on tests is important.

In the classroom, tests enable your teachers to evaluate your knowledge and skills. But what's even more important is that they give you an opportunity to learn. From tests you can learn what your weaknesses are and take steps to overcome them. Do you make errors in reading test questions? If so, you can train yourself to read the questions more carefully. Do you find that test questions ask about things you didn't think were important? If so, you can prepare for the next test by asking yourself questions about the subject matter and by framing questions in the same manner as those on the test. Do you find that your notes don't contain information on which you were tested? Then, you can make up your mind to concentrate harder, to stay alert to key ideas in your reading and classwork. From test questions you can also infer what your teachers consider worth knowing.

The educational value of a test depends in large measure on what you do once the test has been handed back. First, try to look past the grade. (It's perfectly understandable to be concerned primarily with the grades you earn on tests, but if you also try to view tests as opportunities to expand your knowledge and develop your skills, test taking can become an even more crucial part of your education.) You may be temporarily put off by a disappointing grade, but don't take it out on yourself, on your teacher, or on your test paper. Instead of throwing the paper in the garbage, take it with you. After you've cooled off, review the test with an eye toward learning from your mistakes. An essay test is a particularly valuable source of self-evaluation, particularly if the teacher has written extensive comments about the essay. For example, if you found the symbol "dev" in the margin next to several paragraphs, you'd know that in your next essay you should concentrate on the development of paragraphs— that is, providing more details in support of topic sentences. If the teacher has pointed out flaws in your logic or a tendency to base generalizations on scanty evidence, be thankful. Mindful of any concrete criticism that the teacher offers, you'll stay alert to such problems in future essays. To be sure, you may not agree with everything a teacher writes about your work. But consider this: Although you don't accept the teacher's feedback, it is not wrong. As long as the response is honest, think of it as one reader's reaction, and if one reader feels a certain way about your writing, for better or worse, others may feel the same way.

PREPARING FOR QUIZZES AND TESTS

Preparation for quizzes and tests consists mainly of going over the relevant coursework, but the most effective preparation also includes regular, well-organized, day-by-day review. Ideally, such review should include studying a carefully organized notebook, mastering special vocabulary, poring over your class notes, reexamining questions given on previous quizzes and tests, and rereading the highlighted portions of your textbook or reading notes. In addition, try to articulate how the various parts of the curriculum form a unified whole. Partway through a course it may be hard to see the overall design or purpose of each day's work, but by the time of the final exam, you should be able to recognize the master plan for the semester or the year. If in doubt, have a chat with your teacher, who will undoubtedly be impressed by your curiosity and desire to know.

During the weeks before a midterm or final exam listen attentively in class. Even though teachers may continue to add new material to be learned, they often drop direct or indirect hints about matters that you need to know for the approaching exam. Remain vigilant for such statements as:

"In October we studied a case not unlike this one. Remember why it was considered so important." "This is the eighth essential principle we have studied this term. They are all important to an understanding of the course." Teachers often refer in one way or another to almost everything you will see on the examination. Listen for it.

Also keep your eyes open. Remember the story of the teacher who filled the board with French and English sentences, vocabulary words, rates, etc., a week before examination time. Nothing was said to explain why all this had been written there, and no one asked. When the students saw the examination, the reason was self-evident. The examination had been on the board for a whole week. Two students smiled and began writing perfect papers; they had seen. The others had looked too, but hadn't seen.

If you follow the foregoing procedure, you should score high on quizzes and tests—surely higher than if you waited until the last minute and tried to cram everything into your head during an all-night study session. It's hard enough to thoroughly learn even a small amount of material over a long period. To master a large amount in a short time is asking for trouble.

Consistent review should require no more time than doing a regular daily assignment: an hour-long test should not take more than two hours of review. Test review should deal largely with class work or lab work rather than rereading all the assignments. Check the main topics. If you draw a blank, then you'll have to do some rereading, but only enough to jog your memory of what the material says.

Short-answer tests usually require recall of large amounts of information, while essay tests demand recall plus the ability to organize and amplify information. Because maximum recall depends on study spread over time, reviewing for big exams should, whenever possible, be divided into periods of an hour or so, starting no less than ten days to two weeks prior to test day. Review started less than a week before the exam cannot be as thorough and dependable as long-term review. In any case, common sense dictates that hour-long review sessions spread over ten days will prove to be far more beneficial than ten hours of intense study the day before the exam.

HOW TO STUDY FOR AN EXAM

➤ Study in a way that produces the best results. Join a group of classmates or study alone—whichever method works best for you. If possible, do your most difficult studying during the time of day when you are most energized and functioning at your peak.

➤ Choose what is most important to learn and concentrate on that. Don't ignore it, but give less attention to less significant material. Remember that your teacher has only a limited amount of time to test what you know and what you can do. Therefore, keep in mind that some very complicated or time-consuming questions are not likely to show up on exams. On the other hand, play it safe: Know more than what the teacher says is required. Depending on the course, here are some things that typically appear on unit tests, midterms, and finals: general principles related to the coursework, such as use of the scientific method or the use of meter in poetry. In math: definitions, word problems, formulas, theorems, and general concepts. In history: biographical information about famous figures, chronology, reform movements, wars, economic and social trends, civic and political problems, and religious conflict. In English: forms of literature, literary and rhetorical terminology, and rules of grammar and usage. When reviewing a textbook in any subject, pay particular attention to headings in boldface type, to exercises containing questions, and to chapter summaries.

➤ If you haven't already done so, summarize or outline the course or text material in your own words. Writing summaries forces you to think about subject matter in detail. In the process you'll both master the material and identify gaps in your knowledge that call for additional study.

➤ Review by using questions to predict questions. When you have found what you consider important, turn it into a question, or ask yourself how it could be made into a question. This takes discipline, especially because you should be asking questions that you may not be able to answer without further studying. Face it: Easy questions are not really worth asking. Why ask about something when you already know the answer? With practice, you may be able to predict reasonably well up to ninety percent of the questions that will appear on an exam.

➤ Make the terminology of questions part of your review. Although some words appear in question after question, these key words may mean different things to different teachers. Some expect just a short response to a question that asks you to, say, "describe" a character. Others expect a whole paragraph. To prevent any misunderstanding, ask your teachers to define what they mean by such words as *explain, evaluate, state, relate, illustrate, enumerate, describe, interpret, define, diagram, compare, contrast,* and *compare and contrast.*

➤ Substitute understanding for memorization. If you are accustomed to memorizing facts, you may earn credit on quizzes and tests, but nothing can replace a genuine understanding of what you are studying. Memorizing the causes of the Civil War may take you only so far; understanding the true nature of and reasons for the conflict between the North and South will make you a scholar. If you are reviewing history, try to assume the identity of a person who lived through the period you are studying. Accept a role—but not the president, a general, or the hero of the battle—through which you can recreate the feelings of the time. Be a slave, a common soldier, a person in the streets of Richmond or Atlanta. If you are reviewing a foreign language, imagine that in six weeks you will be allowed to use only this language.

Reviewing by changing your identity or point of view can be an intriguing exercise. With imagination you can transform studying into an active and scintillating activity.

TAKING TESTS

By this time in your schooling you are probably familiar with both short-answer and essay tests. Most short-answer tests consist of fill-in-the-blank questions, multiple-choice questions, true/false questions, and matching questions. Essay tests ask you to write out your answers. How much you write depends on the question, of course, but the length may vary between a sentence fragment and several pages of text consisting of thousands of words.

Regardless of the test format, your approach to test-taking should consist of at least the following:

➤ Read the instructions thoroughly and carefully. Pay particularly close attention to instructions that tell you where and how to answer the questions. The reason: Even if you know your stuff, answers that are out of order or in the wrong place may mislead or confuse the grader and cause you to lose credit.

➤ Skim the entire exam for an overview that will help you determine how quickly you need to work. Notice, in particular, if the test offers you a choice of questions to answer.

➤ Don't necessarily answer the questions in the order they appear on the test. Instead, dispose of those you feel confident you can answer quickly and well. Then come back to the more taxing questions.

➤ Before answering a question, *think*. A small investment of time during which you examine each word will pay off in the end. Observe words such as *usually, always, most, never,* and *some*. They may drastically change the meaning of a question.

➤ Do precisely what is requested. Avoid wasting time doing things that will not receive credit. Don't copy problems onto your answer sheet, for instance, unless required to do so. Unless your handwriting is illegible, don't waste time copying over an essay to make it look neater. It's better to use the time editing and proofreading. On the other hand, because certain letters and numbers look alike, strive to be as neat as you can, even when answering objective questions.

➤ Pace yourself so that you'll complete the exam in the allotted time. Spend the appropriate amount of time on questions according to the credit they bear. To spend several minutes on a question worth two points is a misallocation of time and effort. A question worth twenty-five percent of the test should take twenty-five percent of the time.

➤ Check over your answers if you have time, but resist changing answers impulsively. Your first answer may be more reliable unless you are absolutely certain you've made a mistake. If in doubt, leave it alone.

➤ Unless the exam is multiple-choice, remember that a human being is going to grade your paper. Feel free to communicate with the grader, in particular if you are running out of time. Let's say you are writing an essay and still have several things to say when the time is about to run out. Quickly sketch out what you might have written if you could continue. You may earn partial credit for your effort.

Essay, or subjective, tests are more personal than short-answer tests. They provide students with an opportunity to show off and organize what they have learned. They also afford teachers a chance to assess the effectiveness of their instruction. A test that every student fails, for example, could show that the class is full of shirkers, but it could also be illuminating for the teacher because student failure often suggests teacher failure. In any case, when you write an essay, think how you might react to it if you were the teacher.

To improve your chances of writing successful essays on an exam, practice the following:

➤ Read the first question you are going to answer and write a brief outline of your major points in the margin. Think for a minute or two about your answer to check the arrangement of ideas. Make sure your answer includes all important ideas. THINKING BEFORE WRITING will improve your essays as nothing else will.

➤ As you write, restate the question if you can, but at least make the subject of the question the subject of your answer. Never start an answer with a pronoun without an antecedent. "It is when" and "It is because" are weak openings. Always make the subject of the question the subject of your answer. As you read the question for the second time you must constantly watch for anything that will give your answer an element of vagueness.

➤ As you write your answer keep in mind the teacher's preference for style of presentation, use of illustration to show understanding, and elements of a model answer. If the teacher has complimented you on earlier test papers for the way you handled an answer, try to apply this method to as many questions as possible. Ask yourself the question, "What is the teacher's aim in this particular question?" Make your paper easy to mark. Use signal words and numerals to introduce important facts and series. Number questions to the left of the red margin and skip one or two lines between answers. Remember that the neatly written paper has fewer mistakes and is easier for the teacher to mark.

➤ Concentrate on one question at a time, and use a mental system of numbering important points in your answer. Don't overwrite or write away from questions because you have jumped ahead and are thinking of a question to come. The teacher has not asked questions that require repeating subject matter, so be careful to keep all answers within the limits set by the questions. An excellent method for avoiding generalizations and worthless padding is to mentally number important points as you write them down. Illustrations, specific elaboration, important facts, and explanations to clarify your understanding of a definition or event are all necessary parts of a good essay answer.

➤ Check over the completed examination paper before you turn it in. You should reserve several minutes of each examination hour for checking after you have completed the writing. Check for mechanical errors and obvious factual mistakes such as wrong words, incorrect conclusions, transposed characters, etc. As with objective tests, do not change anything in an answer unless you are absolutely sure it is wrong. Rely on your first impression.

➤ You can learn much about writing better examinations and using better methods of study by going over the graded paper after it has been returned. By checking against your book you can see what you omitted that the teacher considered important or how you misinterpreted the qualifying word in a question. If you note such errors carefully, you are not likely to repeat them on the next test.

COLLEGE ENTRANCE EXAMS

Students bound for college will probably take either the SAT I or the ACT Assessment. The SAT I is divided into two parts, verbal and mathematical. The verbal section has two sections, the Critical Reading Test, consisting of multiple-choice questions about several reading passages—some short, some long—and the Writing Exam, containing multiple-choice grammar questions and a written essay. For the essay, you will be assigned a topic and given half an hour to write a response. The exam also includes vocabulary in the form of sentence-completion questions.

The math section of the SAT I assesses mastery of math concepts taught in geometry, Algebra 1, and Algebra 2. You will be given questions asking you to deal with numbers and operations, as well as data analysis, statistics, and probability. Overall, the test measures your ability to reason and to apply mathematical concepts to a variety of situations.

Most students planning to take the SAT I also take the PSAT for practice at the beginning of their junior year. The PSAT is shorter than the SAT I and does not include an essay question. Nor does it have a direct bearing on college admissions. The best preparation for the PSAT and SAT I is a background of wide reading, essay writing experience, and good math courses. Familiarity with the format of each test is also invaluable.

The ACT Assessment is also a multiple-choice exam. It consists of four parts: English, math, reading, and science reasoning. After completing the four sections of the ACT, some students also take the ACT Writing Test, an optional half-hour exam required or recommended by many, but not all, colleges. The writing test consists of a single question to which students respond by writing an essay in thirty minutes.

The English test assesses your mastery of usage and mechanics, including punctuation, basic grammar and usage, and sentence structure. It also tests rhetorical skills, such as writing strategy, organization, and style. The Mathematics test measures knowledge of algebra, geometry, and trigonometry. The Reading test measures your ability to understand materials similar to those read in college courses, and includes passages of prose fiction and nonfiction from the fields of the humanities, social sciences, and natural sciences. The Science Reasoning test assesses your ability to think like a scientist. On the test you must answer questions about sets of scientific information presented in various formats.

To prepare for the ACT, review your math and English skills. Because the reading and science sections of the exam are more like aptitude tests than achievement tests, they are more difficult to prepare for. Reasoning skills do not improve overnight. But it will serve you well to become familiar with the format of the exam. Get a test preparation book and practice answering the questions. The more time you have to prepare before the exam, the better off you'll be on test day.

College entrance achievement tests administered by the College Board are also given on specific subject material. Known as SAT II Subject Tests, they lend themselves to a certain amount of preparation. SAT IIs are offered in many subjects. The colleges you apply to will often ask you to take them, but even if you are not required to take SAT IIs, high scores will enhance your college application. If possible, take SAT IIs in your best subjects. Many colleges ask applicants to take SAT II in Writing, which tests, among other things, your ability to write a short essay. Using a test preparation guide such as that published by Barron's will help you prepare for the exam and give you practice in writing an essay in only twenty minutes.

REVIEWING FOR TESTS: A SUMMARY

1. Concentrate on the important subject matter, but don't ignore the rest.
2. Review by listening for hints and helps given by the teacher just prior to the test.
3. Review by predicting questions for the test. Think how questions can be asked on specific subject matter.
4. Review by reorganizing the subject matter into logical divisions. Keep a sense of unity by being aware of relationships among parts.

5. Review by changing your point of view. Let your imagination add interest to the subject.

6. Review by knowing what *question words* mean. Learn what your teacher expects when certain key words are used.

7. When you take the test or examination, read all questions and instructions carefully and repeatedly until you understand exactly what the answer and the presentation of the answer require.

8. Know the general implications of key and qualifying words in both objective and essay questions. Do not, under any circumstances, make an exception for what the qualifying word asks for.

9. On objective tests give the precise answer; on essay tests give the complete answer. Always remember that quantity is not a substitute for quality.

10. Observe all rules of neatness, mechanics, and clarity. An attractive paper that is easy to read may give you an advantage.

11. Check your paper carefully before you turn it in. Unless you are absolutely sure you have made a mistake, do not change your answers. The first impression, as psychological tests have shown, is usually more reliable.

12. Check all returned papers. Note your errors so you will not repeat them on the next test.

LOOKING BACK

1. What do teachers and test makers mean when they ask you to do the following?
   a. Evaluate
   b. Describe
   c. Compare and contrast

2. Some baseball batters are guess hitters. They guess at the kind of pitch that will be thrown to them (fast ball, curve, slider, change of pace) and then swing. Should you guess about test questions your teacher is likely to ask and prepare for them exclusively?

   Have you ever prepared for a test with a friend who knew more than you did? Have you ever prepared with a friend who knew less? What are the advantages and disadvantages of each?

3. One proven tip for test takers is to check their paper thoroughly before turning it in. What other suggestions would you give to someone seeking advice about how to be a smart test taker?

Chapter 17

Motivation: How to Find It, How to Use It

THE REACH AND THE GRASP

"Ah, but a man's reach should exceed his grasp, Or what's a heaven for?" Thus wrote Robert Browning in his poem, "Andrea del Sarto," in 1855. Although what is within one's reach today has multiplied beyond the vaguest dream of anyone living in Browning's day, it is still a part of natural law that unless one's dreams exceed what one is momentarily capable of grasping, one stops learning. One's life becomes mere survival; finally one is pushed off the stage by a better actor who has developed a greater capacity to reach for dreams. William Golding makes this point in an exciting book entitled *The Inheritors,* in which he describes how slow-witted Neanderthal man was replaced by a person capable of greater vision—Cro-Magnon man.

"But what has this to do with me?" you ask. Well, begin with your natural gifts, namely a work ethic that fuels efforts to be a better performer, not only in the classroom, but on the playing fields, in the family, at your job, as a son or daughter, as a friend, as a dynamic and useful human being. To be a productive person takes effort, but it also gives life greater meaning. Productivity contributes to success or failure. It is impossible to separate productivity from the whole of one's character and it's also difficult to define. It is a combination of interest, ambition, inspiration, moral acceptance of life's importance, a sense of values, and faith in oneself. It is sometimes called by one of the several parts ascribed to it, but generally it is given a name which suggests forward movement and the rhythm of a firm, quick step—*motivation.*

Motivation empowers people to do their best. Without motivation, people atrophy and civilizations wither. You can ponder forever what makes one person succeed and another fail. But if you were asked why great civilizations ultimately fail, a good answer is: "Great civilizations decline not because geography changes but because people's minds change." People become satisfied and cease to be excited about learning. Civilization declines when people do not want to do and to know; when work becomes drudgery and love of learning is replaced by resentment and impatience; when the aim of learning becomes social status rather than truth and ennoblement.

Perhaps we can find how much of the whole concept of motivation is within us by looking at some of its components.

First of all, interest in learning. All the study techniques in the world are useless to someone lacking interest. Interest can transform subject matter from something very dead into something active and alive.

Interest gives work a new dimension. Tom Sawyer discovered it when he had his friends whitewash the fence for him. "Work," he said, "consists of whatever a body is obliged to do, and play consists of whatever a body is not obliged to do." Interest gives obligation the quality and character of privilege. You can use interest to take the feeling of compulsion out of study. Interest will help you do more and better work than is required.

The clockwatcher finds the day long and seemingly endless. The interested worker never has enough time to complete the job. Perhaps interest, as a component of motivation, is captured by the axiom, "If a man does only what is required of him, he is a slave; the moment he does more he is a free man."

Then there is ambition. Ambition is far more than a simple willingness to receive. Through ambition, great deeds are done. Think, for example, of America's heroes, from Lewis and Clark to Amelia Earhart, from Martin Luther King to New York's fire fighters on 9/11. Long ago, Alexander the Great, at the age of twenty, inherited a well-equipped army led by brilliant and devoted generals. If Alexander had been content only to receive, the army would have belonged to the generals.

Ambition, like the other ingredients of motivation, can be measured by the drop or by the barrel. It is within your power to tap into whatever ambition resides within you.

It is easy to make a check list of your ambitions concerning your school work. Much that will pertain to your life's ambitions could be put on your check list while you are still in school.

1. What are my abilities?
2. What will my ambition require of me?
3. What will success mean in the career or job for which I aim?
4. What will defeat mean?
5. Have I put the proper value upon my life and my time?
6. Will my work provide sufficient inspiration and challenge to save me from complacency and stagnation?

We could continue through some explanation of all the components of motivation, but by now you should see what is happening. We have come full circle and are talking about your gifts as described in Chapter 1. Thus, the only way to understand the meaning of motivation is to understand your own gifts and the uses to which they can be put.

Don't stand still if you can walk; don't walk if you can run; don't run if you can fly. There is an old Indian legend of an eaglet that thought it was a prairie chicken and never used its wings. As the story goes, an Indian boy found an eagle's egg and put it in a prairie chicken's nest. The eaglet hatched with the brood of prairie chicks and grew up with them. The changeling eagle, thinking it was a prairie chicken, did what prairie chickens did. It scratched in the dirt for seeds and insects to eat, never flew more than a short distance, and that with an awkward flutter of wings, only a few feet off the ground. After all, that's how prairie chickens were supposed to fly.

Then one day when the eagle was grown, it saw a magnificent bird far above it in the sky. Riding with graceful majesty on the powerful wind currents, it soared with scarcely a beat of its golden wings.

"What a beautiful bird!" said the eagle to one of the prairie chickens. "What is it?"

"That's an eagle, the chief of birds," the prairie chicken replied. "But don't give it a second thought. You could never fly like it."

So the eagle never gave it a second thought, never rose beyond the brief thrashing of wings and the flurry of feathers, and grew old, and died thinking it was a prairie chicken. It's all too easy to go through life thinking we're prairie chickens when we're really eagles.

MOTIVATION—IMPERISHABLE

Let us conclude with two true stories to illustrate a fact: if you show concern for both the better self of which you are capable and your gifts through which you can achieve this better self, motivation will take care of itself.

Not all your papers will be returned with sterling grades. When you have done your best and still get a low grade, there will be moments of discouragement, doubt, and depression. When this happens, remind yourself of the following story.

The first scene of the story is set in the wilderness of Indiana. A small boy trudges through the winter forest to a one-room school. After six weeks the school closed and the boy suffered the first of many deeply felt disappointments. By the time he was twenty-two, he had wandered as an itinerant worker and was now a partner in a crossroads store at the edge of a frontier village in Illinois. The store failed and he lost every penny he had saved from seven years' hard labor.

The lesson had been expensive, but he felt that he had learned by hard experience. He would not fail again. Two years of struggle provided him with enough funds to enter a second partnership. This time he would succeed. But within two years the second store had failed. The young man's partner drank up the profits. The person to whom the partners sold the store failed to make his payments, and when the entire stock of goods had been sold, disappeared with the receipts. When the former partner died the young man was left with debts which seemed impossible to ever pay off.

Now he asked a friend to help him get a job as a surveyor, and he studied mathematics with the village schoolmaster to prepare himself for the job. After he was appointed to the surveyor's job, he borrowed money to buy instruments and a horse; however, he never had a chance to begin work. Creditors from his mercantile failures seized his possessions and he lost both horse and instruments.

Immediately after this the gods dealt him the cruelest blow of all, convincing him that he had been singled out for pain and failure from birth. His sweetheart, perhaps a deep and enduring love, the like of which he did not experience again, suddenly died. He descended to the depths of despair and gloom, often pondering whether the struggle to live was worth it. Long afterward he wrote, "At this period of my life I never dared to carry a pocketknife, fearing I would destroy myself."

Time passes. The man no longer looks young, although he is not yet forty. After ten years of struggle he has paid off the last of his debts. While he worked to pay them off, he also spent long hours trying to satisfy his insatiable hunger to be able to put into words what he felt, to understand the feelings of men around him.

Friends began to suggest that this failure might be a success in the most unexpected of places—politics. So they elected him to Congress. He did not succeed; after two short terms he was defeated for reelection. Nine years later his staunch friends determined to nominate him for the U.S. Senate. However, a split developed in the party and he was forced to step aside in favor of a candidate who could win the number of votes for nomination. This too was failure. Two years later, when he did manage to be nominated and run for the Senate, he was soundly defeated. Of this failure he

said, "I was down and out of politics at the age of 50."
Looking back over thirty years of his life he could not
claim a single personal victory.

The motivating forces of gods and men, of fate, of
dreams and destiny, are beyond prediction and
comprehension. No man knows when he is walking
with destiny, and no man was ever less suspecting than
this long-time loser. For in the fifty-second year of life,
in the thirty-second year of failure, this man was
elected president of the United States. He is usually
listed among the half-dozen greatest men who ever
lived. His name, as you must have guessed by now, is
Abraham Lincoln.

MOTIVATION—A SEED UPON THE GROUND

The second story is really a continuation of the first.
Abraham Lincoln had one thing in common with
Anthony La Manna. Anthony was born on April 14;
the day on which Lincoln was shot. The years were
different, however; Lincoln was shot in 1865 and
Anthony La Manna was born in 1888 in the village of
Valguarnera Caropepe, amid the stone quarries of
Sicily's Monte Erei.

Anthony La Manna, one of eleven children, entered
the quarries as a laborer at the age of twelve. Under the
scorching Sicilian sun, amid the deafening ringing of
hammers and thunderous thuds and rattles of giant slabs
of stone crashing into pits, Anthony La Manna dreamed
of nothing beyond the sulphur and rock-salt mines near
the sea, where the pay was better. But even these mines
seemed far away. They were south over the hills and
past the valley through which ran the Assinarus River.

Tony could wipe the sweat from his brow and scan the jagged horizon, but the hope of better wages from sulphur or rock-salt mines was far away—perhaps too far.

Few ever went from the quarries. The pattern of trudging up the mountain at sunrise and back down at sunset, with an occasional goatherd to offer news from beyond the hills, became for most the center and circumference of a world.

Anthony La Manna, reading the history of his island with his fifth-grade education, and listening to his elders talk, believed that change was against the natural order of things. Sicily, he thought, had really not changed much in the 2,315 years since Nicias and the Athenian army had been destroyed on the banks of the Assinarus River in 415 B.C. The Athenians who were defeated in battle were enslaved in the quarries, where they were scorched by the sun and where they died. Anthony La Manna had also seen men die in the quarries.

When Tony La Manna was sixteen, he followed the valley and the river down to the sea. In the Gulf of Gela a ship was loading goods to carry to America, and Anthony La Manna hired on.

There were times in America when Anthony would have given much to be back on the road which led homeward from the quarry, where the friendly voice of the goatherd broke the loneliness. But his four years in the quarries had given him much skill with a chisel and a hammer on stone; after a short time of digging ditches in the swamps of New Jersey, he became a stonecutter's apprentice in Washington, D.C., and began work on the Lincoln Memorial in 1914.

Day after day, as he worked high on the scaffold, he studied the countenance on the gigantic statue. The sad, tired man, who had begun life in surroundings as humble as those of Tony La Manna, had become a lawyer, and a president. One day at lunch time, as Tony La Manna sat on the end of the high scaffold looking into the middle section of the great monument, where sat the rail splitter from the wilderness of Illinois, the stone splitter from Monte Erei made a sudden decision—Anthony La Manna could make something more of himself. He would become a lawyer. On a piece of planking he wrote "Anthony La Manna" and under his name "Attorney at Law." At the end of the day he brought the piece of board down from the scaffold. His friends laughed—"Another Abe Lincoln, ha! Tony, you've been too long in the hot sun."

It's a long way from a noisy fifth grade class in the little stuccoed school in Caropepe, Sicily, to the National Law Center at George Washington University in Washington, D.C. After ten hours on a scaffold with chisel and hammer, Tony went to night school. And in his canvas bag with chisels, hammer, and salami sandwiches, Tony La Manna carried books. He would hurry through his lunch and begin to read. His friends would laugh, as long before Lincoln's rail-splitting companions had laughed at him, as he sat on a stump with a book in one hand and a slab of salt pork between two chunks of cornbread in the other.

In the midst of his work on the memorial and his studying in night school, Anthony La Manna went off to fight in World War I for democracy and the right to be free and learn and become something in America. When he came back he resumed both his work on the memorial and his studies. At age thirty-two, sixteen years in America, he was chosen to carve the Gettysburg Address on the memorial. He was to inscribe these immortal words of Lincoln in stone for them to be forever enshrined in the hearts of men. While completing that task, Anthony also earned his LL.B. and LL.M.

For nearly forty years he was a successful lawyer in both New York and Washington, and was special counselor to the Veteran's Administration for thirty-two years. When asked to describe what he considered motivation, he said, "Impossible, for each man must discover and define it for himself."

So ends the story, the chapter, and this book. What is motivation and whence does it come? The answer is as difficult to describe as trying to tell the direction of the wind by hearing it move through far-off hills at night. Unless you find your own answer to what motivation is, you will never know. If you have it, you will know; if you do not have it, those around you will know

You can escape neither time nor history. Unless you use the gifts you have been given, time will close many doors which open on long corridors of opportunity through which you will never be permitted to walk. As you turn your back on the closed doors to walk in the tracks you have already made, you will find history gazing upon you, holding you accountable for misappropriation.

"Of what?" you demand.

"Of your talents," answers history.

NOTES

NOTES

NOTES